SUICIDE RISK ™

VOLUME TWO • NIGHTMARE SCENARIO

ROSS RICHIE CEO & Founder • JACK CUMMINS COO & President • MARK SMYLIE Chief Creative Officer • MATT GAGNON Editor-in-Chief • FILIP SABLIK VP of Publishing & Marketing • STEPHEN CHRISTY VP of Development
LANCE KREITER VP of Licensing & Merchandising • PHIL BARBARO VP of Finance • BRYCE CARLSON Managing Editor • MEL CAYLO Marketing Manager • SCOTT NEWMAN Production Design Manager • IRENE BRADISH Operations Manager
DAFNA PLEBAN Editor • SHANNON WATTERS Editor • ERIC HARBURN Editor • REBECCA TAYLOR Editor • IAN BRILL Editor • CHRIS ROSA Assistant Editor • ALEX GALER Assistant Editor • WHITNEY LEOPARD Assistant Editor
JASMINE AMIRI Assistant Editor • CAMERON CHITTOCK Assistant Editor • HANNAH NANCE PARTLOW Production Designer • KELSEY DIETERICH Production Designer • DEVIN FUNCHES E-Commerce & Inventory Coordinator
ANDY LIEGL Event Coordinator • BRIANNA HART Executive Assistant • AARON FERRARA Operations Assistant • JOSÉ MEZA Sales Assistant • ELIZABETH LOUGHRIDGE Accounting Assistant

SUICIDE RISK Volume Two, March 2014. Published by BOOM! Studios, a division of Boom Entertainment, Inc. Suicide Risk is ™ & © 2014 Boom Entertainment, Inc. and Mike
Carey. Originally published in single magazine form as SUICIDE RISK No. 5-9. ™ & © 2013, 2014 Boom Entertainment, Inc., registered in various countries and categories. All rights reserved. BOOM! Studios™
and the BOOM! Studios logo are trademarks of Boom Entertainment, Inc. All characters, events, and institutions depicted herein
are fictional. Any similarity between any of the names, characters, persons, events, and/or institutions in this publication to actual names, characters, and persons, whether living
or dead, events, and/or institutions is unintended and purely coincidental. BOOM! Studios does not read or accept unsolicited submissions of ideas, stories, or artwork.

A catalog record of this book is available from OCLC and from the BOOM! Studios website, www.boom-studios.com, on the Librarians Page.

BOOM! Studios, 5670 Wilshire Boulevard, Suite 450, Los Angeles, CA 90036-5679. Printed in Canada. First Printing. ISBN: 978-1-60886-360-0, eISBN: 978-1-61398-214-3

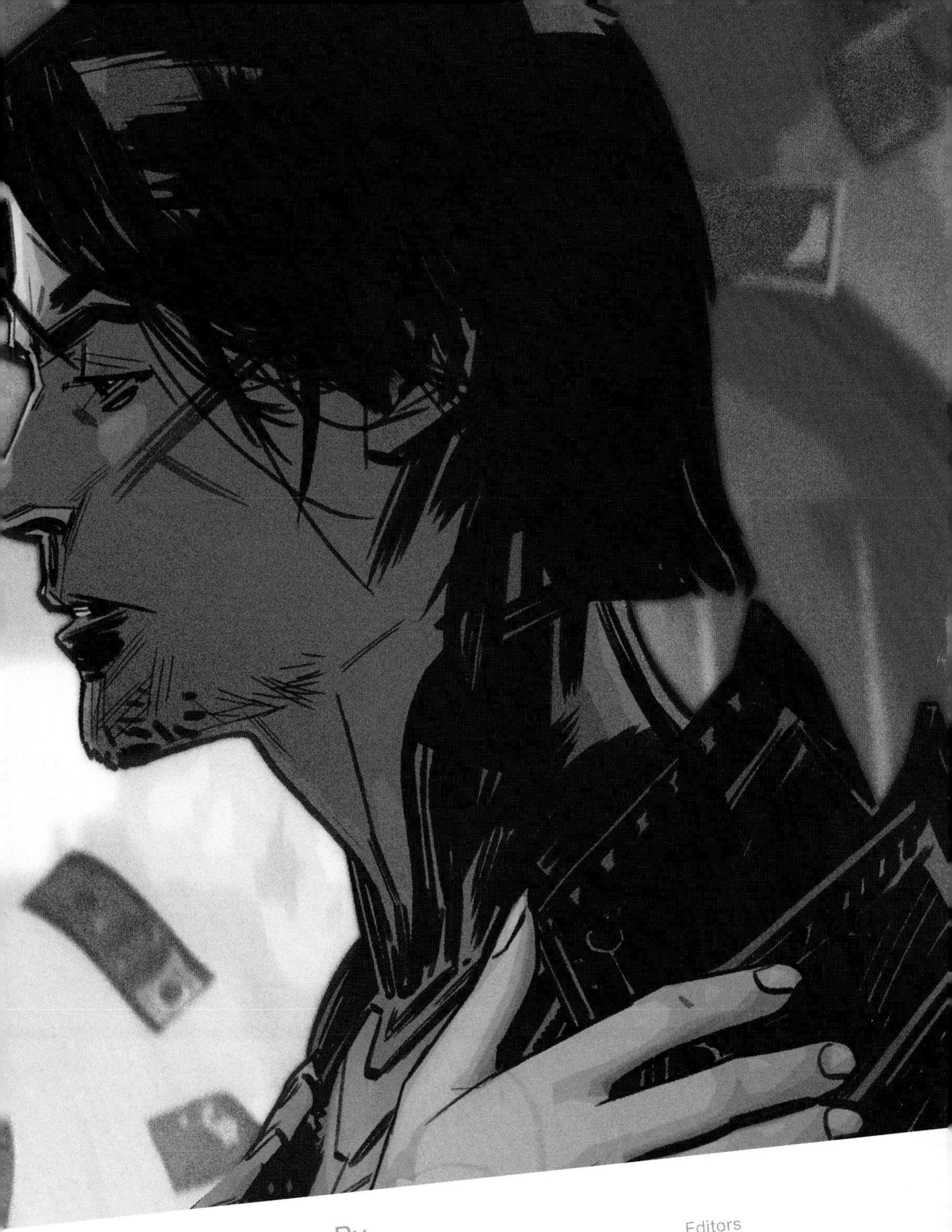

Created & Written By
MIKE CAREY

Art By
ELENA CASAGRANDE
(CHAPTERS 6-9)
JOËLLE JONES
(CHAPTER 5)

Colors By
ANDREW ELDER
(CHAPTERS 6-9)
EMILIO LOPEZ
(CHAPTER 5)

Letters By
ED DUKESHIRE

Cover By
TOMMY LEE EDWARDS

Trade Design By
EMI YONEMURA BROWN

Editors
DAFNA PLEBAN
MATT GAGNON

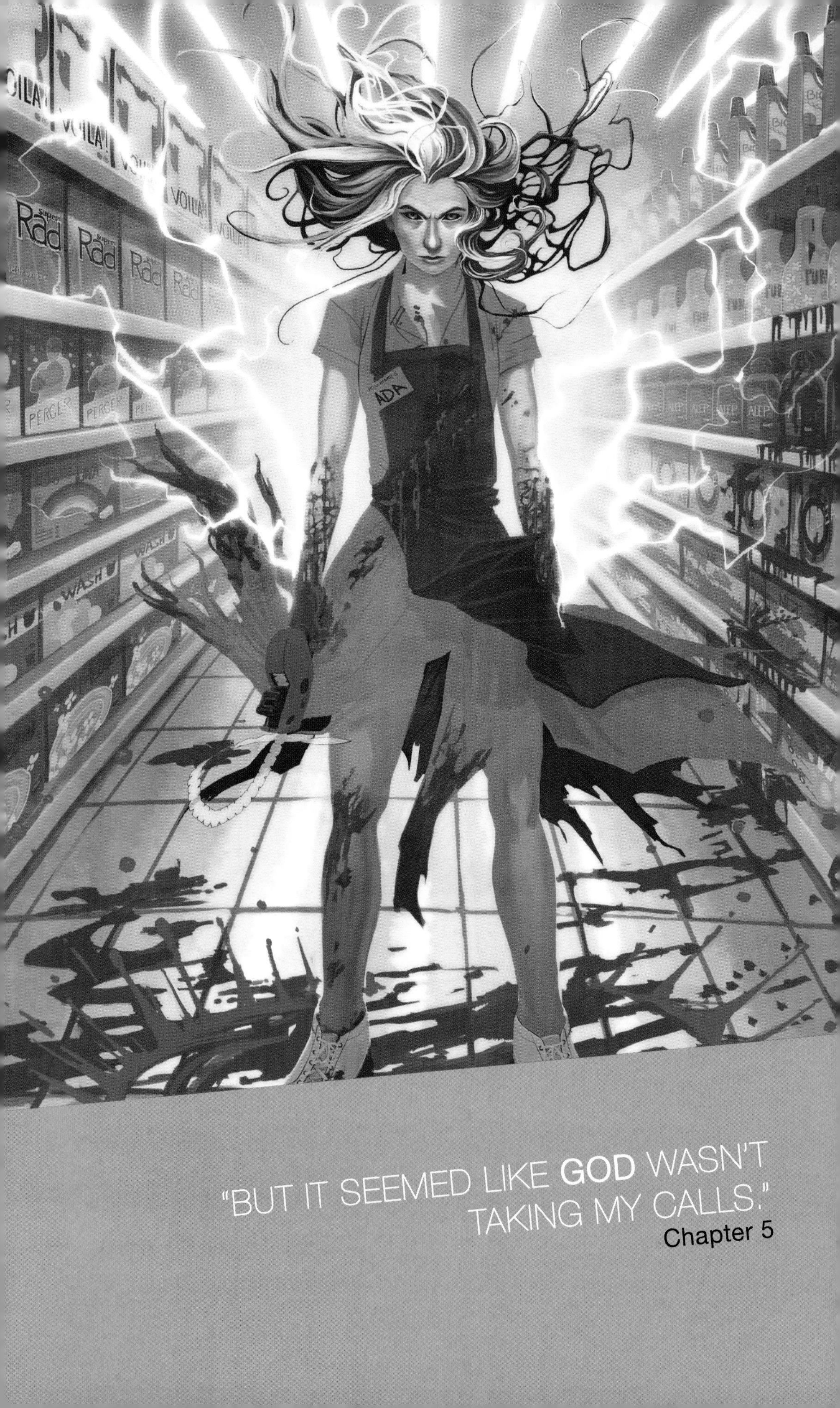
VOILA!
VOILA!
VOILA!
super Rad
Rad
Rad
Rad
PERGER
PERGER
PERGER
WASH
WASH
ALEP
ALEP
ALEP
ALEP
BIG
BIG
ADA

"BUT IT SEEMED LIKE **GOD** WASN'T TAKING MY CALLS."

Chapter 5

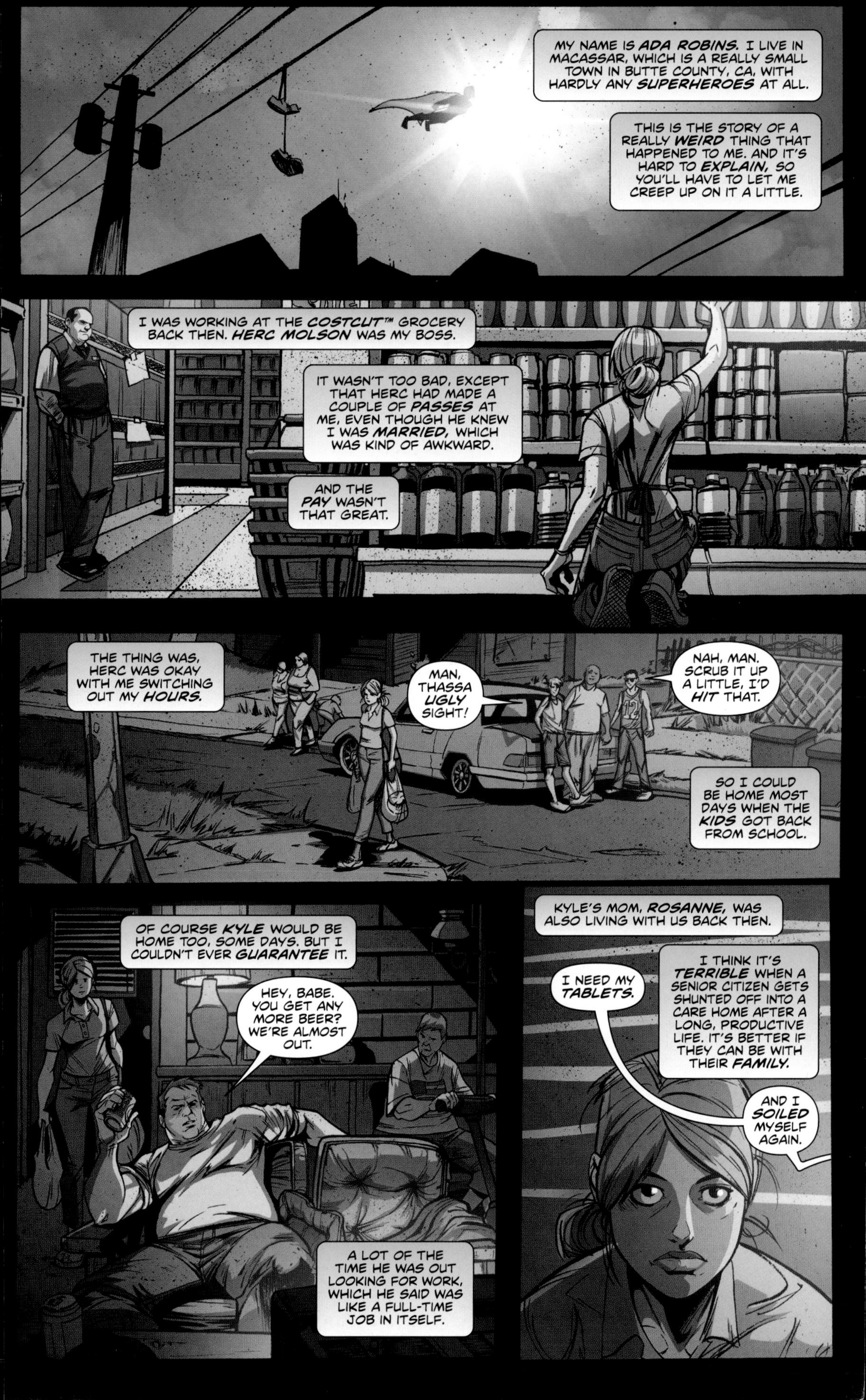
MY NAME IS ADA ROBINS. I LIVE IN MACASSAR, WHICH IS A REALLY SMALL TOWN IN BUTTE COUNTY, CA, WITH HARDLY ANY SUPERHEROES AT ALL.
THIS IS THE STORY OF A REALLY WEIRD THING THAT HAPPENED TO ME. AND IT'S HARD TO EXPLAIN, SO YOU'LL HAVE TO LET ME CREEP UP ON IT A LITTLE.
I WAS WORKING AT THE COSTCUT™ GROCERY BACK THEN. HERC MOLSON WAS MY BOSS.
IT WASN'T TOO BAD, EXCEPT THAT HERC HAD MADE A COUPLE OF PASSES AT ME, EVEN THOUGH HE KNEW I WAS MARRIED, WHICH WAS KIND OF AWKWARD.
AND THE PAY WASN'T THAT GREAT.
THE THING WAS, HERC WAS OKAY WITH ME SWITCHING OUT MY HOURS.
MAN, THASSA UGLY SIGHT!
NAH, MAN. SCRUB IT UP A LITTLE, I'D HIT THAT.
SO I COULD BE HOME MOST DAYS WHEN THE KIDS GOT BACK FROM SCHOOL.
OF COURSE KYLE WOULD BE HOME TOO, SOME DAYS. BUT I COULDN'T EVER GUARANTEE IT.
HEY, BABE. YOU GET ANY MORE BEER? WE'RE ALMOST OUT.
A LOT OF THE TIME HE WAS OUT LOOKING FOR WORK, WHICH HE SAID WAS LIKE A FULL-TIME JOB IN ITSELF.
KYLE'S MOM, ROSANNE, WAS ALSO LIVING WITH US BACK THEN.
I THINK IT'S TERRIBLE WHEN A SENIOR CITIZEN GETS SHUNTED OFF INTO A CARE HOME AFTER A LONG, PRODUCTIVE LIFE. IT'S BETTER IF THEY CAN BE WITH THEIR FAMILY.
I NEED MY TABLETS.
AND I SOILED MYSELF AGAIN.

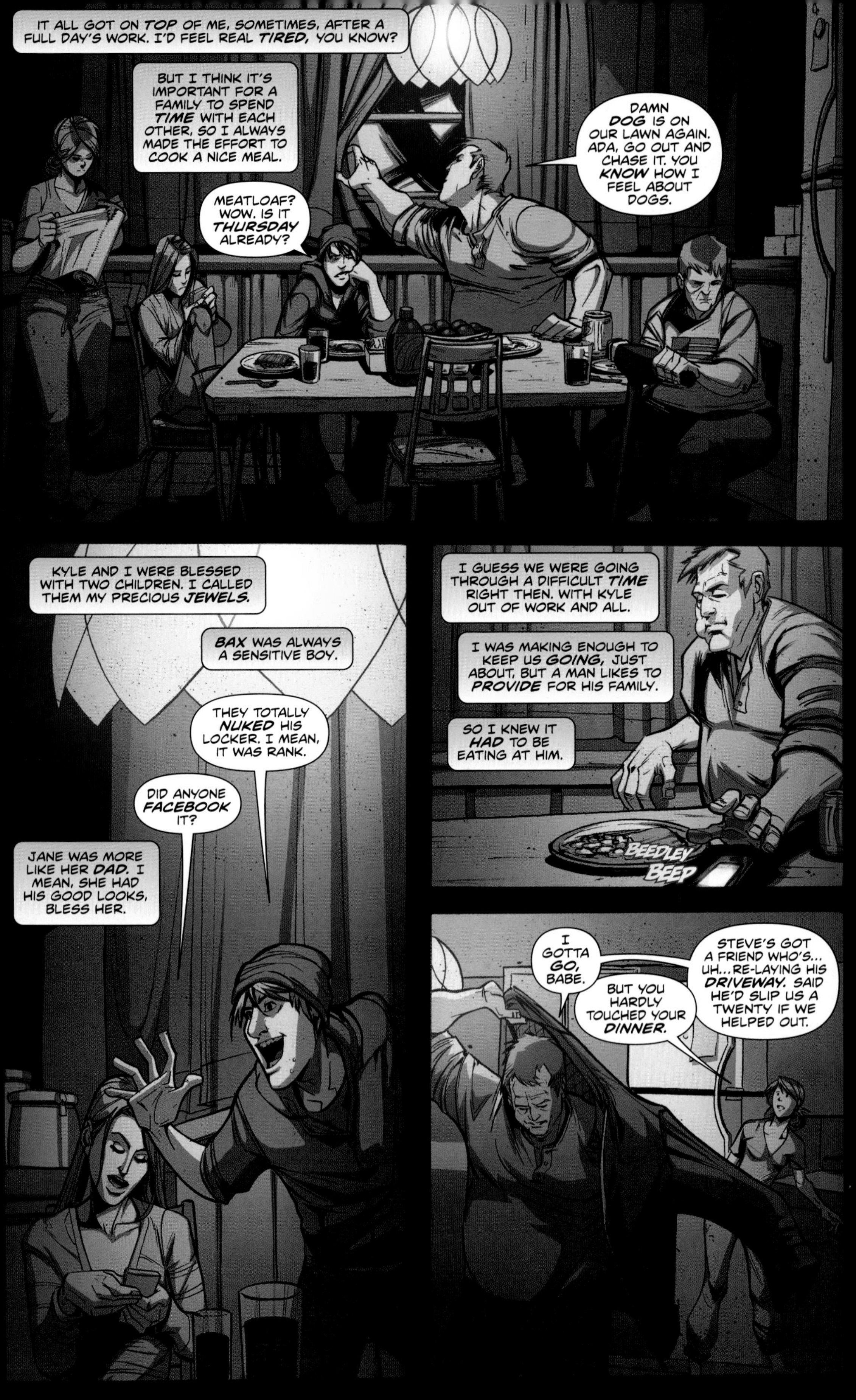

IT ALL GOT ON TOP OF ME, SOMETIMES, AFTER A FULL DAY'S WORK. I'D FEEL REAL TIRED, YOU KNOW?
BUT I THINK IT'S IMPORTANT FOR A FAMILY TO SPEND TIME WITH EACH OTHER, SO I ALWAYS MADE THE EFFORT TO COOK A NICE MEAL.
MEATLOAF? WOW. IS IT THURSDAY ALREADY?
DAMN DOG IS ON OUR LAWN AGAIN. ADA, GO OUT AND CHASE IT. YOU KNOW HOW I FEEL ABOUT DOGS.
KYLE AND I WERE BLESSED WITH TWO CHILDREN. I CALLED THEM MY PRECIOUS JEWELS.
BAX WAS ALWAYS A SENSITIVE BOY.
THEY TOTALLY NUKED HIS LOCKER. I MEAN, IT WAS RANK.
DID ANYONE FACEBOOK IT?
JANE WAS MORE LIKE HER DAD. I MEAN, SHE HAD HIS GOOD LOOKS, BLESS HER.
I GUESS WE WERE GOING THROUGH A DIFFICULT TIME RIGHT THEN. WITH KYLE OUT OF WORK AND ALL.
I WAS MAKING ENOUGH TO KEEP US GOING, JUST ABOUT, BUT A MAN LIKES TO PROVIDE FOR HIS FAMILY.
SO I KNEW IT HAD TO BE EATING AT HIM.
BEEDLEY BEEP
I GOTTA GO, BABE.
BUT YOU HARDLY TOUCHED YOUR DINNER.
STEVE'S GOT A FRIEND WHO'S... UH... RE-LAYING HIS DRIVEWAY. SAID HE'D SLIP US A TWENTY IF WE HELPED OUT.

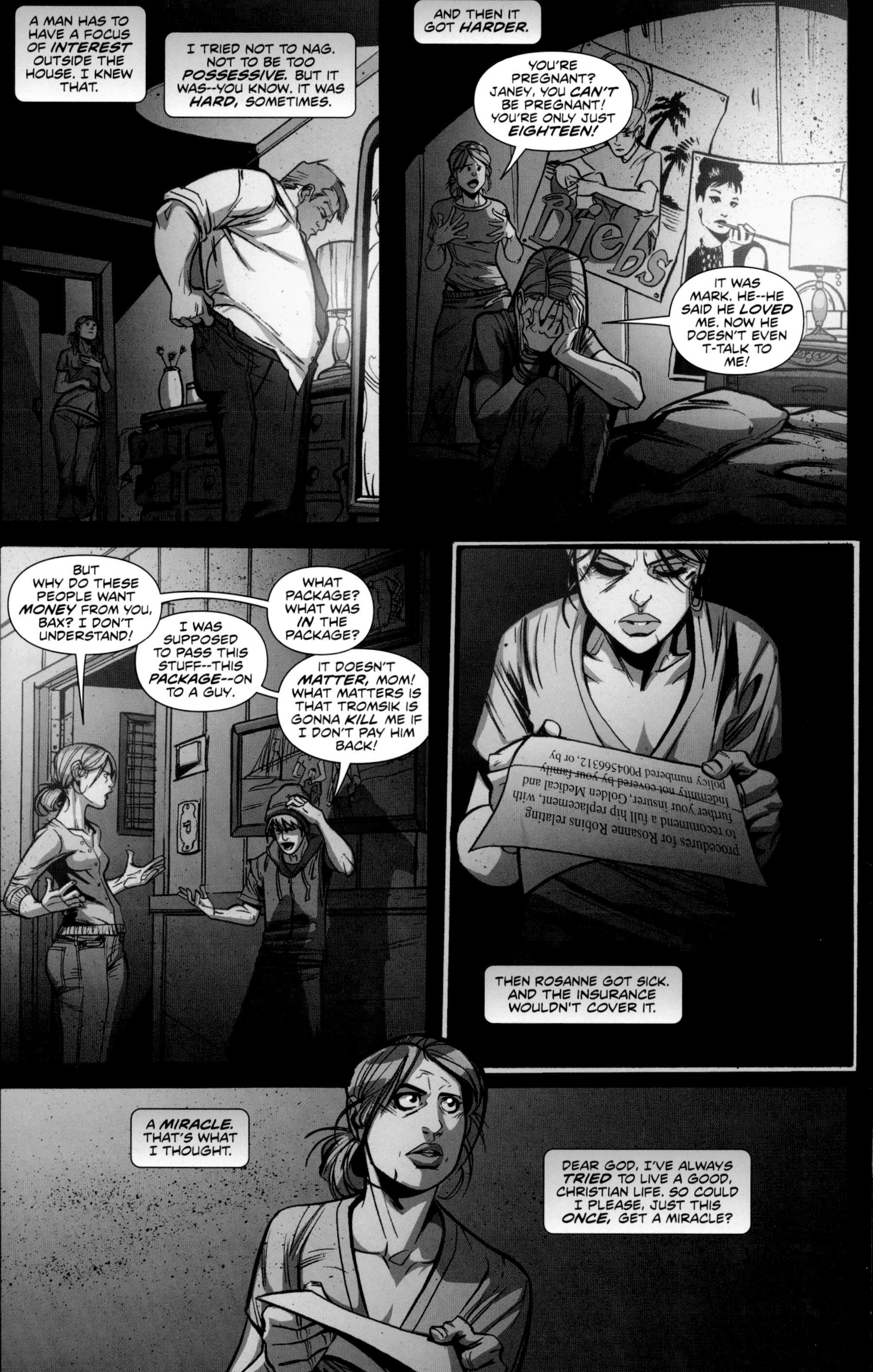
A MAN HAS TO HAVE A FOCUS OF INTEREST OUTSIDE THE HOUSE. I KNEW THAT.
I TRIED NOT TO NAG. NOT TO BE TOO POSSESSIVE. BUT IT WAS--YOU KNOW. IT WAS HARD, SOMETIMES.
AND THEN IT GOT HARDER.
YOU'RE PREGNANT? JANEY, YOU CAN'T BE PREGNANT! YOU'RE ONLY JUST EIGHTEEN!
Biebs
IT WAS MARK. HE--HE SAID HE LOVED ME. NOW HE DOESN'T EVEN T-TALK TO ME!
BUT WHY DO THESE PEOPLE WANT MONEY FROM YOU, BAX? I DON'T UNDERSTAND!
I WAS SUPPOSED TO PASS THIS STUFF--THIS PACKAGE--ON TO A GUY.
WHAT PACKAGE? WHAT WAS IN THE PACKAGE?
IT DOESN'T MATTER, MOM! WHAT MATTERS IS THAT TROMSIK IS GONNA KILL ME IF I DON'T PAY HIM BACK!
procedures for Rosanne Robins relating
to recommend a full hip replacement, with
further your insurer, Golden Medical and
Indemnity not covered by your family
policy numbered P004566312, or by
THEN ROSANNE GOT SICK. AND THE INSURANCE WOULDN'T COVER IT.
A MIRACLE. THAT'S WHAT I THOUGHT.
DEAR GOD, I'VE ALWAYS TRIED TO LIVE A GOOD, CHRISTIAN LIFE. SO COULD I PLEASE, JUST THIS ONCE, GET A MIRACLE?

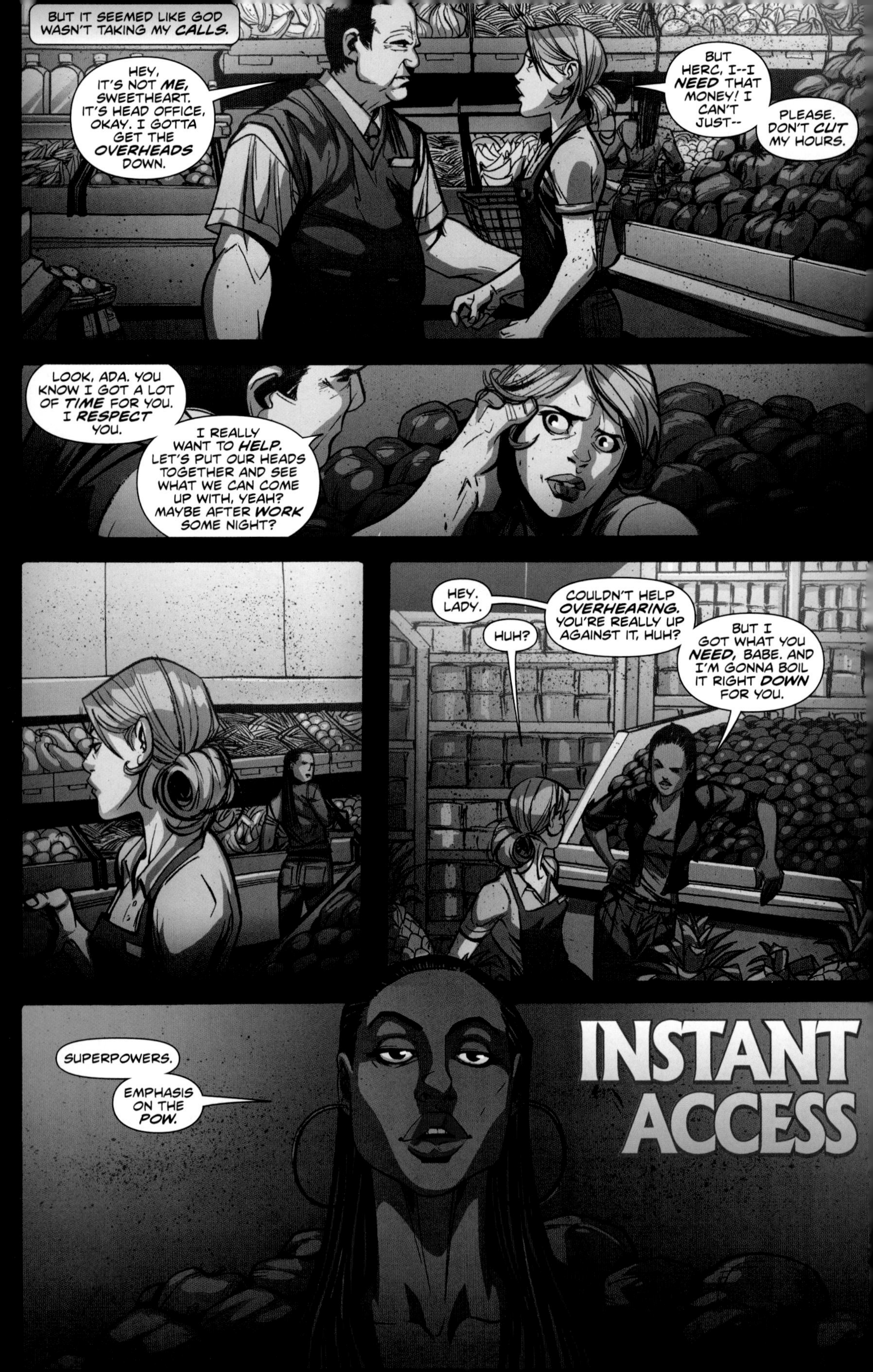
BUT IT SEEMED LIKE GOD WASN'T TAKING MY CALLS.
HEY, IT'S NOT ME, SWEETHEART. IT'S HEAD OFFICE, OKAY. I GOTTA GET THE OVERHEADS DOWN.
BUT HERC, I--I NEED THAT MONEY! I CAN'T JUST--
PLEASE. DON'T CUT MY HOURS.
LOOK, ADA. YOU KNOW I GOT A LOT OF TIME FOR YOU. I RESPECT YOU.
I REALLY WANT TO HELP. LET'S PUT OUR HEADS TOGETHER AND SEE WHAT WE CAN COME UP WITH, YEAH? MAYBE AFTER WORK SOME NIGHT?
HEY. LADY.
COULDN'T HELP OVERHEARING. YOU'RE REALLY UP AGAINST IT, HUH?
HUH?
BUT I GOT WHAT YOU NEED, BABE. AND I'M GONNA BOIL IT RIGHT DOWN FOR YOU.
SUPERPOWERS.
EMPHASIS ON THE POW.
INSTANT ACCESS

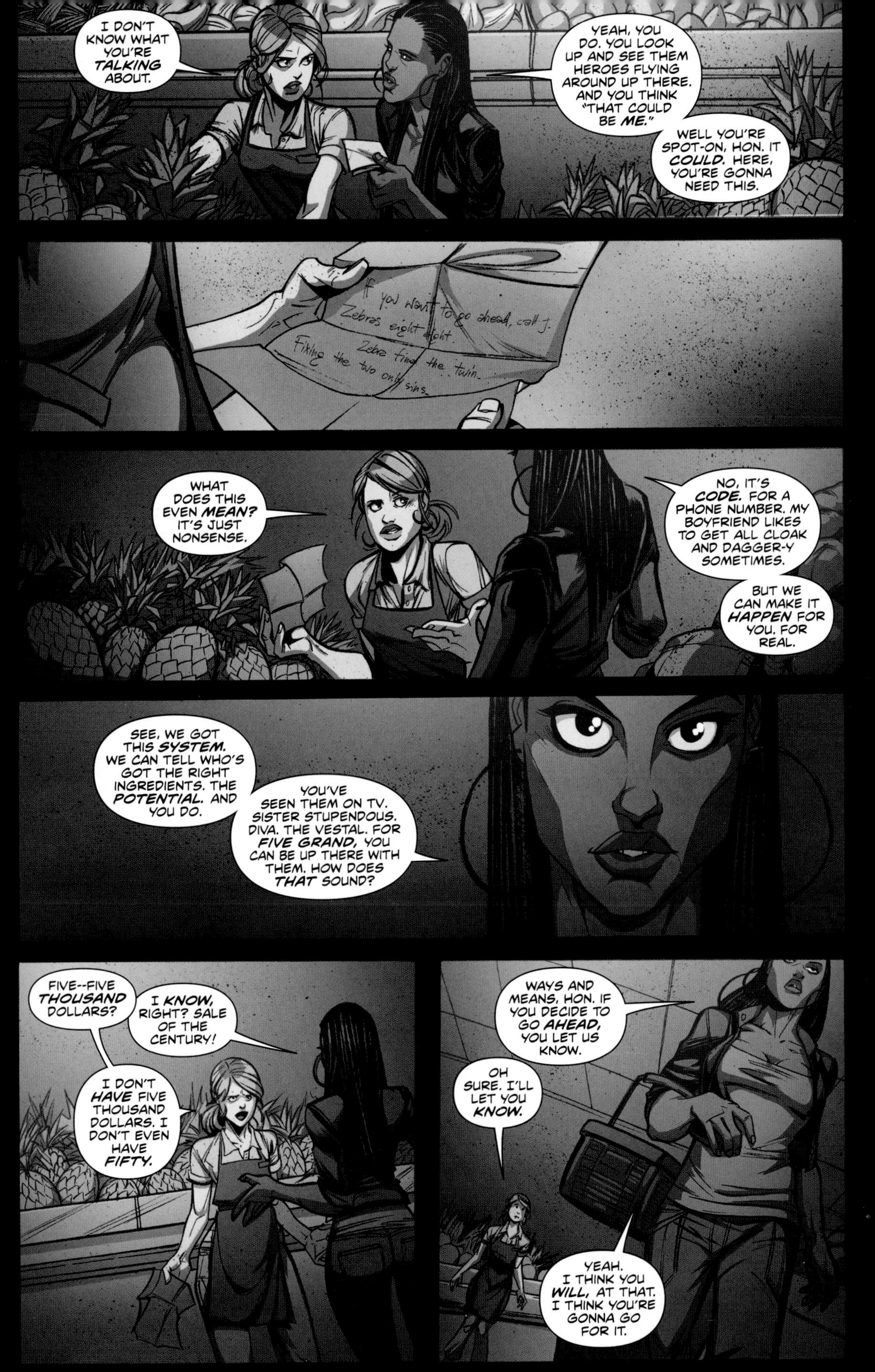
I DON'T KNOW WHAT YOU'RE TALKING ABOUT.
YEAH, YOU DO. YOU LOOK UP AND SEE THEM HEROES FLYING AROUND UP THERE. AND YOU THINK "THAT COULD BE ME."
WELL YOU'RE SPOT-ON, HON. IT COULD. HERE, YOU'RE GONNA NEED THIS.
If you want to go ahead, call J.
Zebras eight eight.
Zebra find the twin.
Fixing the two only sins.
WHAT DOES THIS EVEN MEAN? IT'S JUST NONSENSE.
NO, IT'S CODE. FOR A PHONE NUMBER. MY BOYFRIEND LIKES TO GET ALL CLOAK AND DAGGER-Y SOMETIMES.
BUT WE CAN MAKE IT HAPPEN FOR YOU. FOR REAL.
SEE, WE GOT THIS SYSTEM. WE CAN TELL WHO'S GOT THE RIGHT INGREDIENTS. THE POTENTIAL. AND YOU DO.
YOU'VE SEEN THEM ON TV. SISTER STUPENDOUS. DIVA. THE VESTAL. FOR FIVE GRAND, YOU CAN BE UP THERE WITH THEM. HOW DOES THAT SOUND?
FIVE--FIVE THOUSAND DOLLARS?
I KNOW, RIGHT? SALE OF THE CENTURY!
I DON'T HAVE FIVE THOUSAND DOLLARS. I DON'T EVEN HAVE FIFTY.
WAYS AND MEANS, HON. IF YOU DECIDE TO GO AHEAD, YOU LET US KNOW.
OH SURE. I'LL LET YOU KNOW.
YEAH. I THINK YOU WILL, AT THAT. I THINK YOU'RE GONNA GO FOR IT.

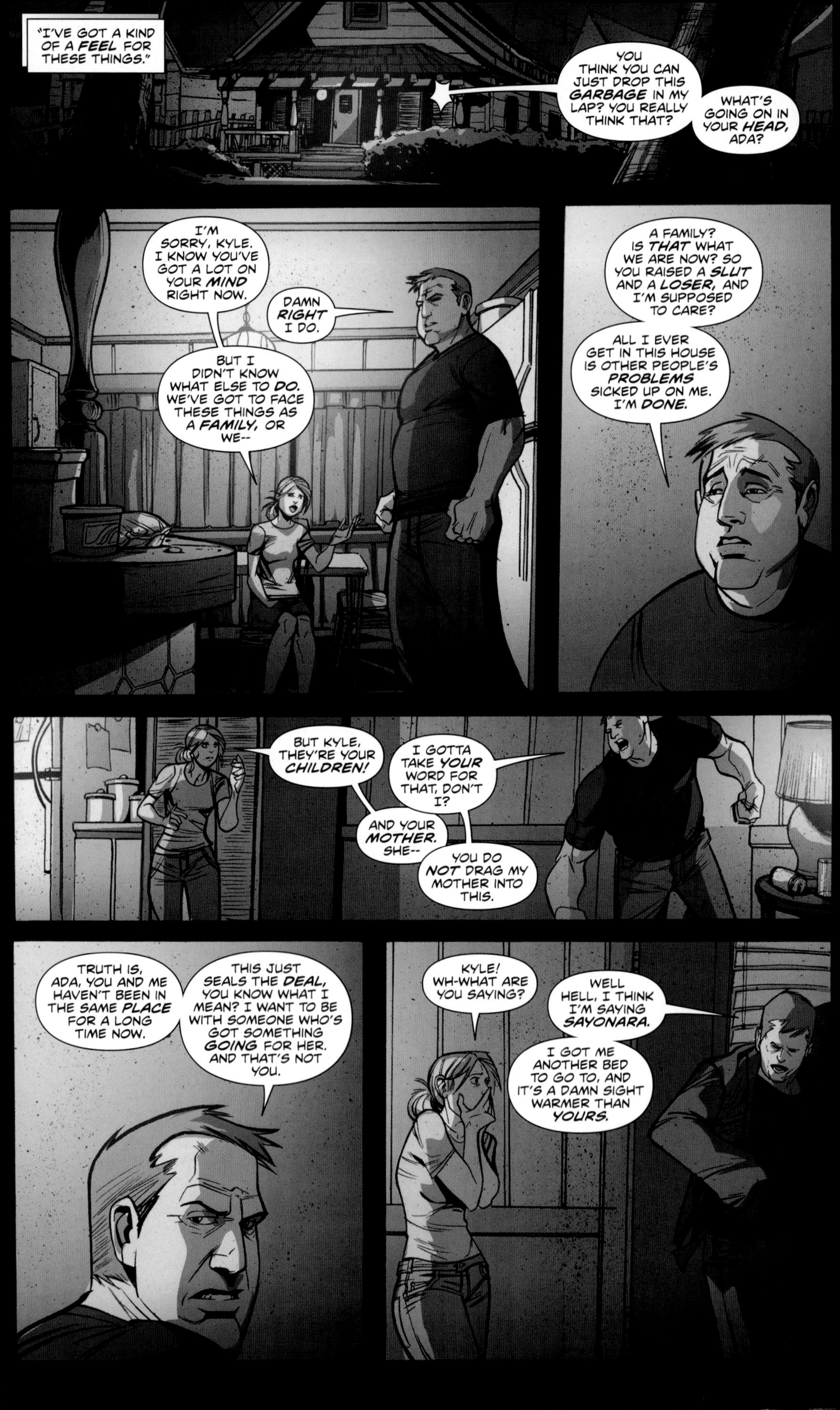
"I'VE GOT A KIND OF A FEEL FOR THESE THINGS."
YOU THINK YOU CAN JUST DROP THIS GARBAGE IN MY LAP? YOU REALLY THINK THAT?
WHAT'S GOING ON IN YOUR HEAD, ADA?
I'M SORRY, KYLE. I KNOW YOU'VE GOT A LOT ON YOUR MIND RIGHT NOW.
DAMN RIGHT I DO.
BUT I DIDN'T KNOW WHAT ELSE TO DO. WE'VE GOT TO FACE THESE THINGS AS A FAMILY, OR WE--
A FAMILY? IS THAT WHAT WE ARE NOW? SO YOU RAISED A SLUT AND A LOSER, AND I'M SUPPOSED TO CARE?
ALL I EVER GET IN THIS HOUSE IS OTHER PEOPLE'S PROBLEMS SICKED UP ON ME. I'M DONE.
BUT KYLE, THEY'RE YOUR CHILDREN!
I GOTTA TAKE YOUR WORD FOR THAT, DON'T I?
AND YOUR MOTHER. SHE--
YOU DO NOT DRAG MY MOTHER INTO THIS.
TRUTH IS, ADA, YOU AND ME HAVEN'T BEEN IN THE SAME PLACE FOR A LONG TIME NOW.
THIS JUST SEALS THE DEAL, YOU KNOW WHAT I MEAN? I WANT TO BE WITH SOMEONE WHO'S GOT SOMETHING GOING FOR HER. AND THAT'S NOT YOU.
KYLE! WH-WHAT ARE YOU SAYING?
WELL HELL, I THINK I'M SAYING SAYONARA.
I GOT ME ANOTHER BED TO GO TO, AND IT'S A DAMN SIGHT WARMER THAN YOURS.

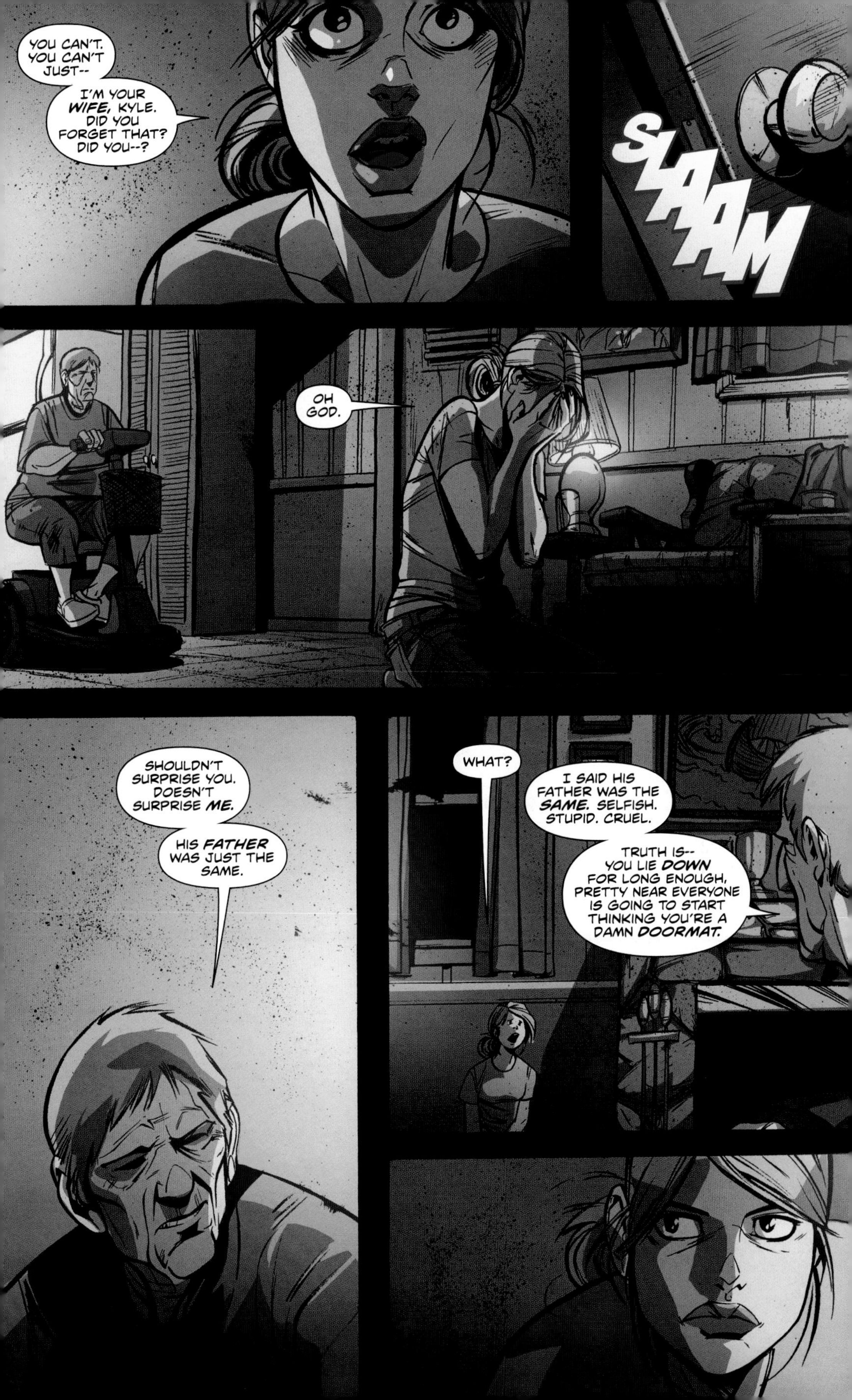

YOU CAN'T. YOU CAN'T JUST--
I'M YOUR WIFE, KYLE. DID YOU FORGET THAT? DID YOU--?
SLAAAM
OH GOD.
SHOULDN'T SURPRISE YOU. DOESN'T SURPRISE ME.
HIS FATHER WAS JUST THE SAME.
WHAT?
I SAID HIS FATHER WAS THE SAME. SELFISH. STUPID. CRUEL.
TRUTH IS-- YOU LIE DOWN FOR LONG ENOUGH, PRETTY NEAR EVERYONE IS GOING TO START THINKING YOU'RE A DAMN DOORMAT.

I HAD A LITTLE **MONEY** PUT AWAY. LESS THAN I THOUGHT, AS IT TURNED OUT, BUT SOME.

AND ROSANNE HAD SEVEN HUNDRED BUCKS IN HER **FUNERAL** FUND. SHE SAID I COULD TAKE IT. SAID IF SHE HAD TO GET BURIED IN A CARDBOARD **BOX**, SHE DIDN'T THINK IT WOULD TROUBLE HER ANY.

WITH NEXT MONTH'S **RENT**, THAT GOT ME TO TWENTY TWO HUNDRED. NOT EVEN **CLOSE**.

SO I TOOK ALL THE CASH CARDS AND THE CREDIT CARDS OUT FOR A LITTLE **EXERCISE**. MOST OF THEM WERE DEAD OR BLOCKED, BUT I GOT **LUCKY** ON A COUPLE.

A GRAND HERE, A COUPLE OF HUNDRED THERE, IT ALL ADDS **UP**.

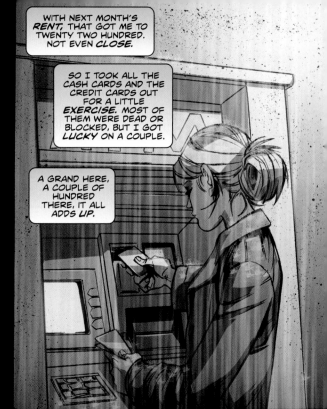

SPECIFICALLY--

--IT ADDS UP TO **$4623.17**.

HERC, I NEED AN **ADVANCE** ON MY NEXT PAY CHECK.

OH YEAH?

WELL, I GOT **NEEDS** TOO, ADA.

YES. I KNOW.

IT WASN'T EVEN THAT **BAD**, REALLY.

IT WAS JUST THAT I COULDN'T GET **CLEAN** AFTERWARDS. NOT PROPERLY.

NOT EVEN WITH **BLEACH**.

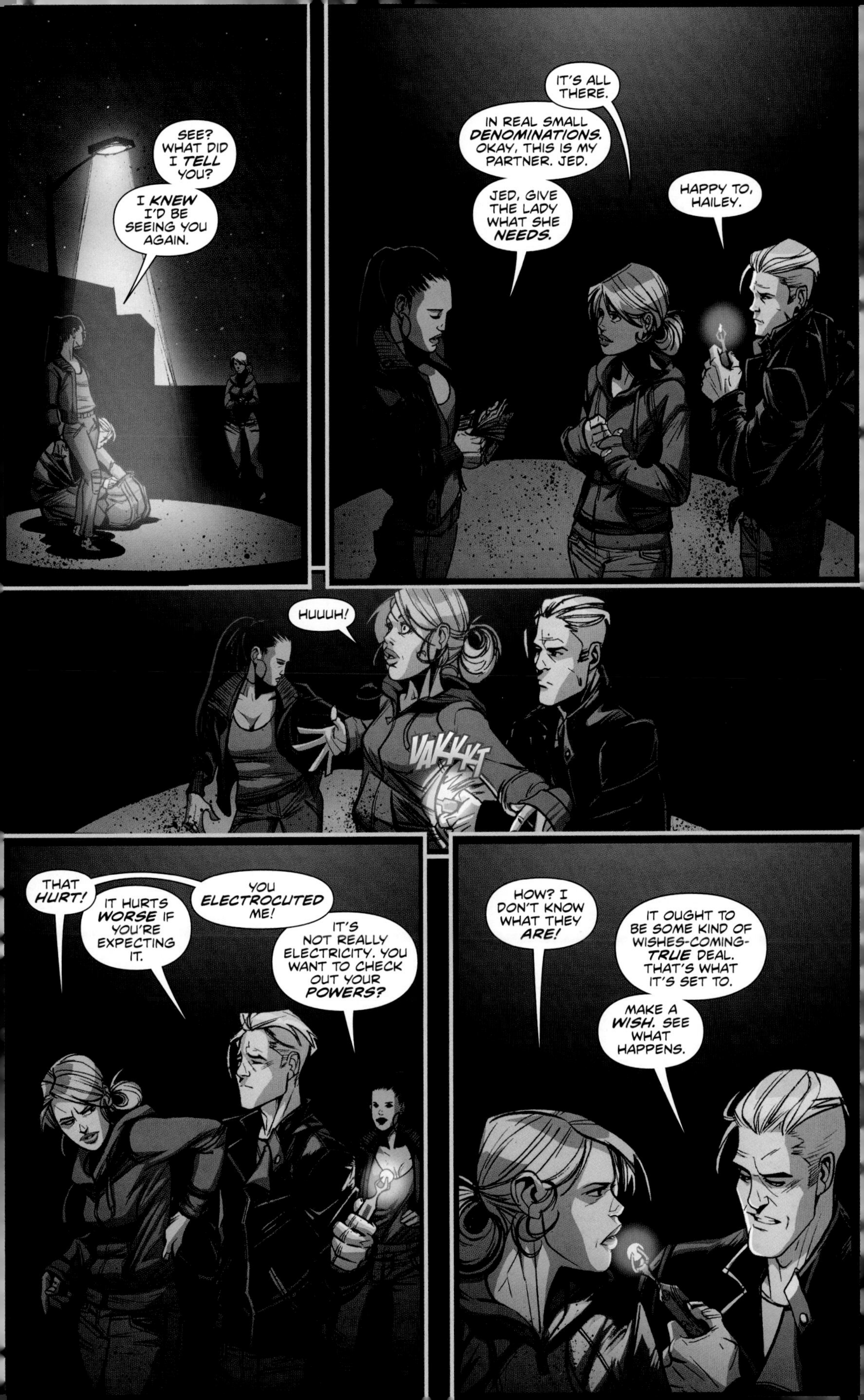
SEE? WHAT DID I TELL YOU?
I KNEW I'D BE SEEING YOU AGAIN.
IT'S ALL THERE.
IN REAL SMALL DENOMINATIONS. OKAY, THIS IS MY PARTNER. JED.
JED, GIVE THE LADY WHAT SHE NEEDS.
HAPPY TO, HAILEY.
HUUUH!
VAKKKT
THAT HURT!
YOU ELECTROCUTED ME!
IT HURTS WORSE IF YOU'RE EXPECTING IT.
IT'S NOT REALLY ELECTRICITY. YOU WANT TO CHECK OUT YOUR POWERS?
HOW? I DON'T KNOW WHAT THEY ARE!
IT OUGHT TO BE SOME KIND OF WISHES-COMING-TRUE DEAL. THAT'S WHAT IT'S SET TO.
MAKE A WISH. SEE WHAT HAPPENS.

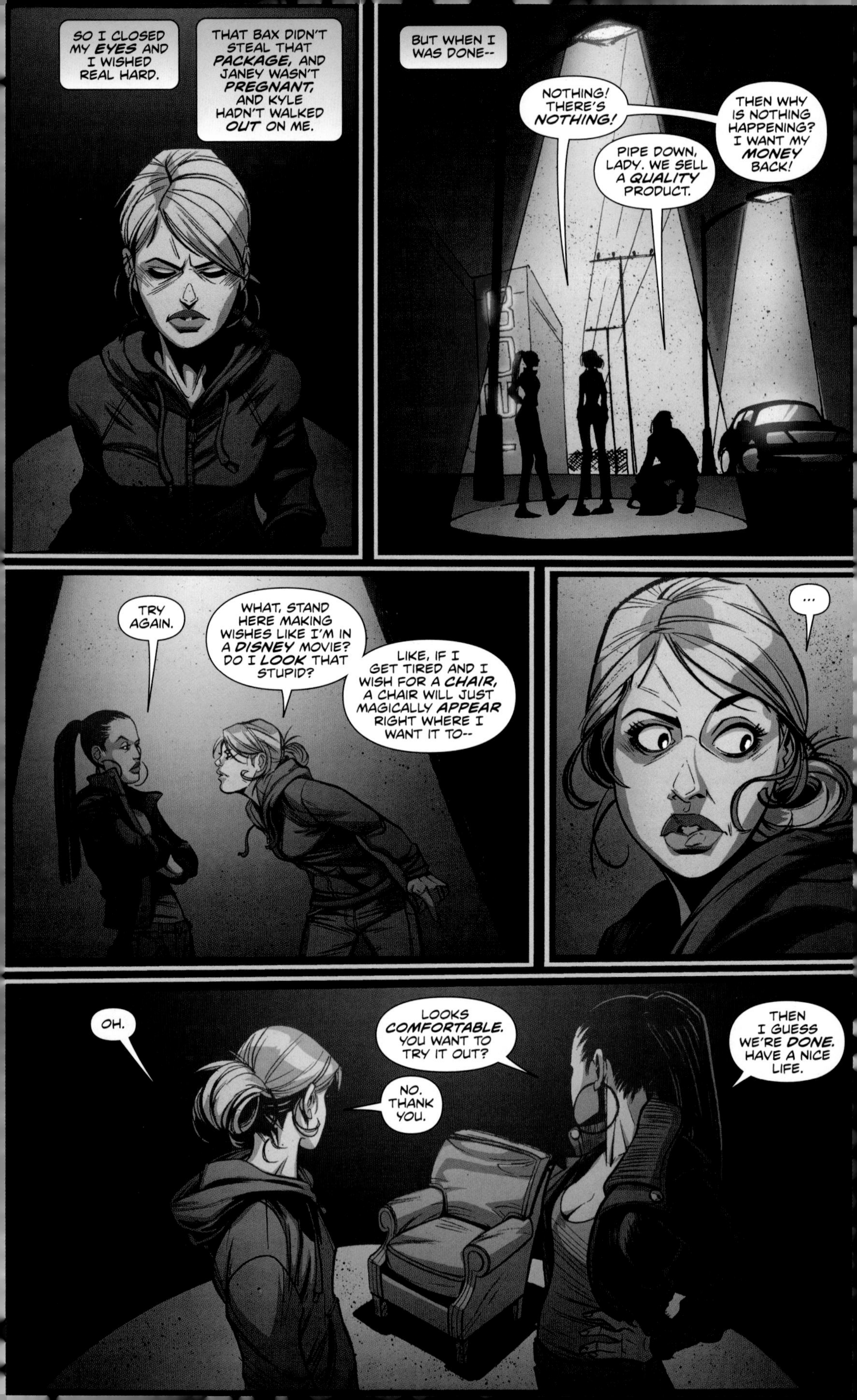
SO I CLOSED MY EYES AND I WISHED REAL HARD.
THAT BAX DIDN'T STEAL THAT PACKAGE, AND JANEY WASN'T PREGNANT, AND KYLE HADN'T WALKED OUT ON ME.
BUT WHEN I WAS DONE--
NOTHING! THERE'S NOTHING!
THEN WHY IS NOTHING HAPPENING? I WANT MY MONEY BACK!
PIPE DOWN, LADY. WE SELL A QUALITY PRODUCT.
TRY AGAIN.
WHAT, STAND HERE MAKING WISHES LIKE I'M IN A DISNEY MOVIE? DO I LOOK THAT STUPID?
LIKE, IF I GET TIRED AND I WISH FOR A CHAIR, A CHAIR WILL JUST MAGICALLY APPEAR RIGHT WHERE I WANT IT TO--
...
OH.
LOOKS COMFORTABLE. YOU WANT TO TRY IT OUT?
NO. THANK YOU.
THEN I GUESS WE'RE DONE. HAVE A NICE LIFE.

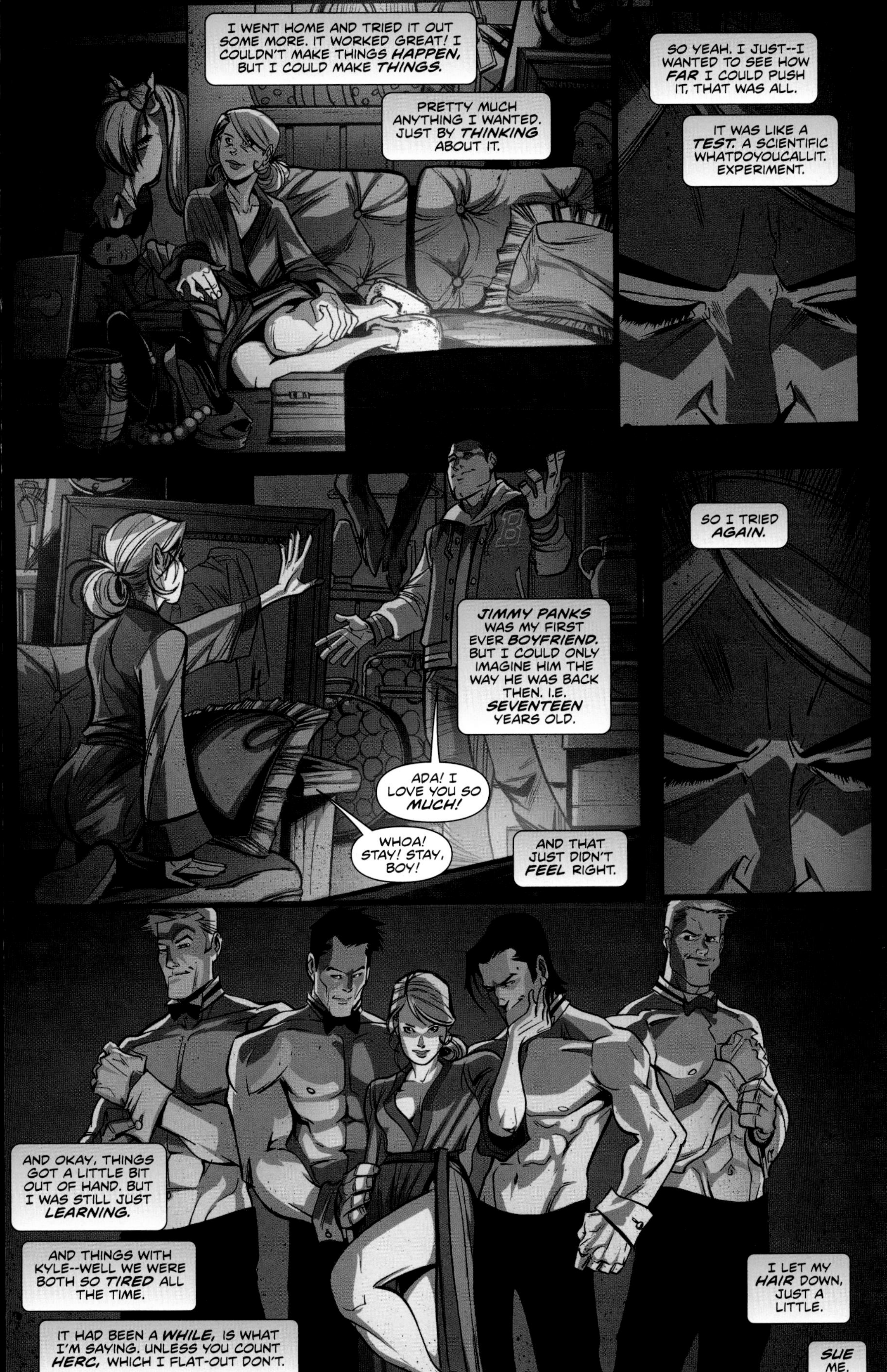

I WENT HOME AND TRIED IT OUT SOME MORE. IT WORKED GREAT! I COULDN'T MAKE THINGS *HAPPEN,* BUT I COULD MAKE *THINGS.*
PRETTY MUCH ANYTHING I WANTED. JUST BY *THINKING* ABOUT IT.
SO YEAH. I JUST--I WANTED TO SEE HOW *FAR* I COULD PUSH IT, THAT WAS ALL.
IT WAS LIKE A *TEST.* A SCIENTIFIC WHATDOYOUCALLIT. EXPERIMENT.
JIMMY PANKS WAS MY FIRST EVER *BOYFRIEND.* BUT I COULD ONLY IMAGINE HIM THE WAY HE WAS BACK THEN. I.E. *SEVENTEEN* YEARS OLD.
ADA! I LOVE YOU SO *MUCH!*
WHOA! STAY! STAY, BOY!
AND THAT JUST DIDN'T *FEEL* RIGHT.
SO I TRIED *AGAIN.*
AND OKAY, THINGS GOT A LITTLE BIT OUT OF HAND. BUT I WAS STILL JUST *LEARNING.*
AND THINGS WITH KYLE--WELL WE WERE BOTH SO *TIRED* ALL THE TIME.
IT HAD BEEN A *WHILE,* IS WHAT I'M SAYING. UNLESS YOU COUNT *HERC,* WHICH I FLAT-OUT DON'T.
I LET MY *HAIR* DOWN, JUST A LITTLE.
SUE ME.

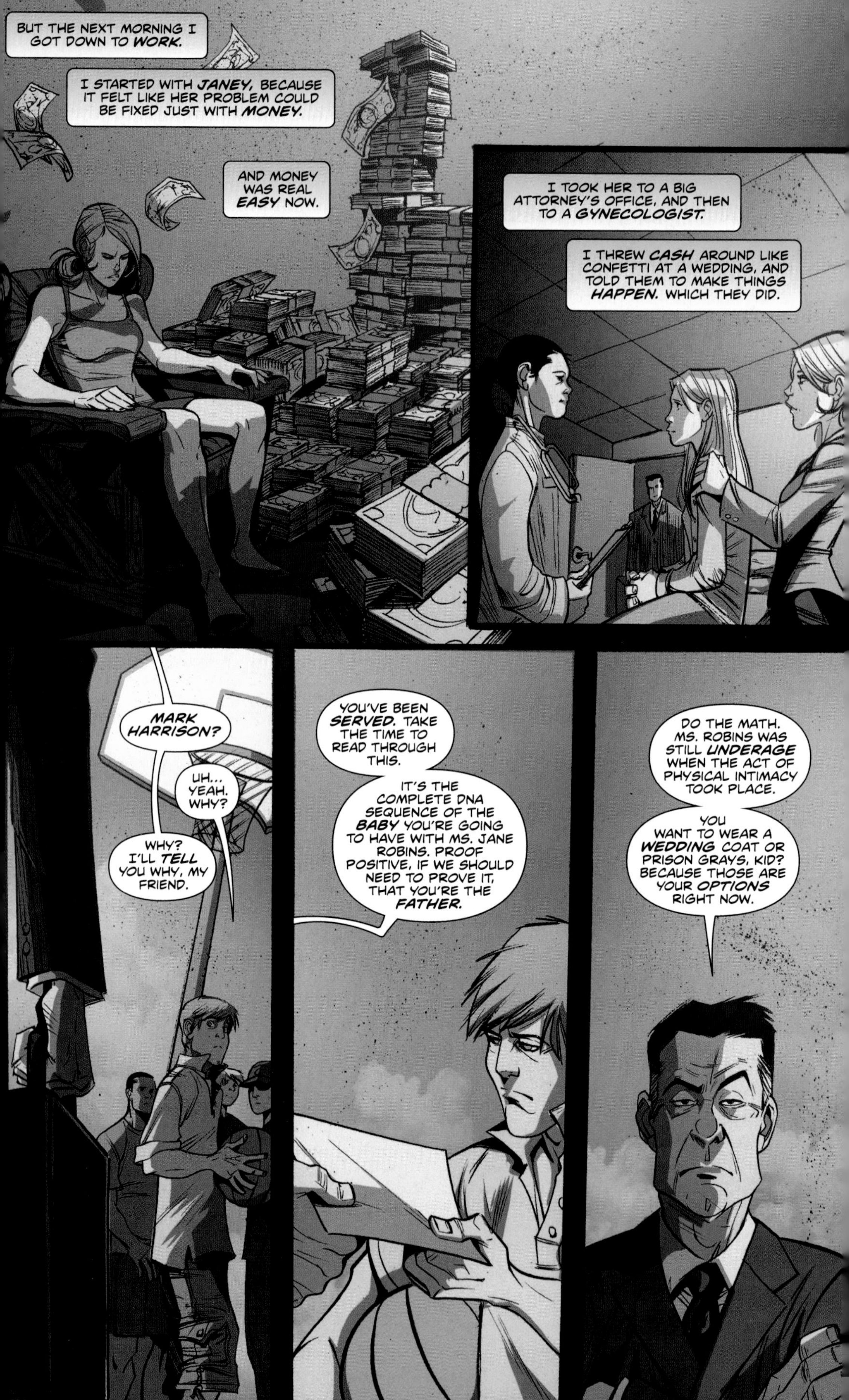
BUT THE NEXT MORNING I GOT DOWN TO WORK.
I STARTED WITH JANEY, BECAUSE IT FELT LIKE HER PROBLEM COULD BE FIXED JUST WITH MONEY.
AND MONEY WAS REAL EASY NOW.
I TOOK HER TO A BIG ATTORNEY'S OFFICE, AND THEN TO A GYNECOLOGIST.
I THREW CASH AROUND LIKE CONFETTI AT A WEDDING, AND TOLD THEM TO MAKE THINGS HAPPEN. WHICH THEY DID.
MARK HARRISON?
UH... YEAH. WHY?
WHY? I'LL TELL YOU WHY, MY FRIEND.
YOU'VE BEEN SERVED. TAKE THE TIME TO READ THROUGH THIS.
IT'S THE COMPLETE DNA SEQUENCE OF THE BABY YOU'RE GOING TO HAVE WITH MS. JANE ROBINS. PROOF POSITIVE, IF WE SHOULD NEED TO PROVE IT, THAT YOU'RE THE FATHER.
DO THE MATH. MS. ROBINS WAS STILL UNDERAGE WHEN THE ACT OF PHYSICAL INTIMACY TOOK PLACE.
YOU WANT TO WEAR A WEDDING COAT OR PRISON GRAYS, KID? BECAUSE THOSE ARE YOUR OPTIONS RIGHT NOW.

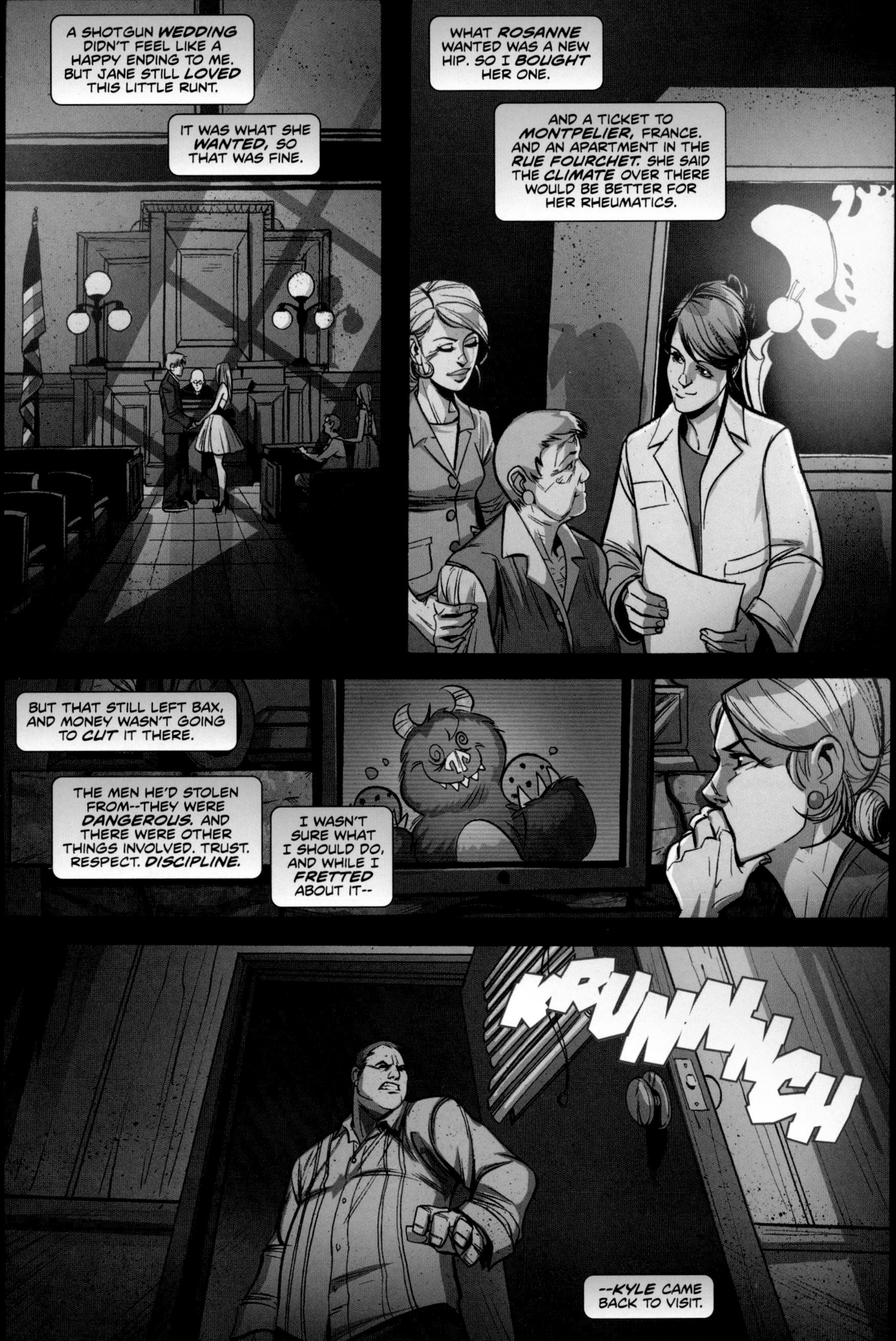
A SHOTGUN WEDDING DIDN'T FEEL LIKE A HAPPY ENDING TO ME. BUT JANE STILL LOVED THIS LITTLE RUNT.
IT WAS WHAT SHE WANTED, SO THAT WAS FINE.
WHAT ROSANNE WANTED WAS A NEW HIP. SO I BOUGHT HER ONE.
AND A TICKET TO MONTPELIER, FRANCE. AND AN APARTMENT IN THE RUE FOURCHET. SHE SAID THE CLIMATE OVER THERE WOULD BE BETTER FOR HER RHEUMATICS.
BUT THAT STILL LEFT BAX, AND MONEY WASN'T GOING TO CUT IT THERE.
THE MEN HE'D STOLEN FROM--THEY WERE DANGEROUS. AND THERE WERE OTHER THINGS INVOLVED. TRUST. RESPECT. DISCIPLINE.
I WASN'T SURE WHAT I SHOULD DO, AND WHILE I FRETTED ABOUT IT--
KRUNNNCH
--KYLE CAME BACK TO VISIT.

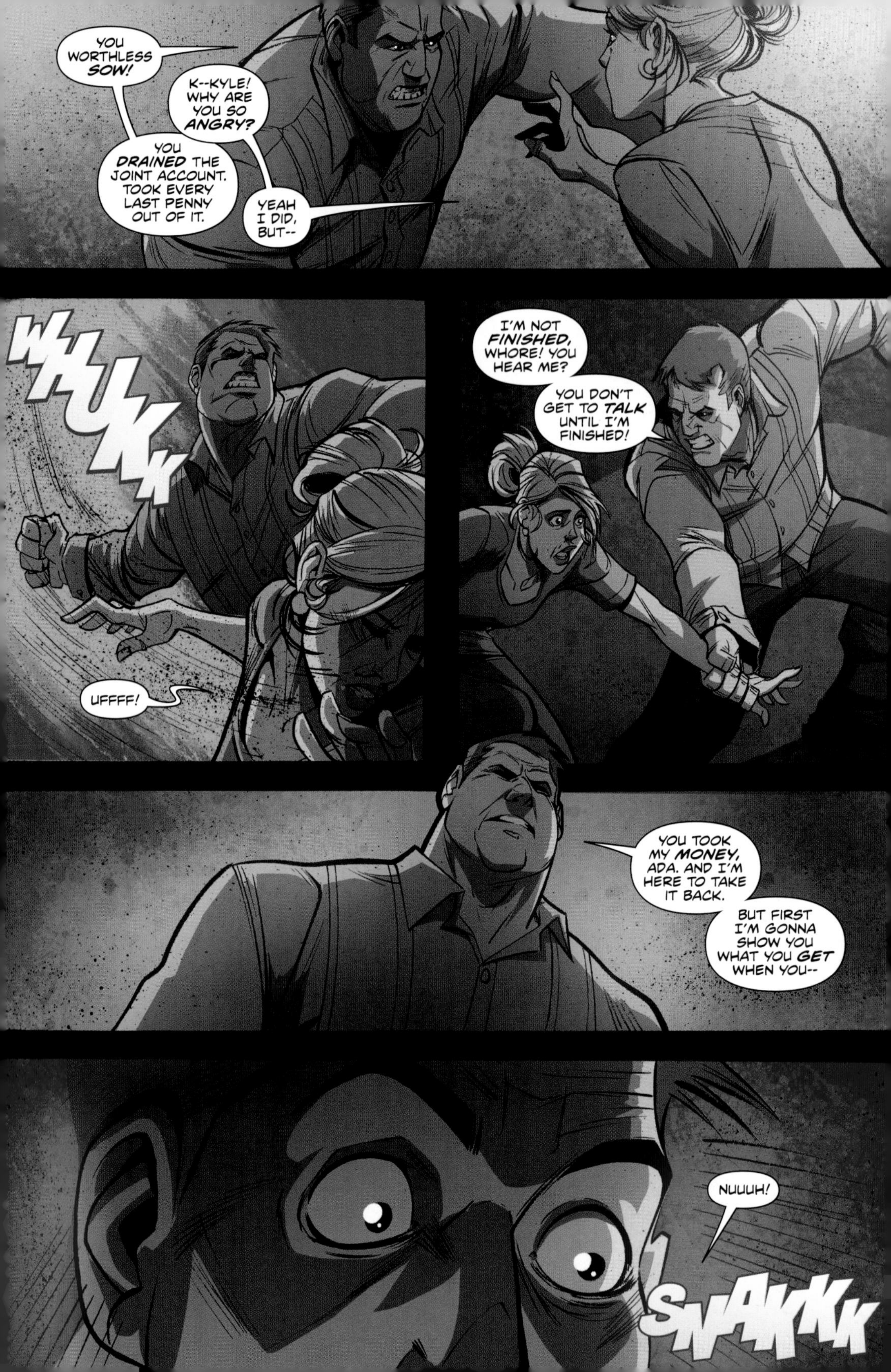
YOU WORTHLESS SOW!
K--KYLE! WHY ARE YOU SO ANGRY?
YOU DRAINED THE JOINT ACCOUNT. TOOK EVERY LAST PENNY OUT OF IT.
YEAH I DID, BUT--
WHUKK
UFFFF!
I'M NOT FINISHED, WHORE! YOU HEAR ME?
YOU DON'T GET TO TALK UNTIL I'M FINISHED!
YOU TOOK MY MONEY, ADA. AND I'M HERE TO TAKE IT BACK.
BUT FIRST I'M GONNA SHOW YOU WHAT YOU GET WHEN YOU--
NUUUH!
SNAKKK

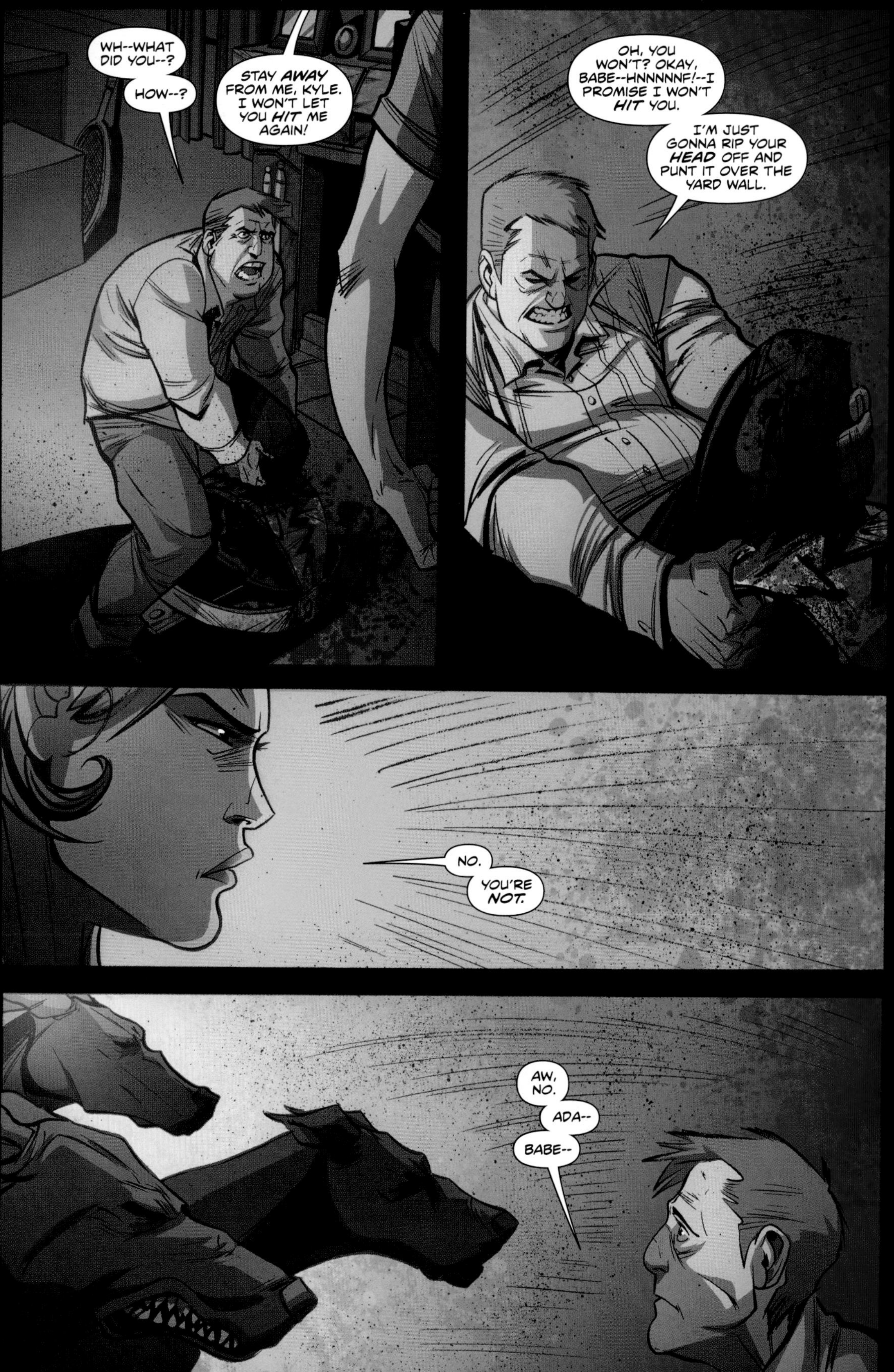
WH--WHAT DID YOU--?
HOW--?
STAY AWAY FROM ME, KYLE. I WON'T LET YOU HIT ME AGAIN!
OH, YOU WON'T? OKAY, BABE--HNNNNNF!--I PROMISE I WON'T HIT YOU.
I'M JUST GONNA RIP YOUR HEAD OFF AND PUNT IT OVER THE YARD WALL.
NO.
YOU'RE NOT.
AW, NO.
ADA--
BABE--

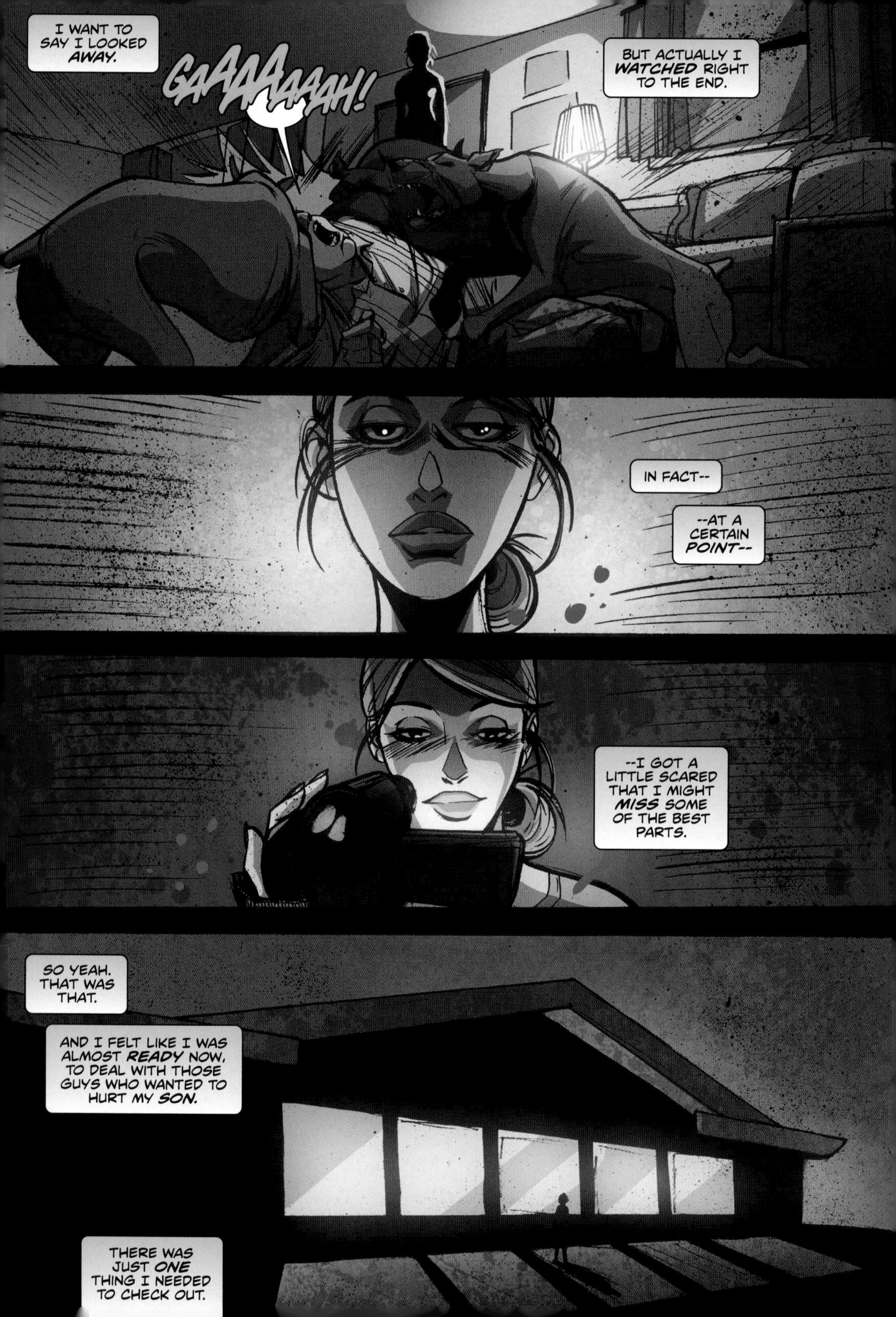
I WANT TO SAY I LOOKED AWAY.
GAAAAAAAAH!
BUT ACTUALLY I WATCHED RIGHT TO THE END.
IN FACT--
--AT A CERTAIN POINT--
--I GOT A LITTLE SCARED THAT I MIGHT MISS SOME OF THE BEST PARTS.
SO YEAH. THAT WAS THAT.
AND I FELT LIKE I WAS ALMOST READY NOW, TO DEAL WITH THOSE GUYS WHO WANTED TO HURT MY SON.
THERE WAS JUST ONE THING I NEEDED TO CHECK OUT.

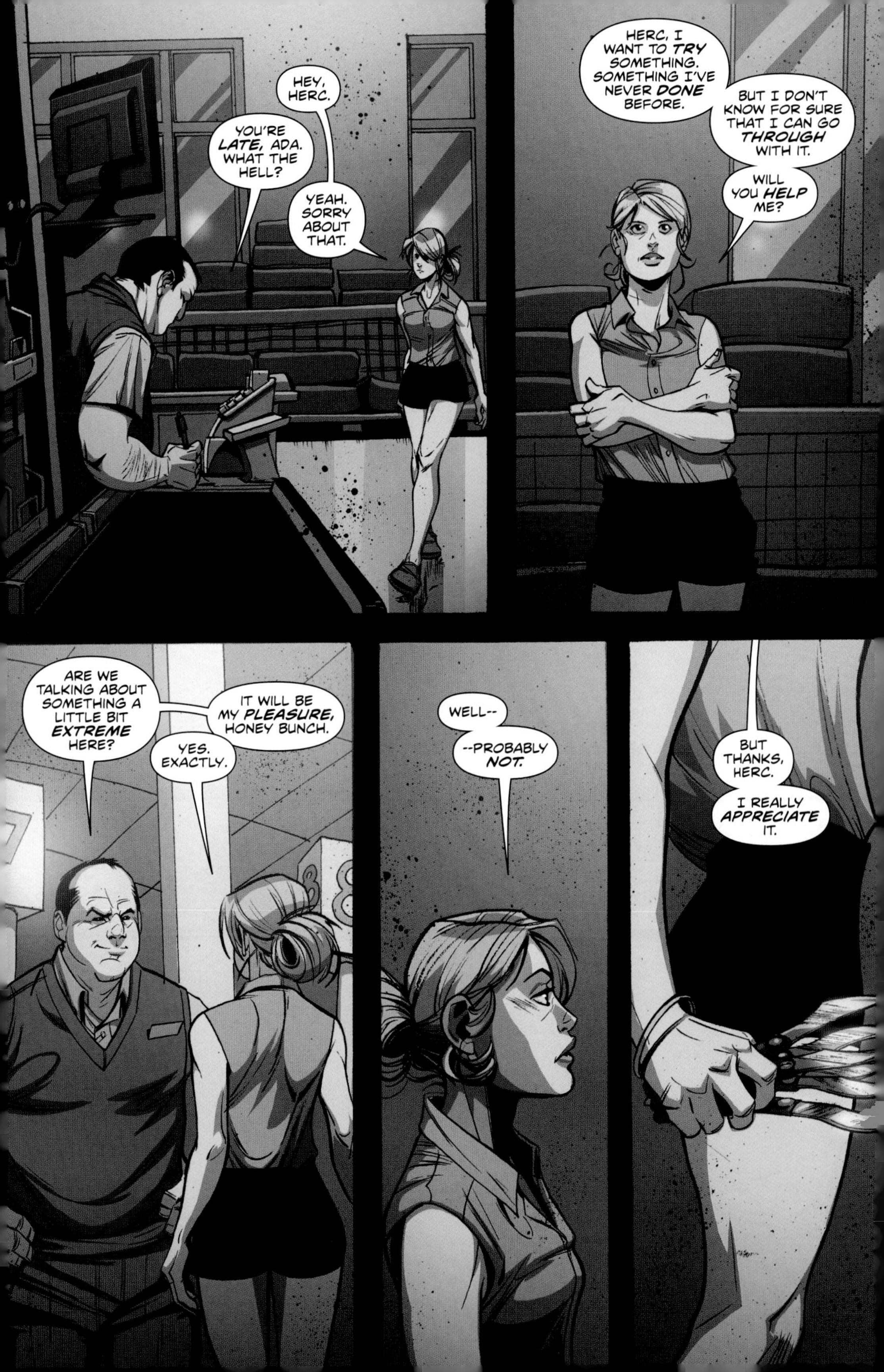
HEY, HERC.
YOU'RE LATE, ADA. WHAT THE HELL?
YEAH. SORRY ABOUT THAT.
HERC, I WANT TO TRY SOMETHING. SOMETHING I'VE NEVER DONE BEFORE.
BUT I DON'T KNOW FOR SURE THAT I CAN GO THROUGH WITH IT.
WILL YOU HELP ME?
ARE WE TALKING ABOUT SOMETHING A LITTLE BIT EXTREME HERE?
YES. EXACTLY.
IT WILL BE MY PLEASURE, HONEY BUNCH.
WELL--
--PROBABLY NOT.
BUT THANKS, HERC.
I REALLY APPRECIATE IT.

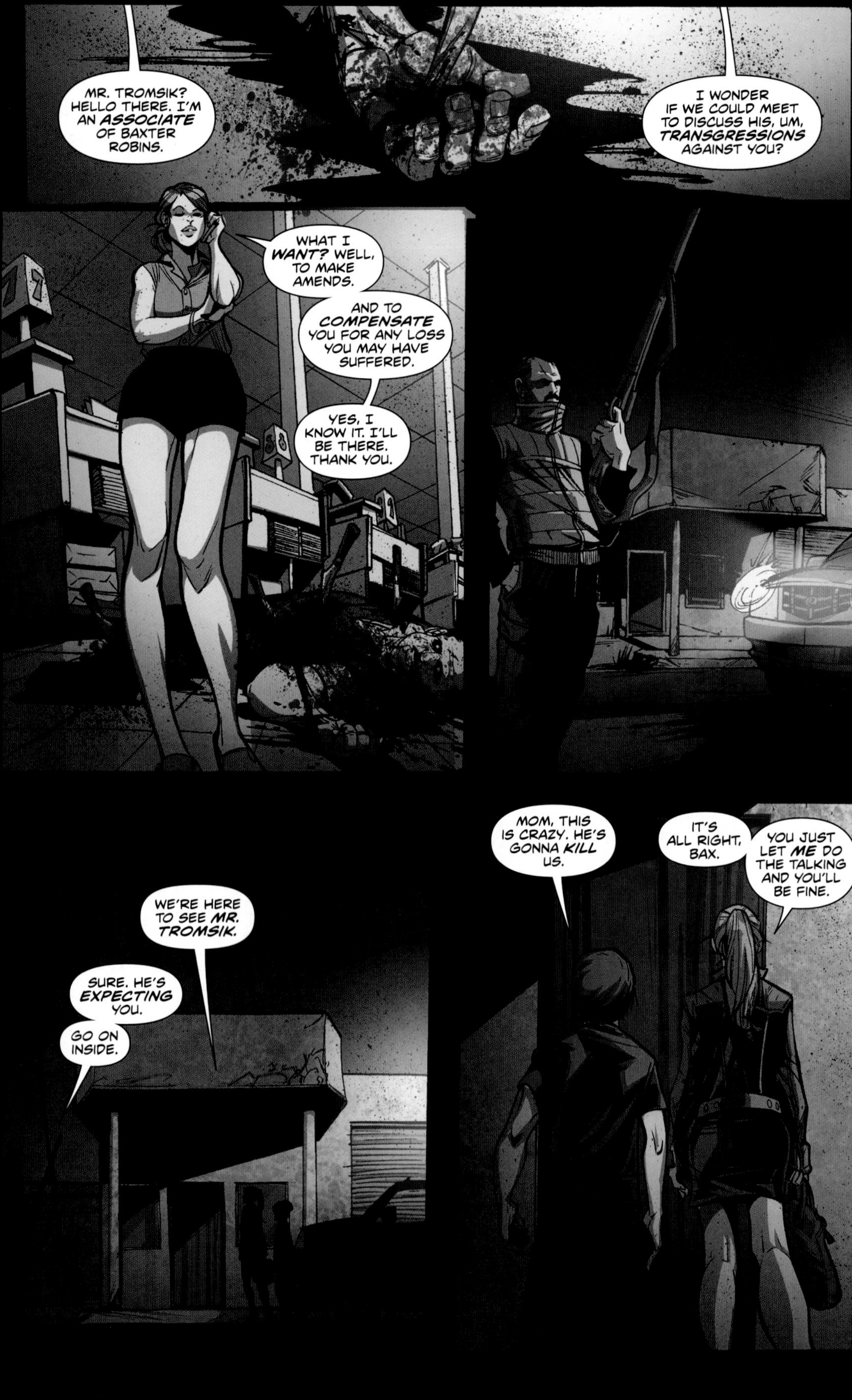
MR. TROMSIK? HELLO THERE. I'M AN ASSOCIATE OF BAXTER ROBINS.
I WONDER IF WE COULD MEET TO DISCUSS HIS, UM, TRANSGRESSIONS AGAINST YOU?
WHAT I WANT? WELL, TO MAKE AMENDS.
AND TO COMPENSATE YOU FOR ANY LOSS YOU MAY HAVE SUFFERED.
YES, I KNOW IT. I'LL BE THERE. THANK YOU.
WE'RE HERE TO SEE MR. TROMSIK.
SURE. HE'S EXPECTING YOU.
GO ON INSIDE.
MOM, THIS IS CRAZY. HE'S GONNA KILL US.
IT'S ALL RIGHT, BAX.
YOU JUST LET ME DO THE TALKING AND YOU'LL BE FINE.

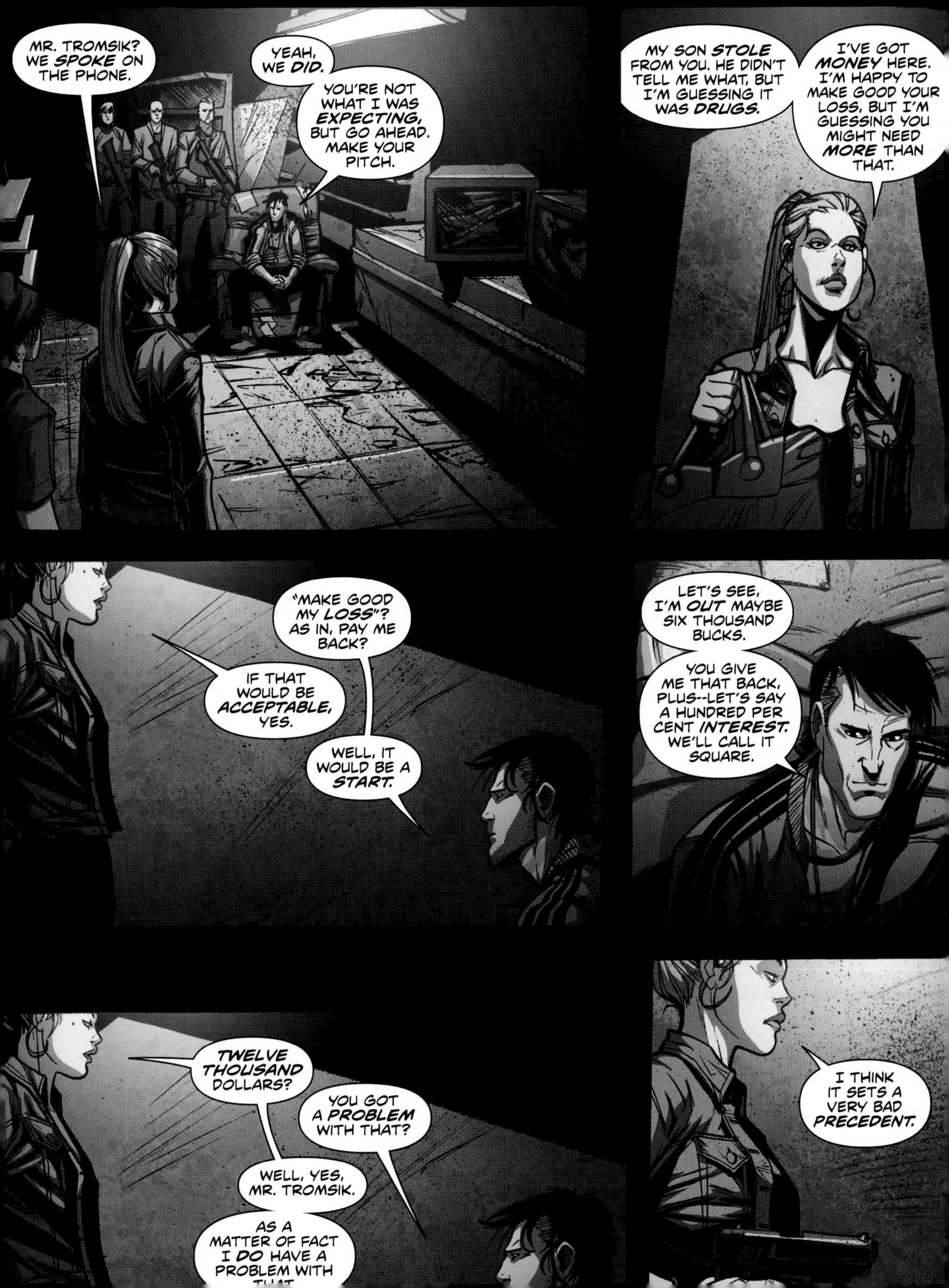
MR. TROMSIK? WE SPOKE ON THE PHONE.
YEAH, WE DID.
YOU'RE NOT WHAT I WAS EXPECTING, BUT GO AHEAD. MAKE YOUR PITCH.
MY SON STOLE FROM YOU. HE DIDN'T TELL ME WHAT, BUT I'M GUESSING IT WAS DRUGS.
I'VE GOT MONEY HERE. I'M HAPPY TO MAKE GOOD YOUR LOSS, BUT I'M GUESSING YOU MIGHT NEED MORE THAN THAT.
"MAKE GOOD MY LOSS"? AS IN, PAY ME BACK?
IF THAT WOULD BE ACCEPTABLE, YES.
WELL, IT WOULD BE A START.
LET'S SEE, I'M OUT MAYBE SIX THOUSAND BUCKS.
YOU GIVE ME THAT BACK, PLUS--LET'S SAY A HUNDRED PER CENT INTEREST. WE'LL CALL IT SQUARE.
TWELVE THOUSAND DOLLARS?
YOU GOT A PROBLEM WITH THAT?
WELL, YES, MR. TROMSIK.
AS A MATTER OF FACT I DO HAVE A PROBLEM WITH
I THINK IT SETS A VERY BAD PRECEDENT.

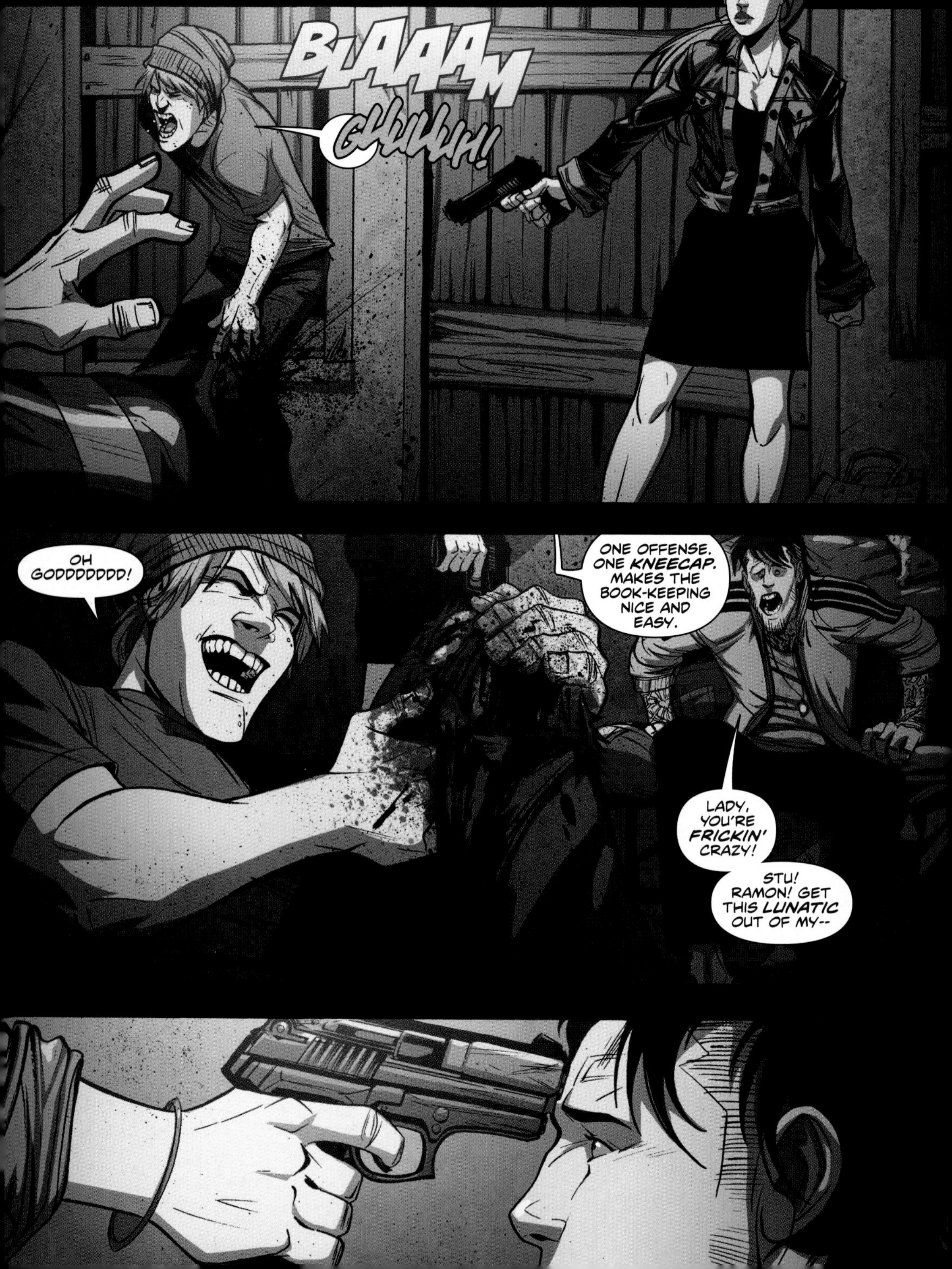
BLAAAAM
GHUUUUH!
OH GODDDDDDDD!
ONE OFFENSE. ONE KNEECAP. MAKES THE BOOK-KEEPING NICE AND EASY.
LADY, YOU'RE FRICKIN' CRAZY!
STU! RAMON! GET THIS LUNATIC OUT OF MY--

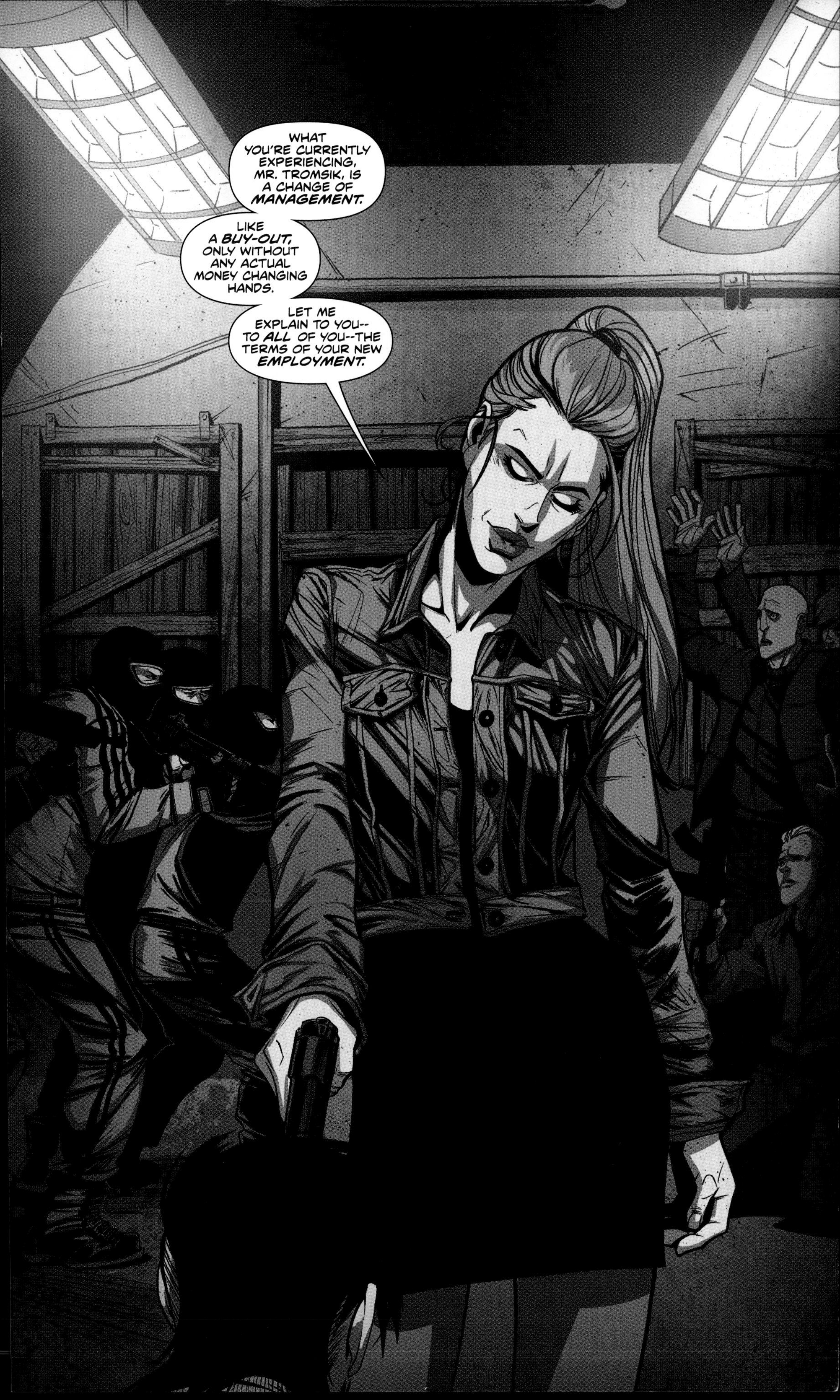
WHAT YOU'RE CURRENTLY EXPERIENCING, MR. TROMSIK, IS A CHANGE OF MANAGEMENT.
LIKE A BUY-OUT, ONLY WITHOUT ANY ACTUAL MONEY CHANGING HANDS.
LET ME EXPLAIN TO YOU-- TO ALL OF YOU--THE TERMS OF YOUR NEW EMPLOYMENT.

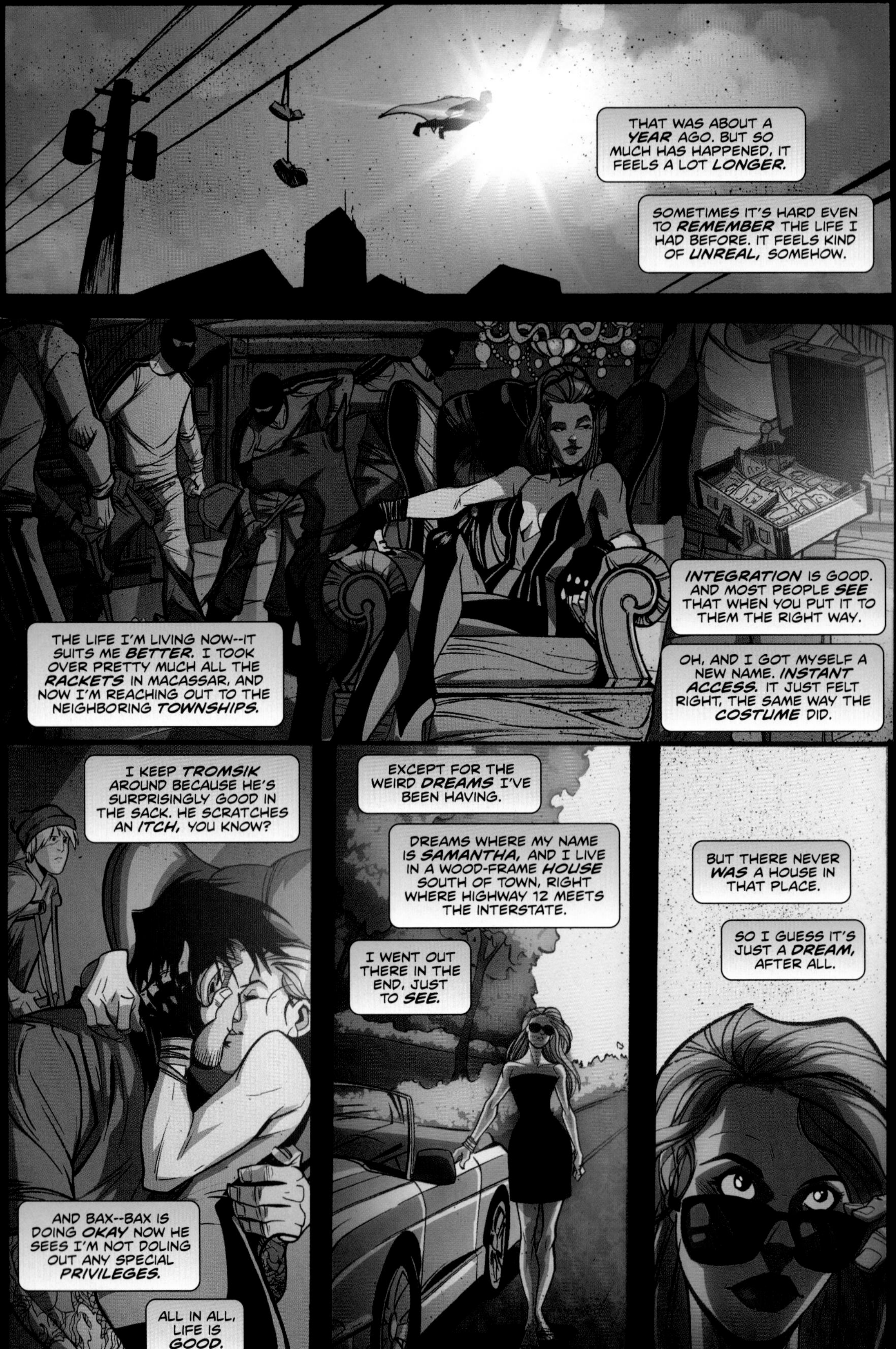
THAT WAS ABOUT A YEAR AGO. BUT SO MUCH HAS HAPPENED, IT FEELS A LOT LONGER.
SOMETIMES IT'S HARD EVEN TO REMEMBER THE LIFE I HAD BEFORE. IT FEELS KIND OF UNREAL, SOMEHOW.
THE LIFE I'M LIVING NOW--IT SUITS ME BETTER. I TOOK OVER PRETTY MUCH ALL THE RACKETS IN MACASSAR, AND NOW I'M REACHING OUT TO THE NEIGHBORING TOWNSHIPS.
INTEGRATION IS GOOD. AND MOST PEOPLE SEE THAT WHEN YOU PUT IT TO THEM THE RIGHT WAY.
OH, AND I GOT MYSELF A NEW NAME. INSTANT ACCESS. IT JUST FELT RIGHT, THE SAME WAY THE COSTUME DID.
I KEEP TROMSIK AROUND BECAUSE HE'S SURPRISINGLY GOOD IN THE SACK. HE SCRATCHES AN ITCH, YOU KNOW?
AND BAX--BAX IS DOING OKAY NOW HE SEES I'M NOT DOLING OUT ANY SPECIAL PRIVILEGES.
ALL IN ALL, LIFE IS GOOD.
EXCEPT FOR THE WEIRD DREAMS I'VE BEEN HAVING.
DREAMS WHERE MY NAME IS SAMANTHA, AND I LIVE IN A WOOD-FRAME HOUSE SOUTH OF TOWN, RIGHT WHERE HIGHWAY 12 MEETS THE INTERSTATE.
I WENT OUT THERE IN THE END, JUST TO SEE.
BUT THERE NEVER WAS A HOUSE IN THAT PLACE.
SO I GUESS IT'S JUST A DREAM, AFTER ALL.

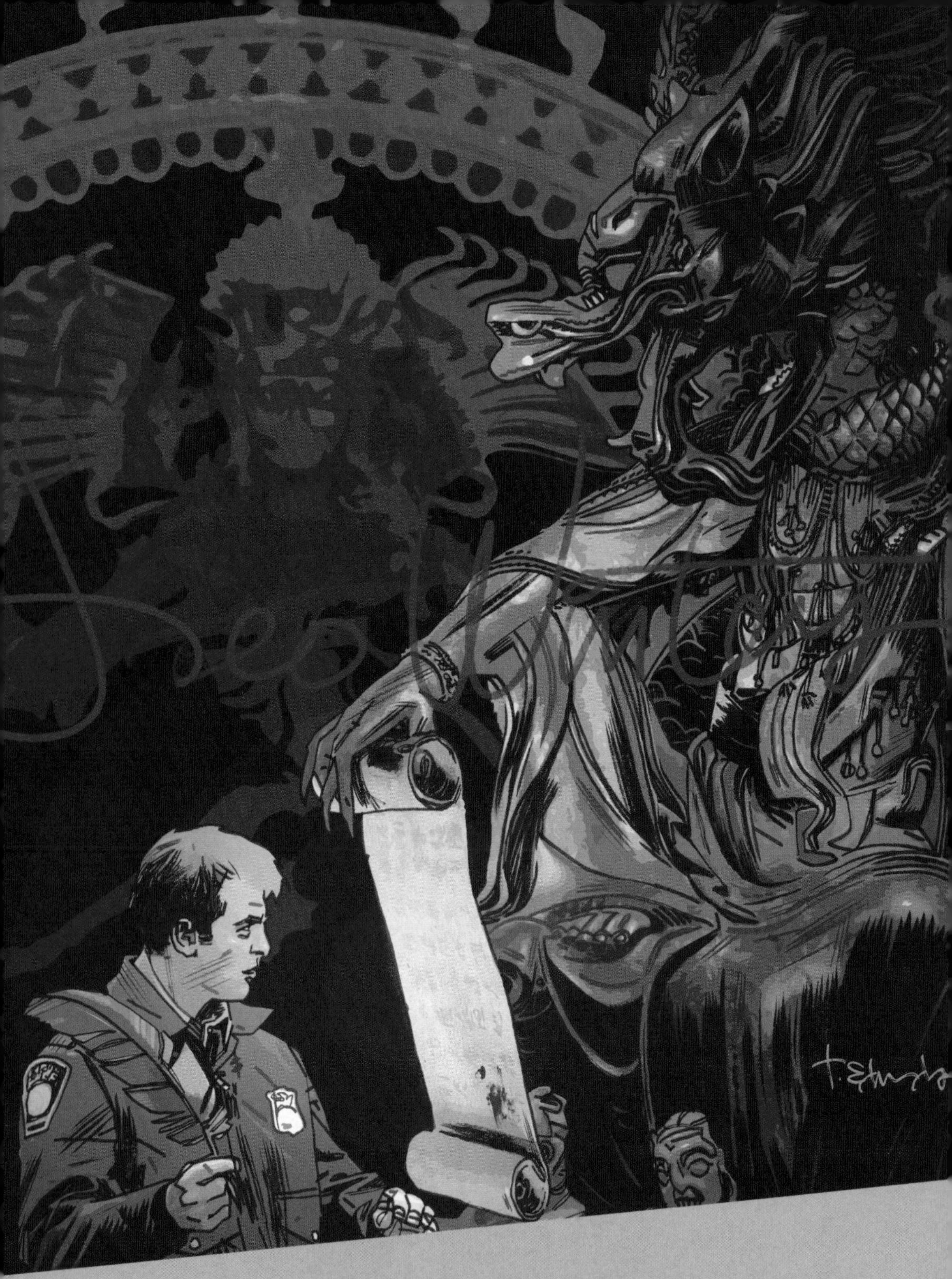

"SO WE'VE COME TO THE HOUR OF **RECKONING.**"

Chapter 6

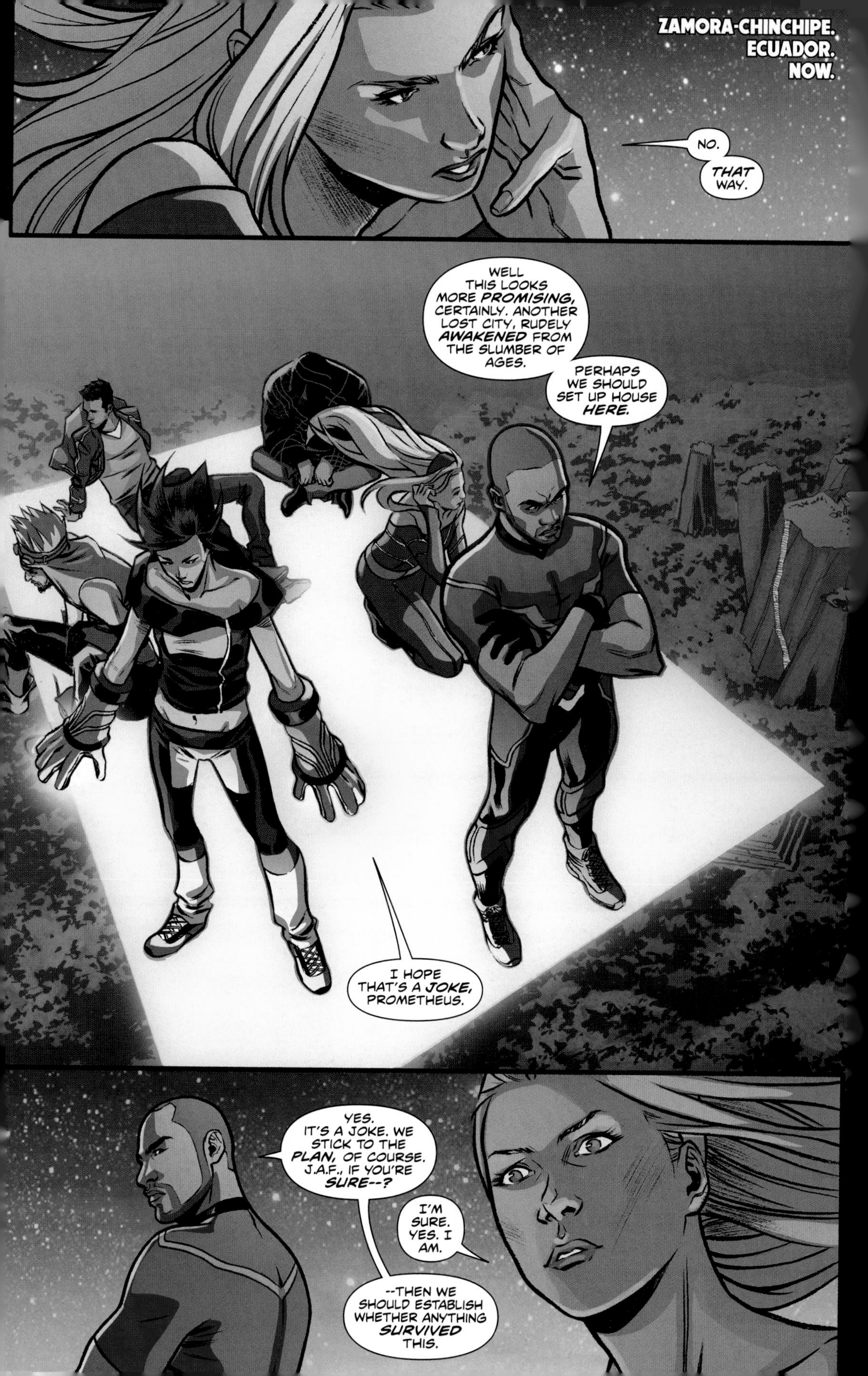
ZAMORA-CHINCHIPE. ECUADOR. NOW.
NO. THAT WAY.
WELL THIS LOOKS MORE PROMISING, CERTAINLY. ANOTHER LOST CITY, RUDELY AWAKENED FROM THE SLUMBER OF AGES.
PERHAPS WE SHOULD SET UP HOUSE HERE.
I HOPE THAT'S A JOKE, PROMETHEUS.
YES. IT'S A JOKE. WE STICK TO THE PLAN, OF COURSE. J.A.F., IF YOU'RE SURE--?
I'M SURE. YES. I AM.
--THEN WE SHOULD ESTABLISH WHETHER ANYTHING SURVIVED THIS.

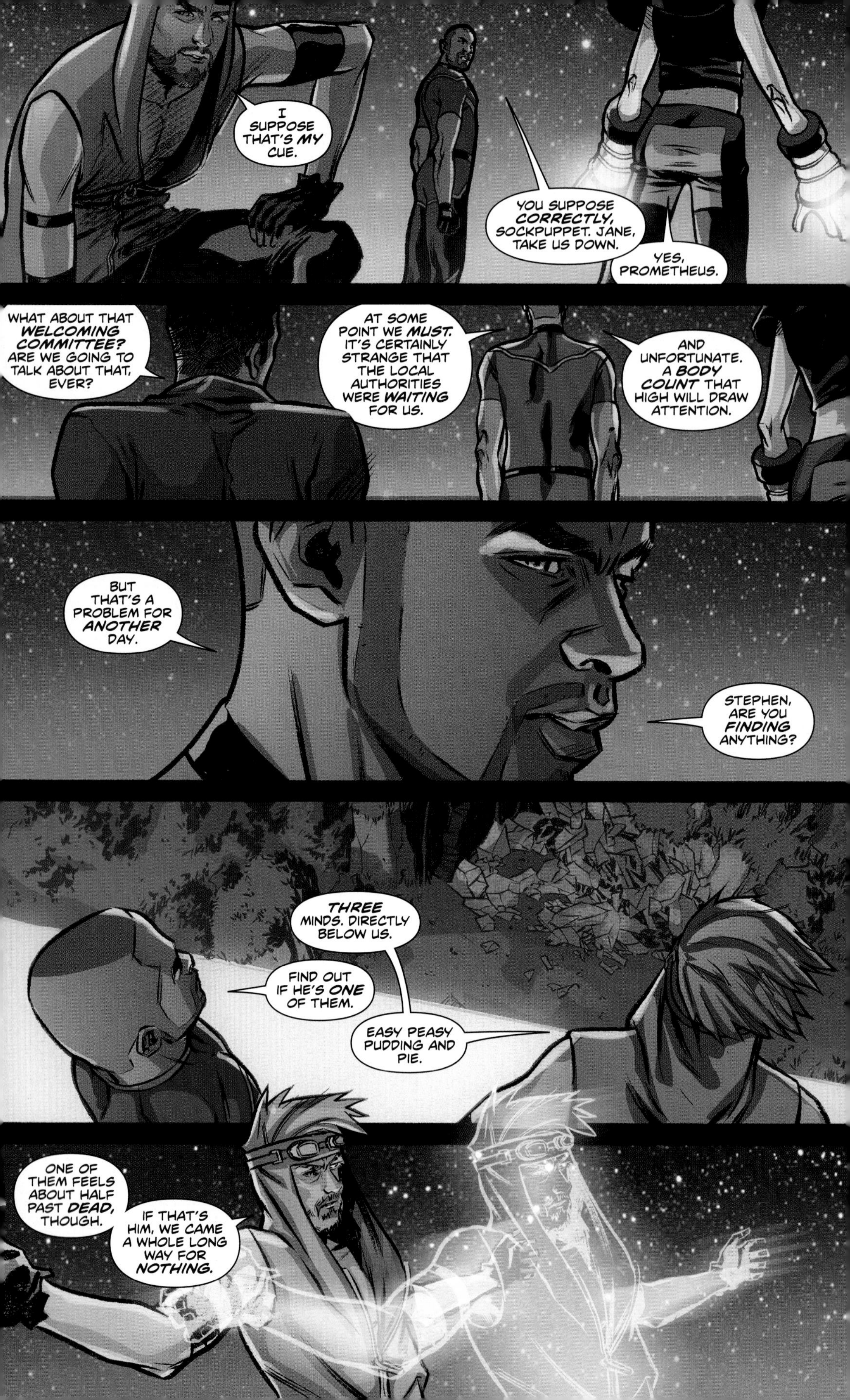

I SUPPOSE THAT'S MY CUE.
YOU SUPPOSE CORRECTLY, SOCKPUPPET. JANE, TAKE US DOWN.
YES, PROMETHEUS.
WHAT ABOUT THAT WELCOMING COMMITTEE? ARE WE GOING TO TALK ABOUT THAT, EVER?
AT SOME POINT WE MUST. IT'S CERTAINLY STRANGE THAT THE LOCAL AUTHORITIES WERE WAITING FOR US.
AND UNFORTUNATE. A BODY COUNT THAT HIGH WILL DRAW ATTENTION.
BUT THAT'S A PROBLEM FOR ANOTHER DAY.
STEPHEN, ARE YOU FINDING ANYTHING?
THREE MINDS. DIRECTLY BELOW US.
FIND OUT IF HE'S ONE OF THEM.
EASY PEASY PUDDING AND PIE.
ONE OF THEM FEELS ABOUT HALF PAST DEAD, THOUGH.
IF THAT'S HIM, WE CAME A WHOLE LONG WAY FOR NOTHING.

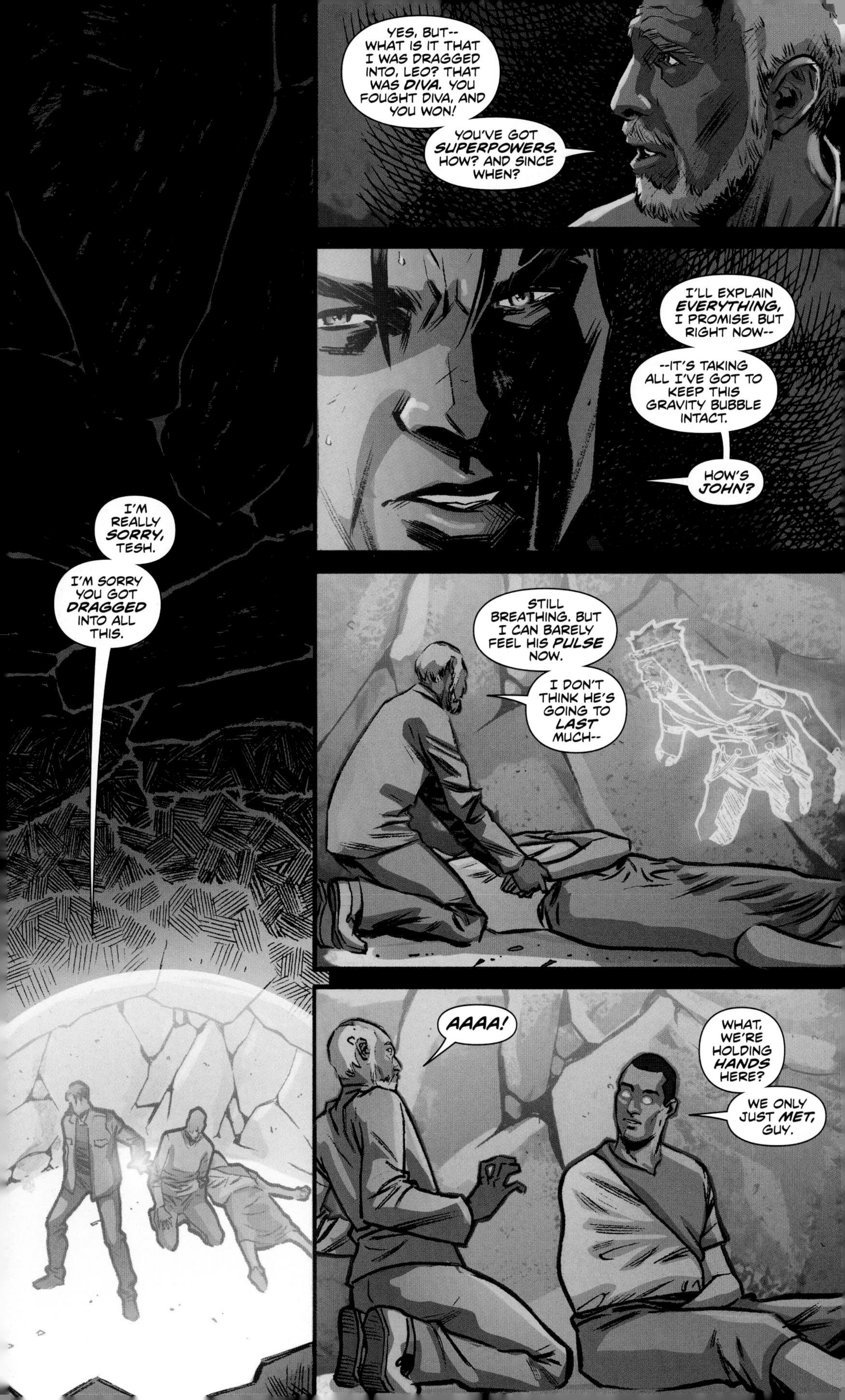
YES, BUT-- WHAT IS IT THAT I WAS DRAGGED INTO, LEO? THAT WAS DIVA. YOU FOUGHT DIVA, AND YOU WON!
YOU'VE GOT SUPERPOWERS. HOW? AND SINCE WHEN?
I'LL EXPLAIN EVERYTHING, I PROMISE. BUT RIGHT NOW--
--IT'S TAKING ALL I'VE GOT TO KEEP THIS GRAVITY BUBBLE INTACT.
HOW'S JOHN?
I'M REALLY SORRY, TESH.
I'M SORRY YOU GOT DRAGGED INTO ALL THIS.
STILL BREATHING. BUT I CAN BARELY FEEL HIS PULSE NOW.
I DON'T THINK HE'S GOING TO LAST MUCH--
AAAA!
WHAT, WE'RE HOLDING HANDS HERE?
WE ONLY JUST MET, GUY.

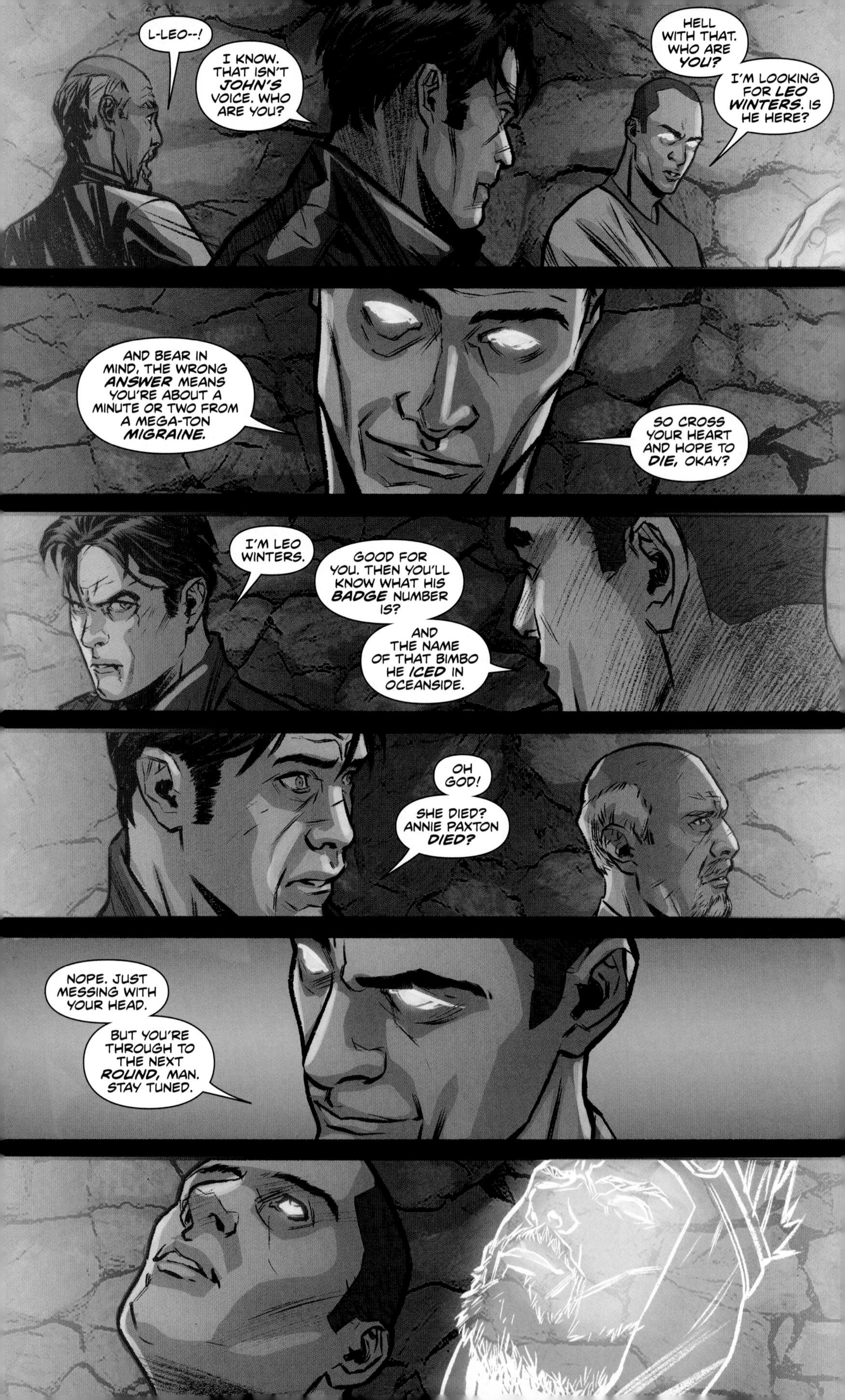

L-LEO--!
I KNOW. THAT ISN'T JOHN'S VOICE. WHO ARE YOU?
HELL WITH THAT. WHO ARE YOU?
I'M LOOKING FOR LEO WINTERS. IS HE HERE?
AND BEAR IN MIND, THE WRONG ANSWER MEANS YOU'RE ABOUT A MINUTE OR TWO FROM A MEGA-TON MIGRAINE.
SO CROSS YOUR HEART AND HOPE TO DIE, OKAY?
I'M LEO WINTERS.
GOOD FOR YOU. THEN YOU'LL KNOW WHAT HIS BADGE NUMBER IS?
AND THE NAME OF THAT BIMBO HE ICED IN OCEANSIDE.
OH GOD!
SHE DIED? ANNIE PAXTON DIED?
NOPE. JUST MESSING WITH YOUR HEAD.
BUT YOU'RE THROUGH TO THE NEXT ROUND, MAN. STAY TUNED.

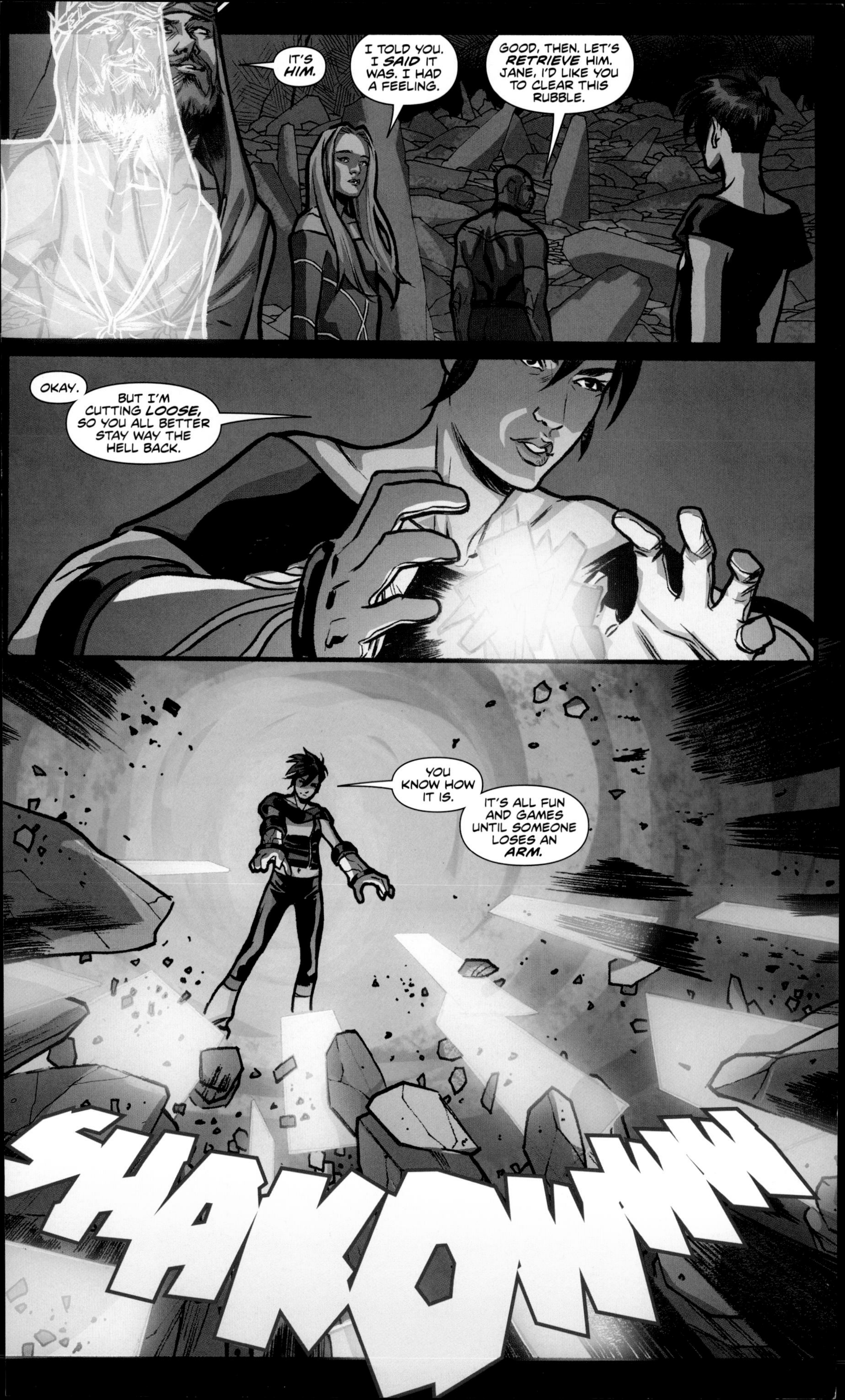
IT'S HIM.
I TOLD YOU. I SAID IT WAS. I HAD A FEELING.
GOOD, THEN. LET'S RETRIEVE HIM. JANE, I'D LIKE YOU TO CLEAR THIS RUBBLE.
OKAY.
BUT I'M CUTTING LOOSE, SO YOU ALL BETTER STAY WAY THE HELL BACK.
YOU KNOW HOW IT IS.
IT'S ALL FUN AND GAMES UNTIL SOMEONE LOSES AN ARM.
SHAKOWWW

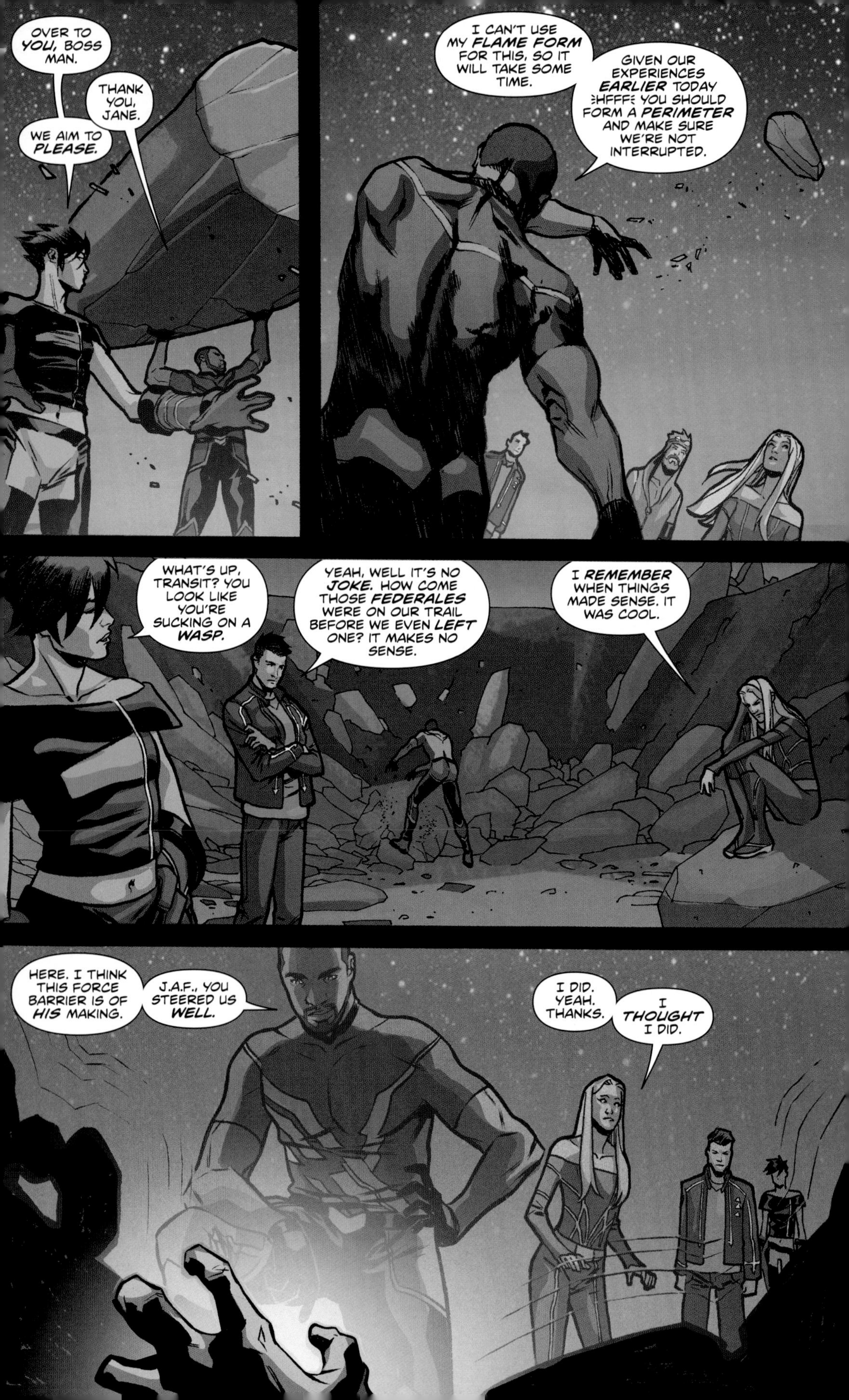
OVER TO YOU, BOSS MAN.
THANK YOU, JANE.
WE AIM TO PLEASE.
I CAN'T USE MY FLAME FORM FOR THIS, SO IT WILL TAKE SOME TIME.
GIVEN OUR EXPERIENCES EARLIER TODAY HFFF YOU SHOULD FORM A PERIMETER AND MAKE SURE WE'RE NOT INTERRUPTED.
WHAT'S UP, TRANSIT? YOU LOOK LIKE YOU'RE SUCKING ON A WASP.
YEAH, WELL IT'S NO JOKE. HOW COME THOSE FEDERALES WERE ON OUR TRAIL BEFORE WE EVEN LEFT ONE? IT MAKES NO SENSE.
I REMEMBER WHEN THINGS MADE SENSE. IT WAS COOL.
HERE. I THINK THIS FORCE BARRIER IS OF HIS MAKING.
J.A.F., YOU STEERED US WELL.
I DID. YEAH. THANKS.
I THOUGHT I DID.

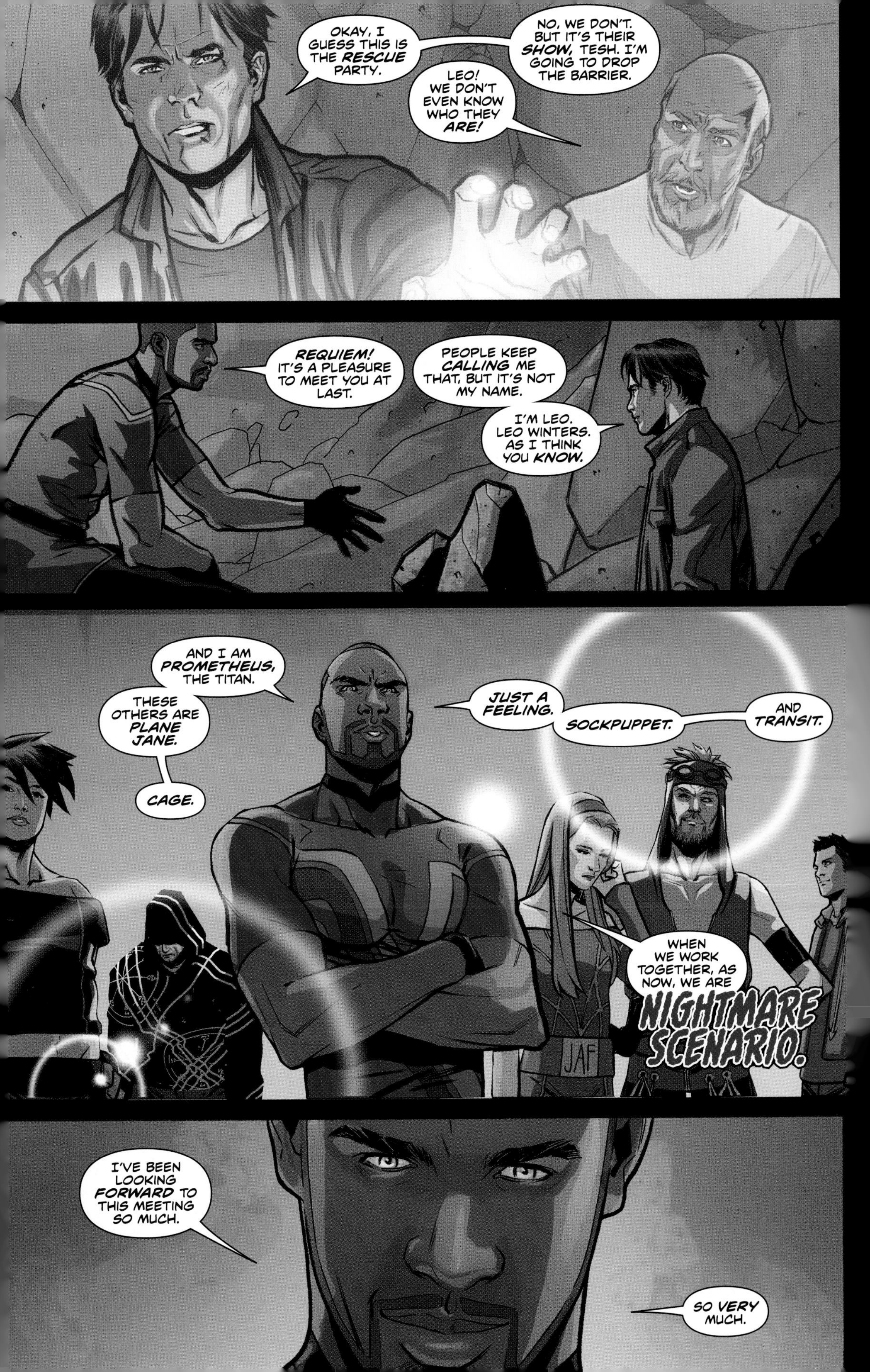
OKAY, I GUESS THIS IS THE RESCUE PARTY.
LEO! WE DON'T EVEN KNOW WHO THEY ARE!
NO, WE DON'T. BUT IT'S THEIR SHOW, TESH. I'M GOING TO DROP THE BARRIER.
REQUIEM! IT'S A PLEASURE TO MEET YOU AT LAST.
PEOPLE KEEP CALLING ME THAT, BUT IT'S NOT MY NAME.
I'M LEO. LEO WINTERS. AS I THINK YOU KNOW.
AND I AM PROMETHEUS, THE TITAN.
JUST A FEELING.
THESE OTHERS ARE PLANE JANE.
CAGE.
SOCKPUPPET.
AND TRANSIT.
WHEN WE WORK TOGETHER, AS NOW, WE ARE
NIGHTMARE SCENARIO.
JAF
I'VE BEEN LOOKING FORWARD TO THIS MEETING SO MUCH.
SO VERY MUCH.

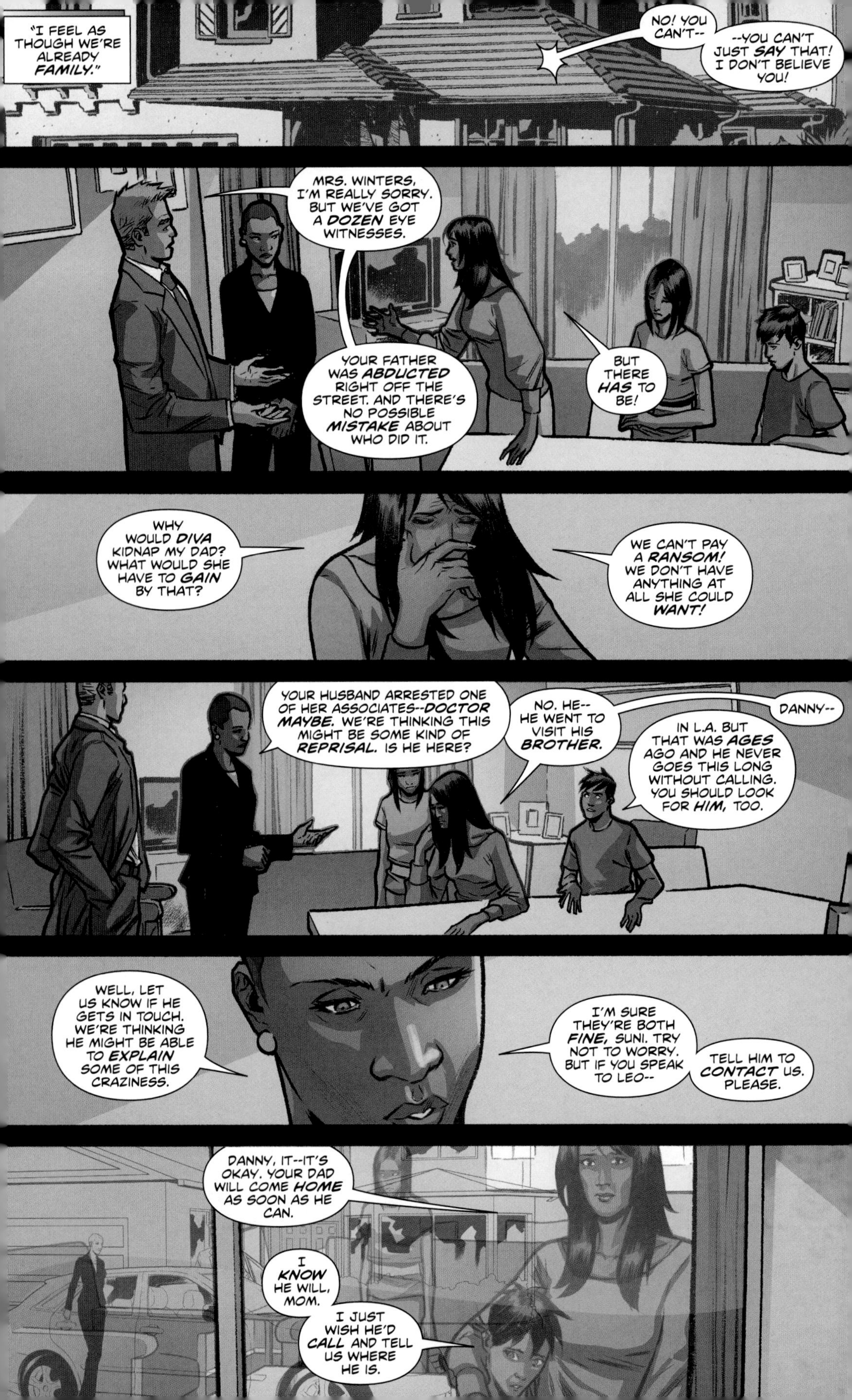

"I FEEL AS THOUGH WE'RE ALREADY FAMILY."
NO! YOU CAN'T--
--YOU CAN'T JUST SAY THAT! I DON'T BELIEVE YOU!
MRS. WINTERS, I'M REALLY SORRY. BUT WE'VE GOT A DOZEN EYE WITNESSES.
YOUR FATHER WAS ABDUCTED RIGHT OFF THE STREET. AND THERE'S NO POSSIBLE MISTAKE ABOUT WHO DID IT.
BUT THERE HAS TO BE!
WHY WOULD DIVA KIDNAP MY DAD? WHAT WOULD SHE HAVE TO GAIN BY THAT?
WE CAN'T PAY A RANSOM! WE DON'T HAVE ANYTHING AT ALL SHE COULD WANT!
YOUR HUSBAND ARRESTED ONE OF HER ASSOCIATES--DOCTOR MAYBE. WE'RE THINKING THIS MIGHT BE SOME KIND OF REPRISAL. IS HE HERE?
NO. HE-- HE WENT TO VISIT HIS BROTHER.
DANNY--
IN L.A. BUT THAT WAS AGES AGO AND HE NEVER GOES THIS LONG WITHOUT CALLING. YOU SHOULD LOOK FOR HIM, TOO.
WELL, LET US KNOW IF HE GETS IN TOUCH. WE'RE THINKING HE MIGHT BE ABLE TO EXPLAIN SOME OF THIS CRAZINESS.
I'M SURE THEY'RE BOTH FINE, SUNI. TRY NOT TO WORRY. BUT IF YOU SPEAK TO LEO--
TELL HIM TO CONTACT US. PLEASE.
DANNY, IT--IT'S OKAY. YOUR DAD WILL COME HOME AS SOON AS HE CAN.
I KNOW HE WILL, MOM.
I JUST WISH HE'D CALL AND TELL US WHERE HE IS.

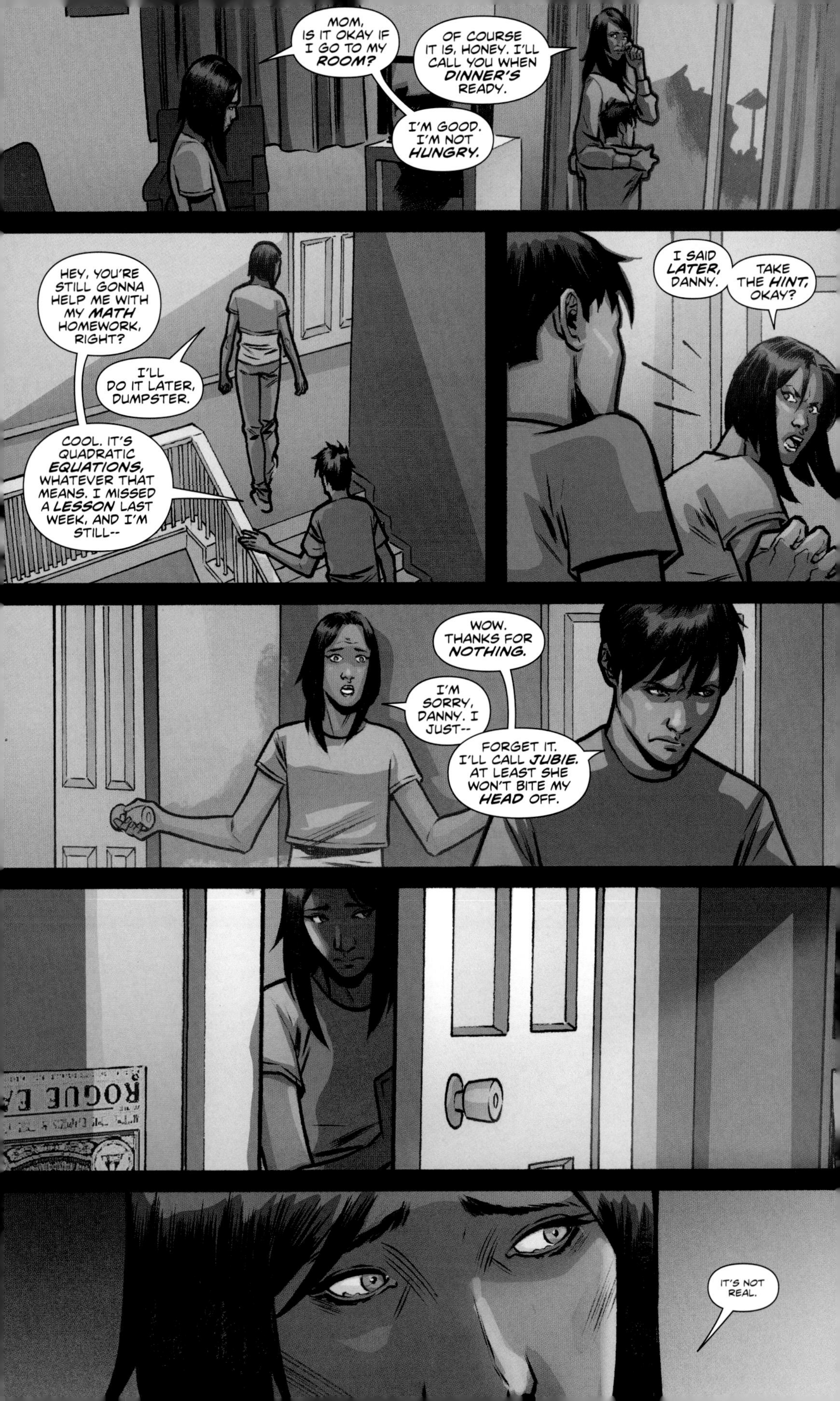

MOM, IS IT OKAY IF I GO TO MY ROOM?
OF COURSE IT IS, HONEY. I'LL CALL YOU WHEN DINNER'S READY.
I'M GOOD. I'M NOT HUNGRY.
HEY, YOU'RE STILL GONNA HELP ME WITH MY MATH HOMEWORK, RIGHT?
I'LL DO IT LATER, DUMPSTER.
COOL. IT'S QUADRATIC EQUATIONS, WHATEVER THAT MEANS. I MISSED A LESSON LAST WEEK, AND I'M STILL--
I SAID LATER, DANNY.
TAKE THE HINT, OKAY?
WOW. THANKS FOR NOTHING.
I'M SORRY, DANNY. I JUST--
FORGET IT. I'LL CALL JUBIE. AT LEAST SHE WON'T BITE MY HEAD OFF.
ROGUE
IT'S NOT REAL.

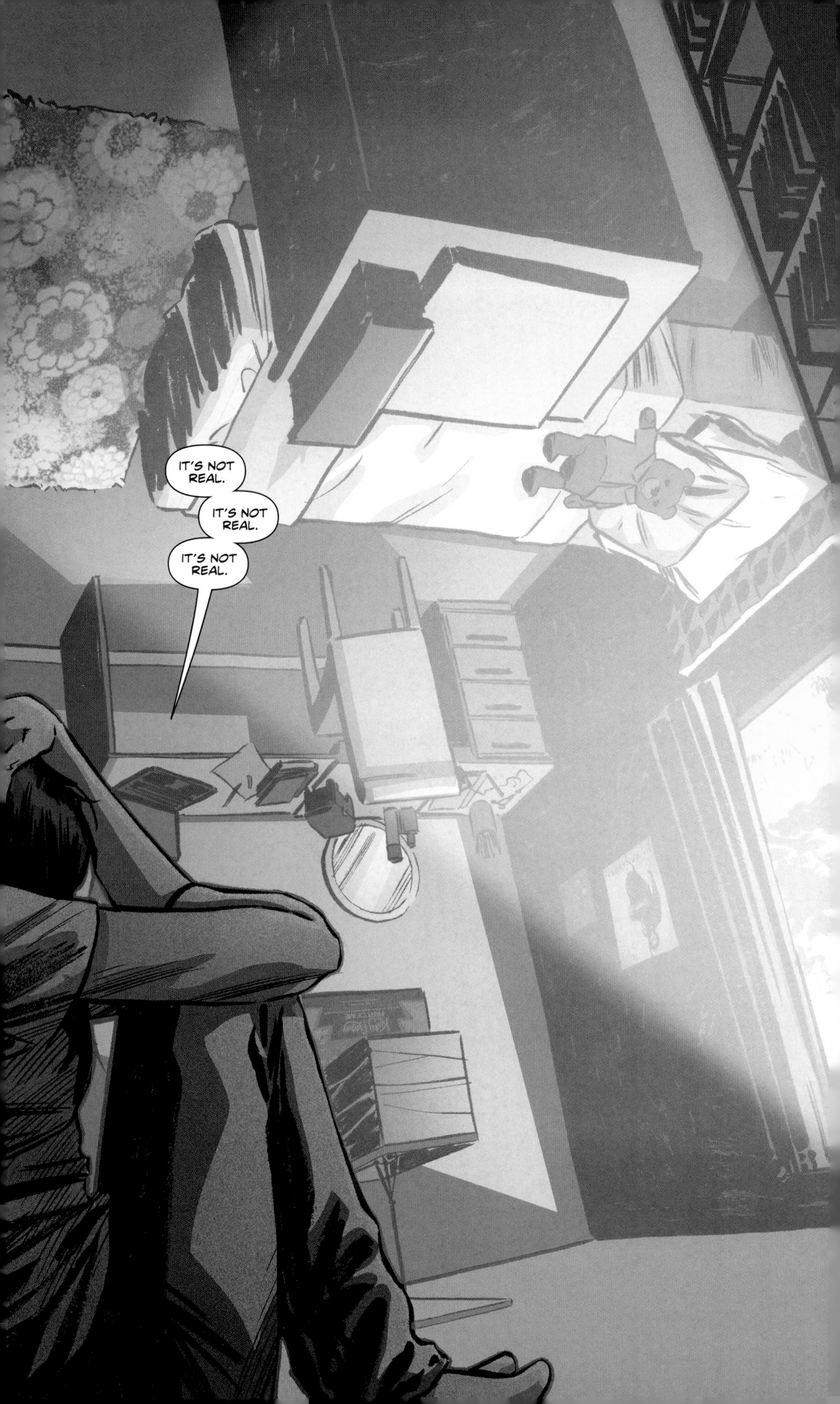
IT'S NOT REAL.
IT'S NOT REAL.
IT'S NOT REAL.

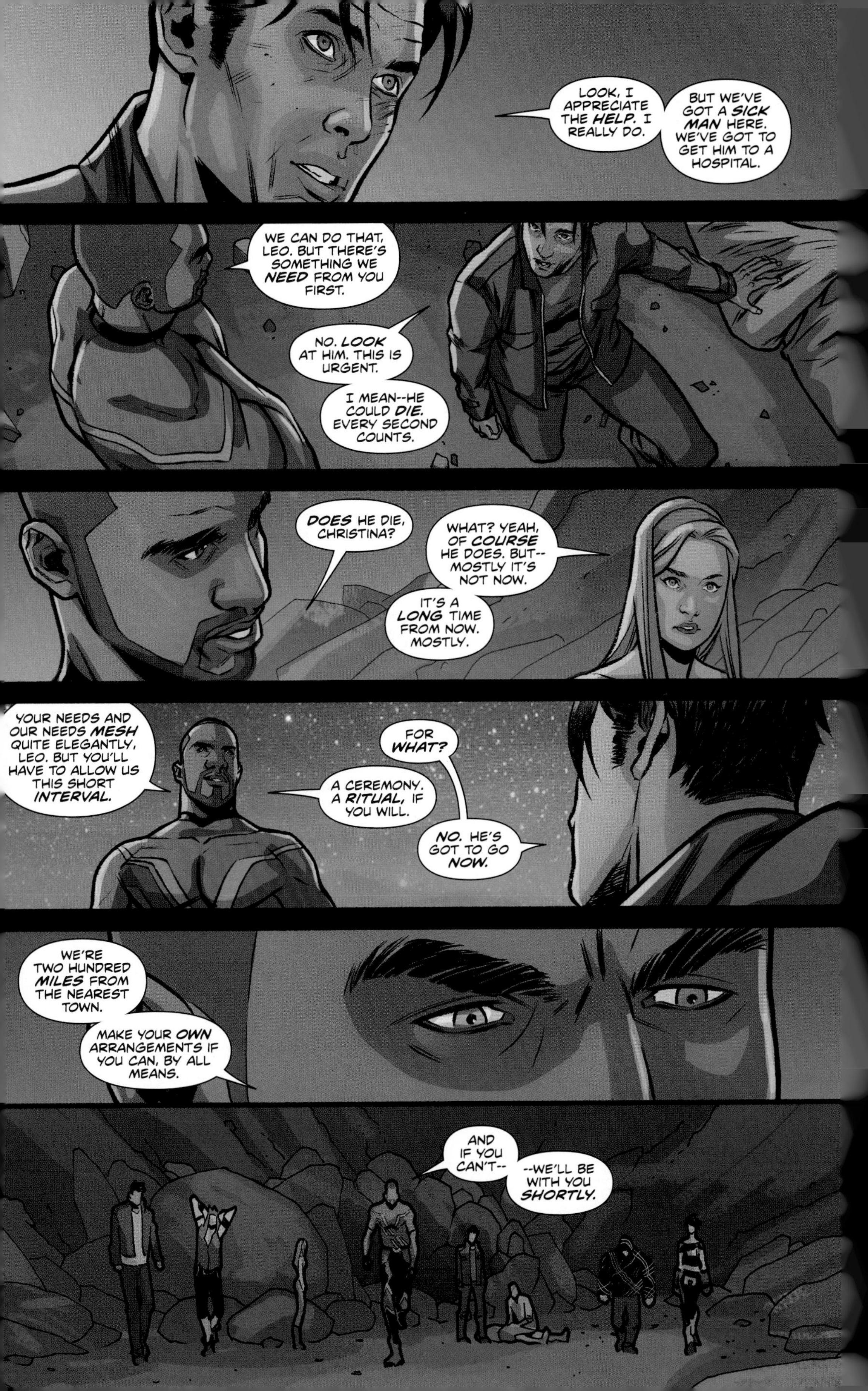
LOOK, I APPRECIATE THE HELP. I REALLY DO.
BUT WE'VE GOT A SICK MAN HERE. WE'VE GOT TO GET HIM TO A HOSPITAL.
WE CAN DO THAT, LEO. BUT THERE'S SOMETHING WE NEED FROM YOU FIRST.
NO. LOOK AT HIM. THIS IS URGENT.
I MEAN--HE COULD DIE. EVERY SECOND COUNTS.
DOES HE DIE, CHRISTINA?
WHAT? YEAH, OF COURSE HE DOES. BUT--MOSTLY IT'S NOT NOW.
IT'S A LONG TIME FROM NOW. MOSTLY.
YOUR NEEDS AND OUR NEEDS MESH QUITE ELEGANTLY, LEO. BUT YOU'LL HAVE TO ALLOW US THIS SHORT INTERVAL.
FOR WHAT?
A CEREMONY. A RITUAL, IF YOU WILL.
NO. HE'S GOT TO GO NOW.
WE'RE TWO HUNDRED MILES FROM THE NEAREST TOWN.
MAKE YOUR OWN ARRANGEMENTS IF YOU CAN, BY ALL MEANS.
AND IF YOU CAN'T--
--WE'LL BE WITH YOU SHORTLY.

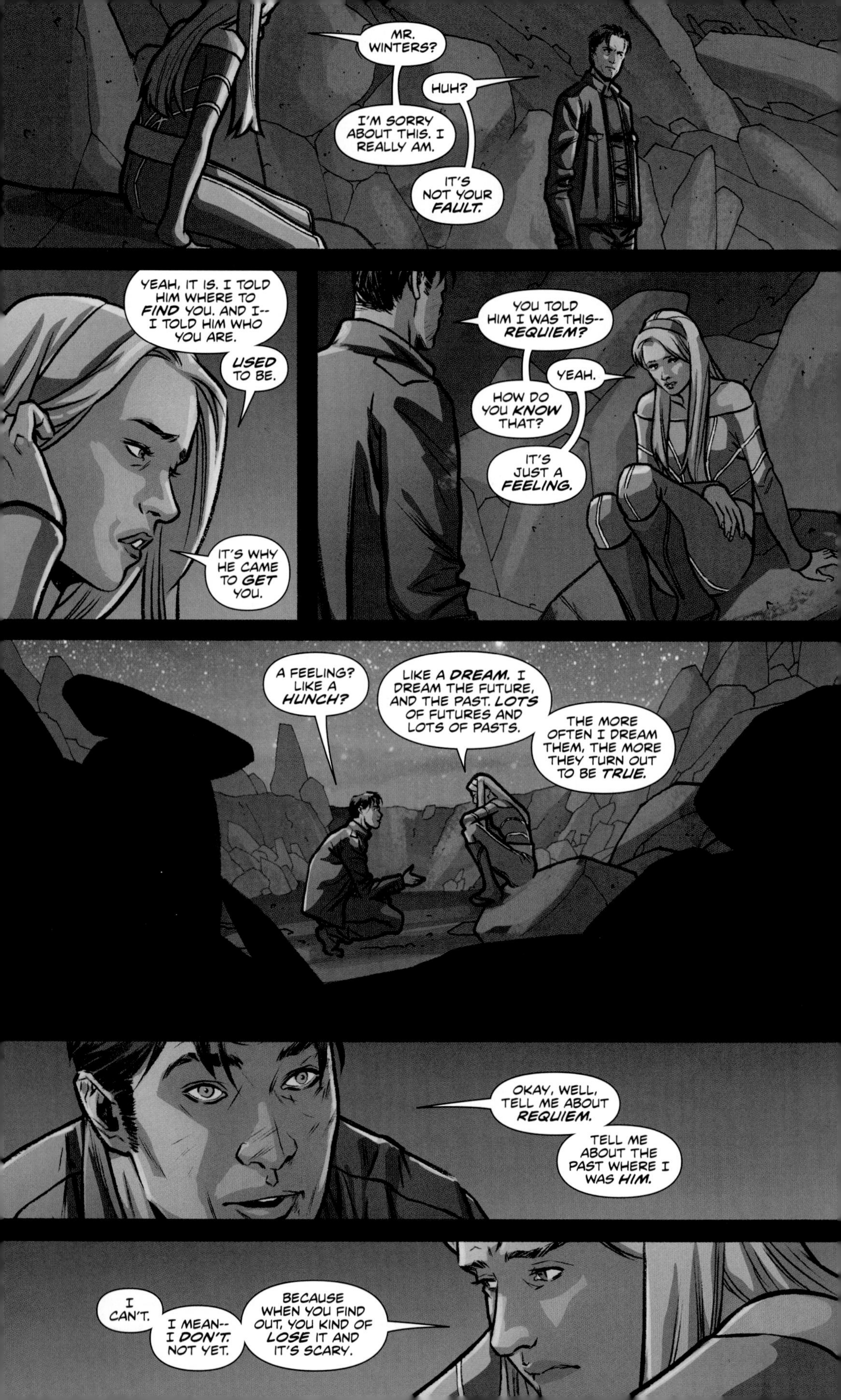

MR. WINTERS?
HUH?
I'M SORRY ABOUT THIS. I REALLY AM.
IT'S NOT YOUR FAULT.
YEAH, IT IS. I TOLD HIM WHERE TO FIND YOU. AND I-- I TOLD HIM WHO YOU ARE.
USED TO BE.
IT'S WHY HE CAME TO GET YOU.
YOU TOLD HIM I WAS THIS-- REQUIEM?
YEAH.
HOW DO YOU KNOW THAT?
IT'S JUST A FEELING.
A FEELING? LIKE A HUNCH?
LIKE A DREAM. I DREAM THE FUTURE, AND THE PAST. LOTS OF FUTURES AND LOTS OF PASTS.
THE MORE OFTEN I DREAM THEM, THE MORE THEY TURN OUT TO BE TRUE.
OKAY, WELL, TELL ME ABOUT REQUIEM.
TELL ME ABOUT THE PAST WHERE I WAS HIM.
I CAN'T.
I MEAN-- I DON'T. NOT YET.
BECAUSE WHEN YOU FIND OUT, YOU KIND OF LOSE IT AND IT'S SCARY.

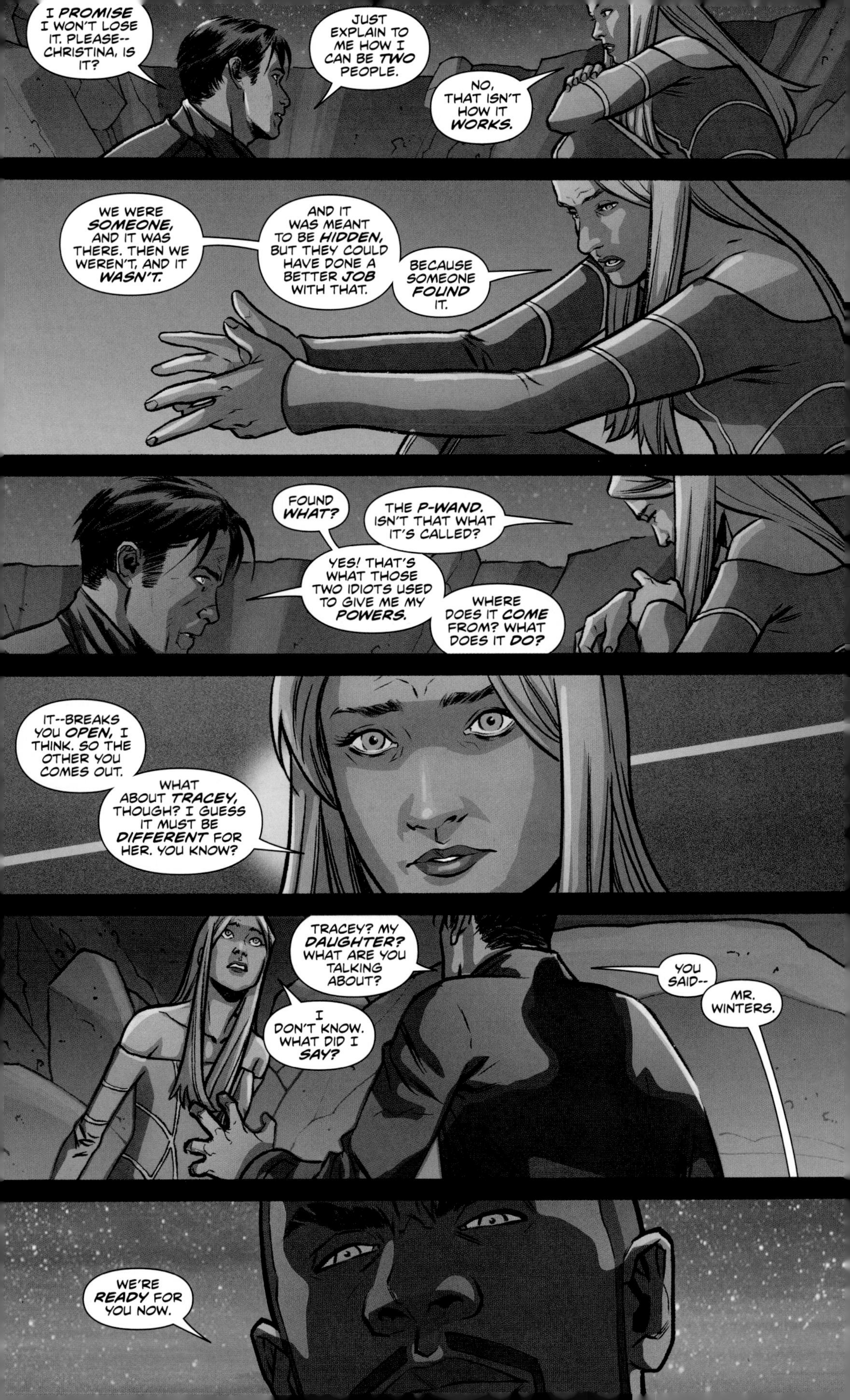
I PROMISE I WON'T LOSE IT. PLEASE-- CHRISTINA, IS IT?
JUST EXPLAIN TO ME HOW I CAN BE TWO PEOPLE.
NO, THAT ISN'T HOW IT WORKS.
WE WERE SOMEONE, AND IT WAS THERE. THEN WE WEREN'T, AND IT WASN'T.
AND IT WAS MEANT TO BE HIDDEN, BUT THEY COULD HAVE DONE A BETTER JOB WITH THAT.
BECAUSE SOMEONE FOUND IT.
FOUND WHAT?
THE P-WAND. ISN'T THAT WHAT IT'S CALLED?
YES! THAT'S WHAT THOSE TWO IDIOTS USED TO GIVE ME MY POWERS.
WHERE DOES IT COME FROM? WHAT DOES IT DO?
IT--BREAKS YOU OPEN, I THINK. SO THE OTHER YOU COMES OUT.
WHAT ABOUT TRACEY, THOUGH? I GUESS IT MUST BE DIFFERENT FOR HER. YOU KNOW?
TRACEY? MY DAUGHTER? WHAT ARE YOU TALKING ABOUT?
I DON'T KNOW. WHAT DID I SAY?
YOU SAID--
MR. WINTERS.
WE'RE READY FOR YOU NOW.

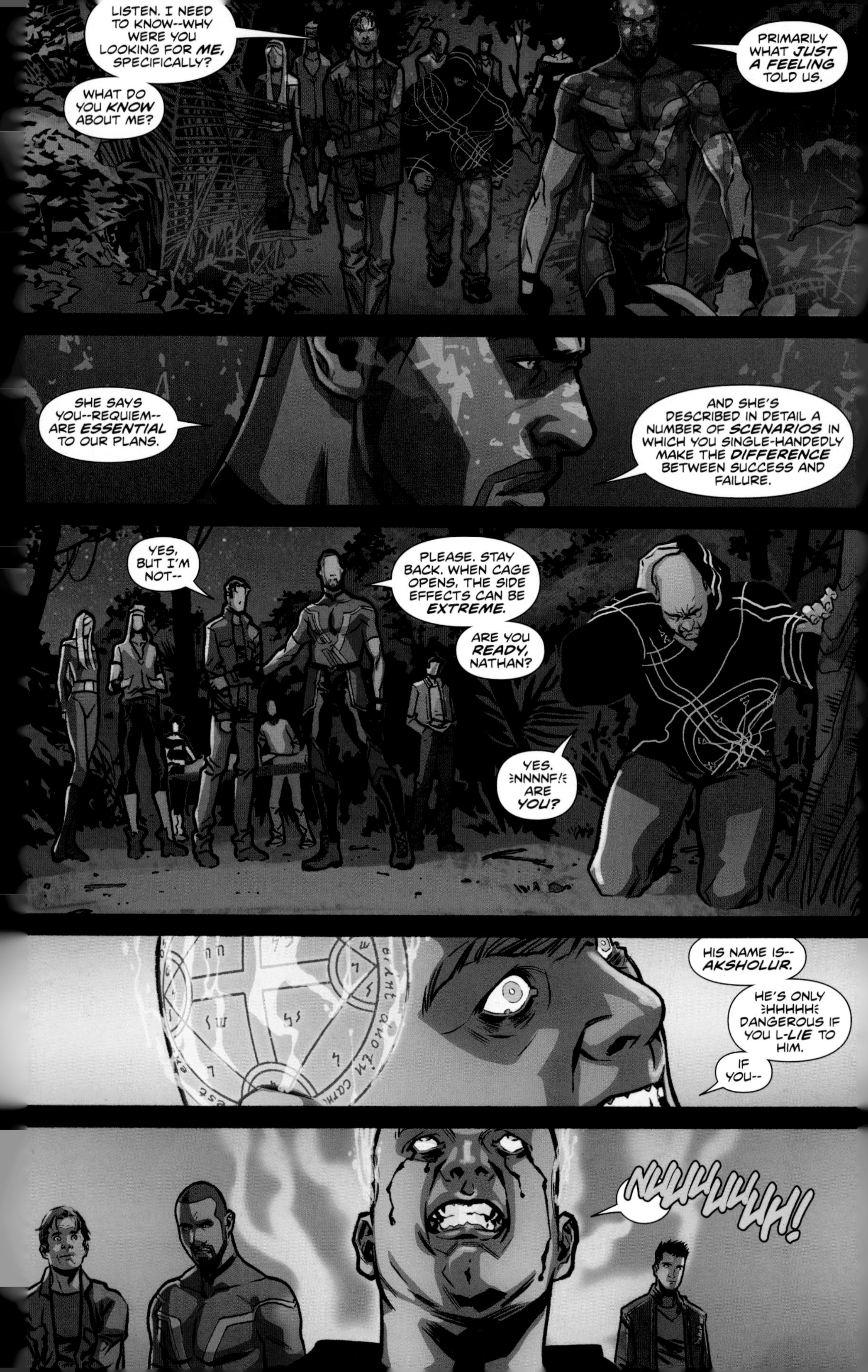
LISTEN. I NEED TO KNOW--WHY WERE YOU LOOKING FOR *ME*, SPECIFICALLY?
WHAT DO YOU *KNOW* ABOUT ME?
PRIMARILY WHAT *JUST A FEELING* TOLD US.
SHE SAYS YOU--REQUIEM--ARE *ESSENTIAL* TO OUR PLANS.
AND SHE'S DESCRIBED IN DETAIL A NUMBER OF *SCENARIOS* IN WHICH YOU SINGLE-HANDEDLY MAKE THE *DIFFERENCE* BETWEEN SUCCESS AND FAILURE.
YES, BUT I'M NOT--
PLEASE. STAY BACK. WHEN CAGE OPENS, THE SIDE EFFECTS CAN BE *EXTREME*.
ARE YOU *READY*, NATHAN?
YES. NNNNF! ARE *YOU*?
HIS NAME IS--*AKSHOLUR*.
HE'S ONLY HHHHH DANGEROUS IF YOU L-*LIE* TO HIM.
IF YOU--
NUUUUUUH!

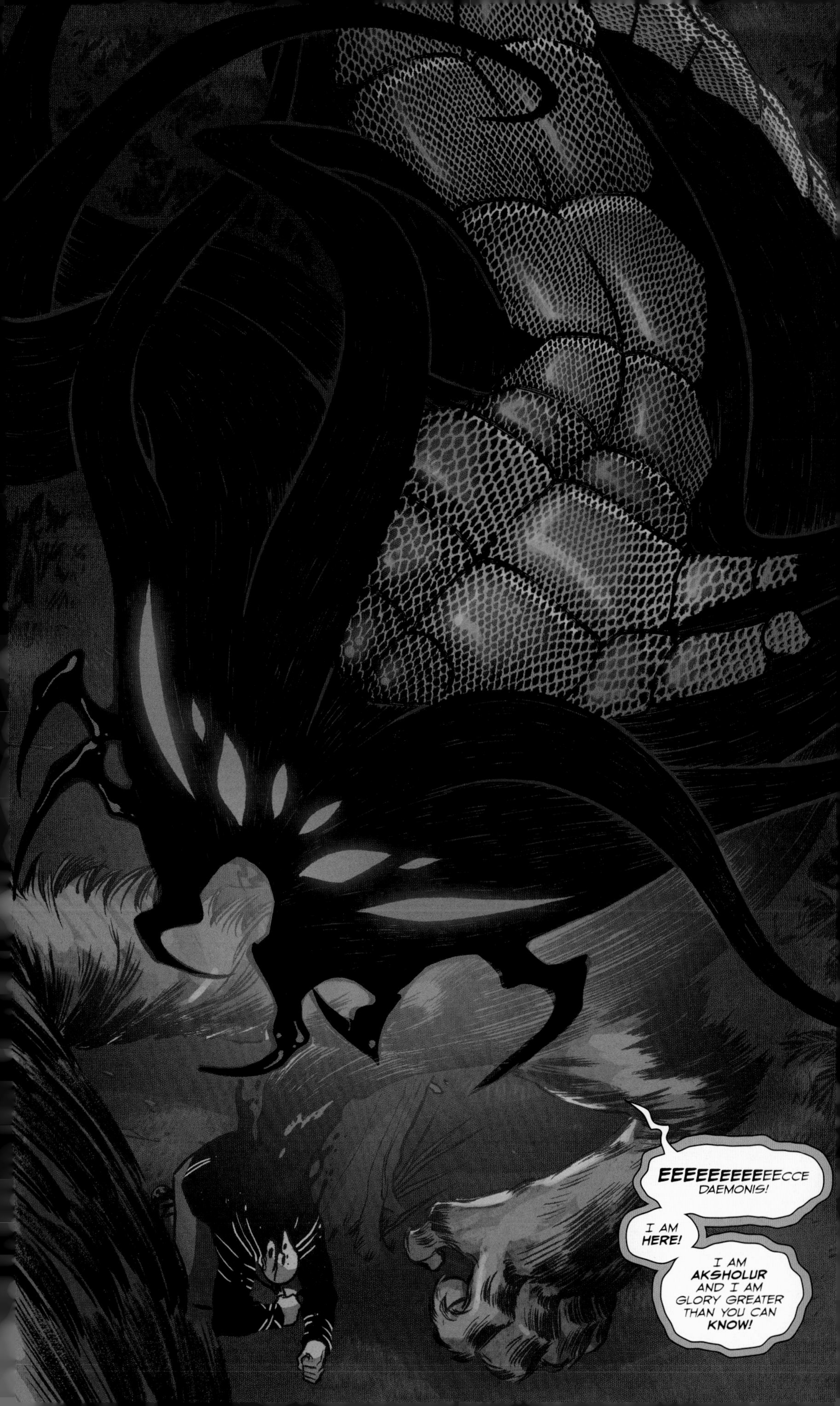
EEEEEEEEEEECCE DAEMONIS!
I AM HERE!
I AM AKSHOLUR AND I AM GLORY GREATER THAN YOU CAN KNOW!

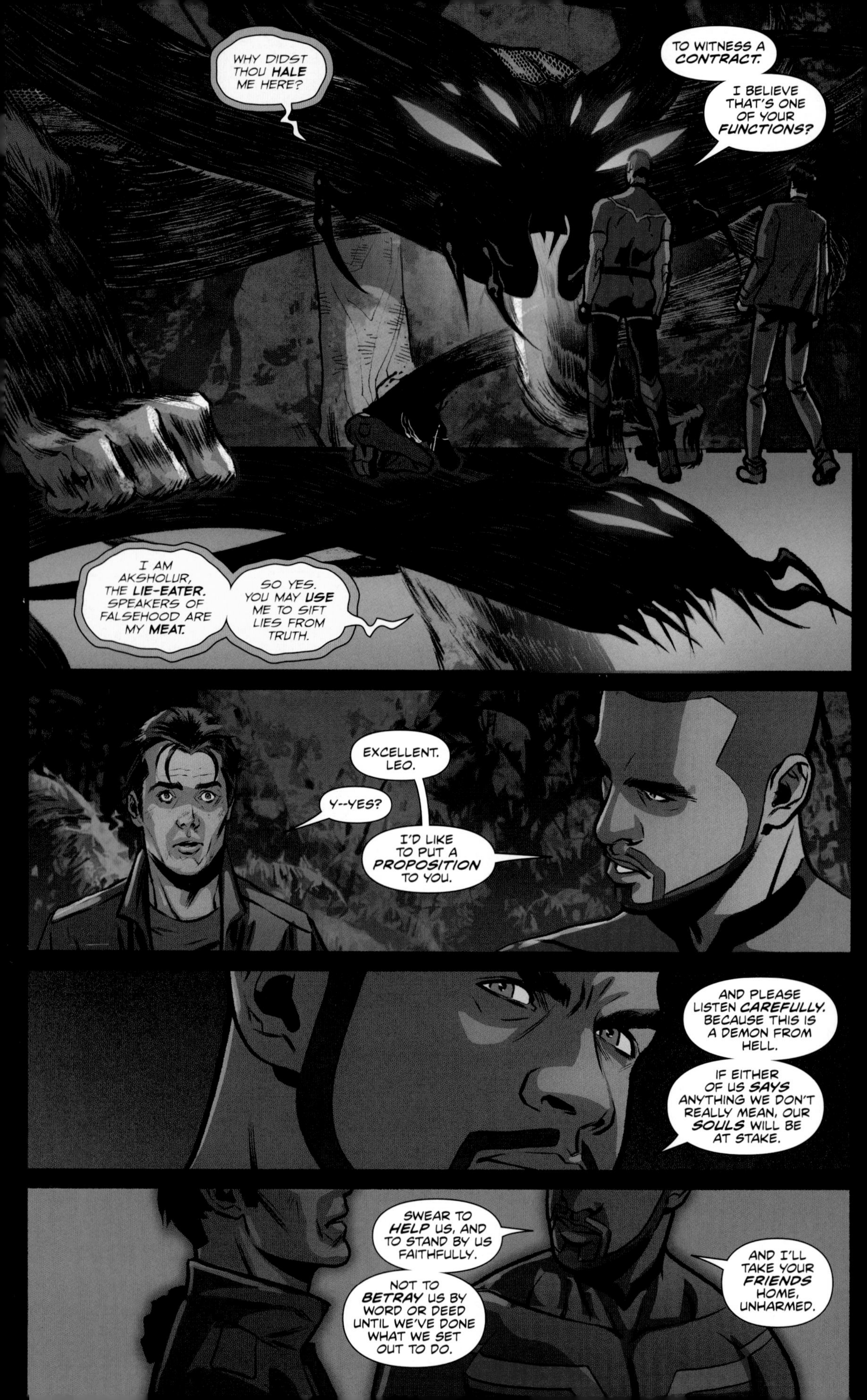
WHY DIDST THOU HALE ME HERE?
TO WITNESS A CONTRACT.
I BELIEVE THAT'S ONE OF YOUR FUNCTIONS?
I AM AKSHOLUR, THE LIE-EATER. SPEAKERS OF FALSEHOOD ARE MY MEAT.
SO YES. YOU MAY USE ME TO SIFT LIES FROM TRUTH.
EXCELLENT. LEO.
Y--YES?
I'D LIKE TO PUT A PROPOSITION TO YOU.
AND PLEASE LISTEN CAREFULLY. BECAUSE THIS IS A DEMON FROM HELL.
IF EITHER OF US SAYS ANYTHING WE DON'T REALLY MEAN, OUR SOULS WILL BE AT STAKE.
SWEAR TO HELP US, AND TO STAND BY US FAITHFULLY.
NOT TO BETRAY US BY WORD OR DEED UNTIL WE'VE DONE WHAT WE SET OUT TO DO.
AND I'LL TAKE YOUR FRIENDS HOME, UNHARMED.

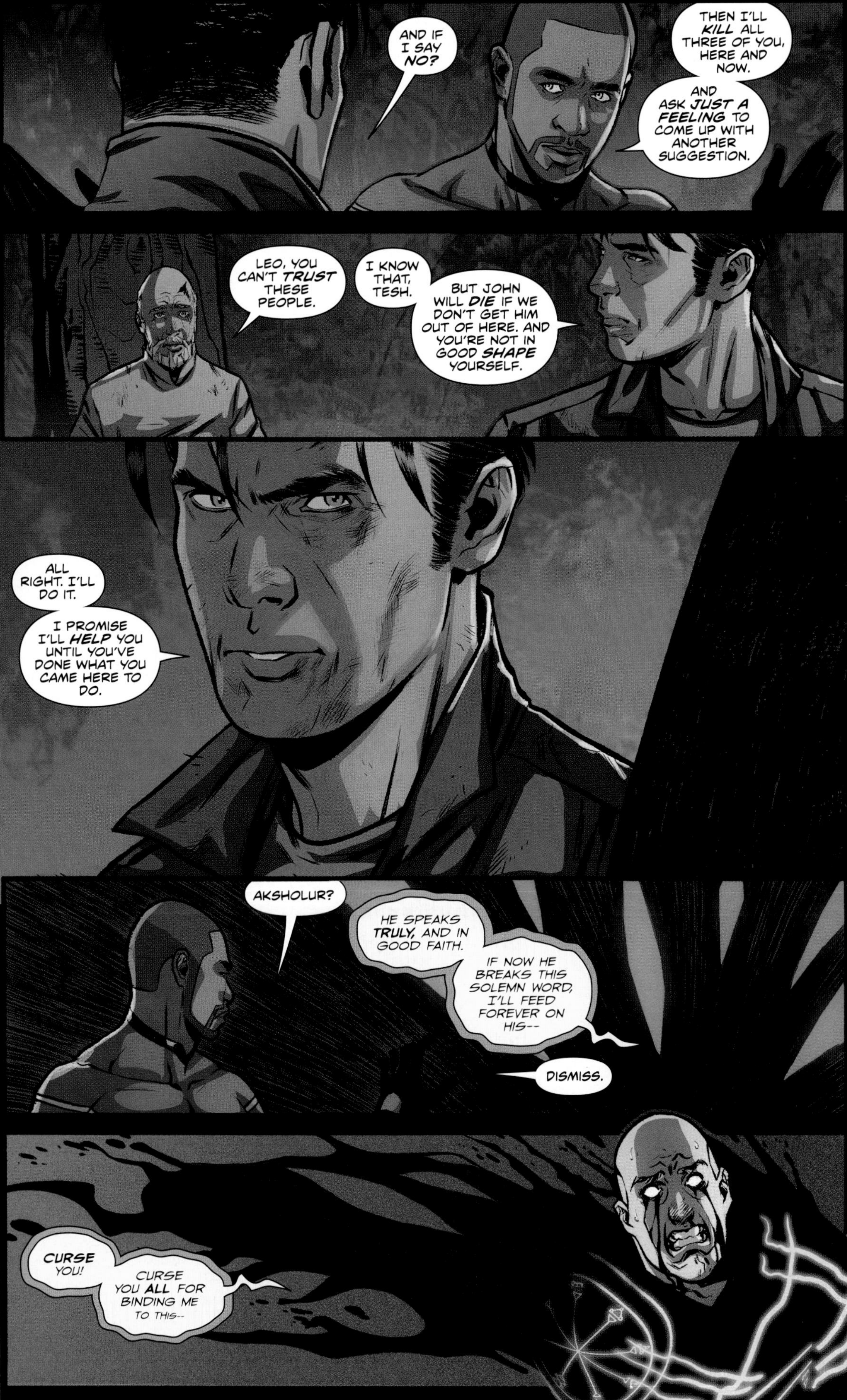
AND IF I SAY NO?
THEN I'LL KILL ALL THREE OF YOU, HERE AND NOW.
AND ASK JUST A FEELING TO COME UP WITH ANOTHER SUGGESTION.
LEO, YOU CAN'T TRUST THESE PEOPLE.
I KNOW THAT, TESH.
BUT JOHN WILL DIE IF WE DON'T GET HIM OUT OF HERE. AND YOU'RE NOT IN GOOD SHAPE YOURSELF.
ALL RIGHT. I'LL DO IT.
I PROMISE I'LL HELP YOU UNTIL YOU'VE DONE WHAT YOU CAME HERE TO DO.
AKSHOLUR?
HE SPEAKS TRULY, AND IN GOOD FAITH.
IF NOW HE BREAKS THIS SOLEMN WORD, I'LL FEED FOREVER ON HIS--
DISMISS.
CURSE YOU!
CURSE YOU ALL FOR BINDING ME TO THIS--

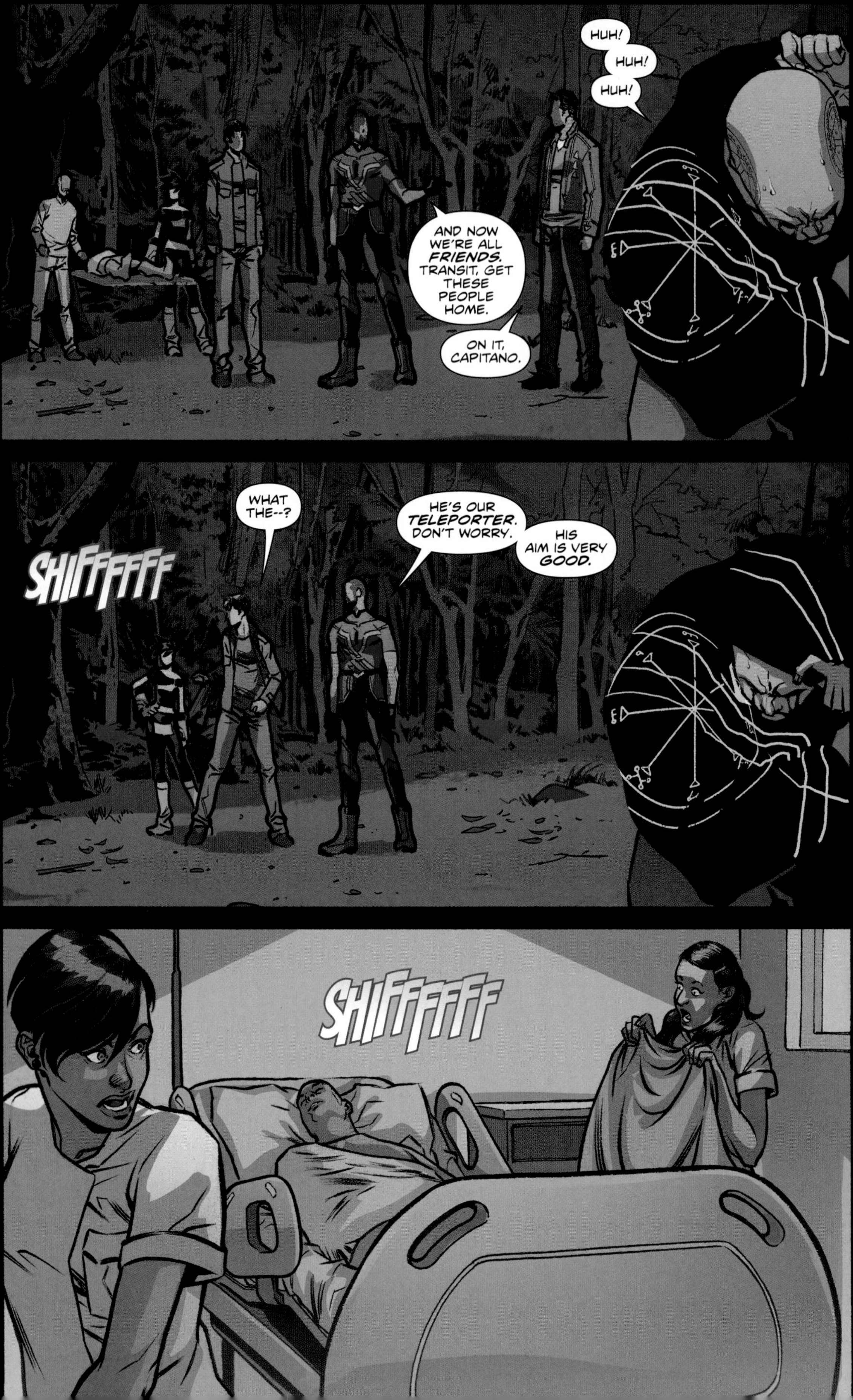
HUH!
HUH!
HUH!
AND NOW WE'RE ALL FRIENDS. TRANSIT, GET THESE PEOPLE HOME.
ON IT, CAPITANO.
SHIFFFFFF
WHAT THE--?
HE'S OUR TELEPORTER. DON'T WORRY.
HIS AIM IS VERY GOOD.
SHIFFFFFF

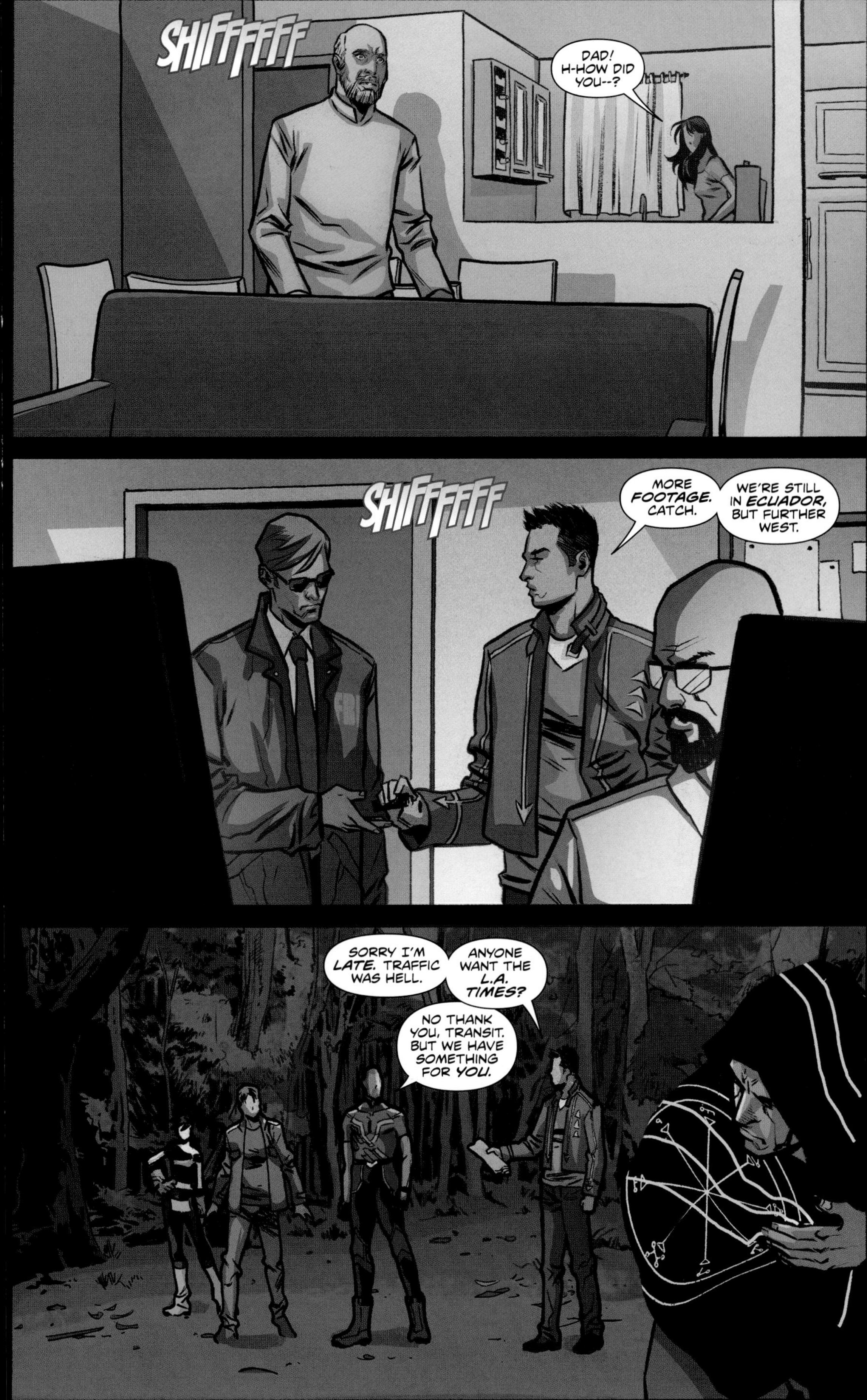
SHIFFFFFF
DAD! H-HOW DID YOU--?
SHIFFFFFF
MORE FOOTAGE. CATCH.
WE'RE STILL IN ECUADOR, BUT FURTHER WEST.
SORRY I'M LATE. TRAFFIC WAS HELL.
ANYONE WANT THE L.A. TIMES?
NO THANK YOU, TRANSIT. BUT WE HAVE SOMETHING FOR YOU.

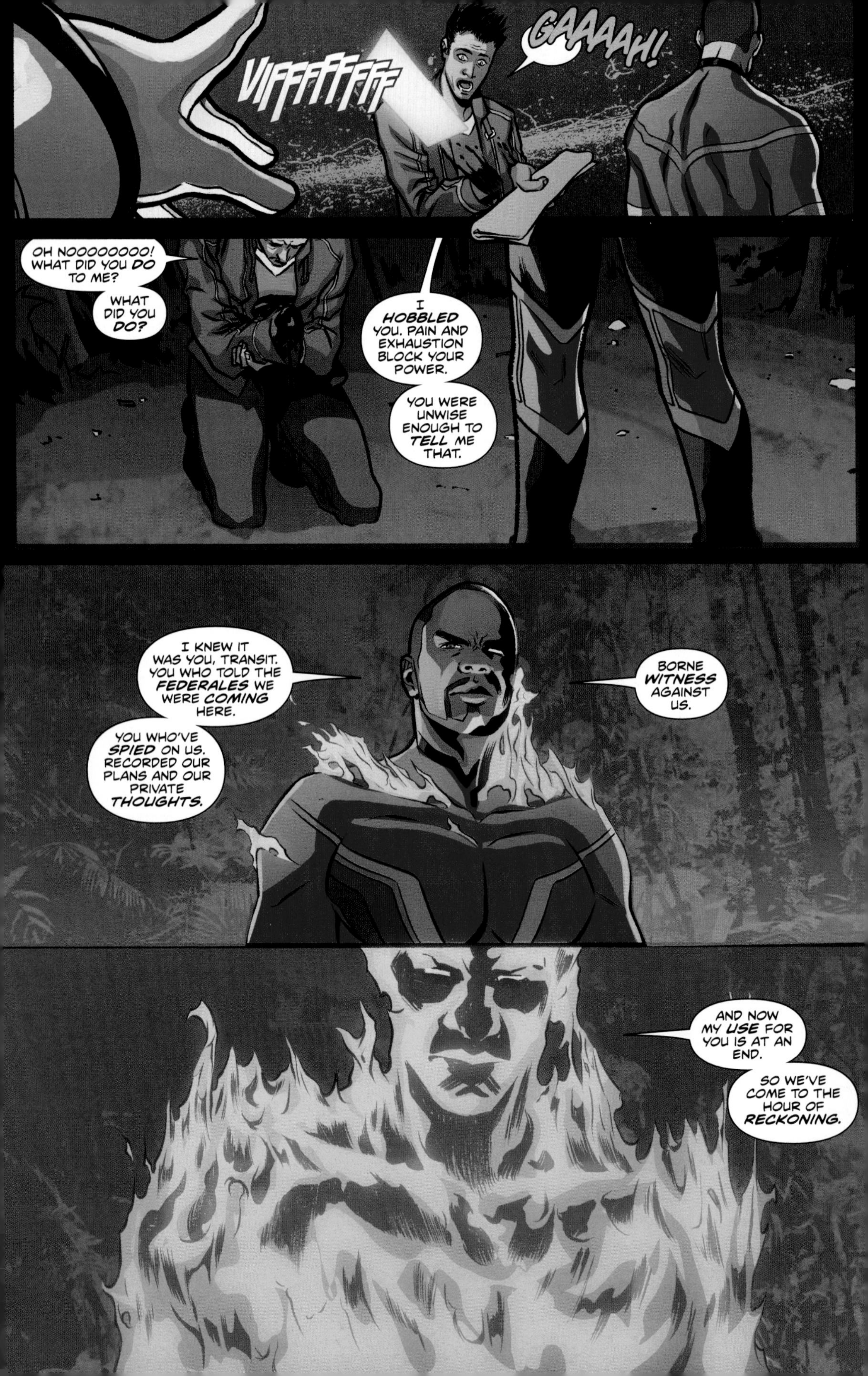
VIFFFFFFFF
GAAAAAH!
OH NOOOOOOOO! WHAT DID YOU DO TO ME?
WHAT DID YOU DO?
I HOBBLED YOU. PAIN AND EXHAUSTION BLOCK YOUR POWER.
YOU WERE UNWISE ENOUGH TO TELL ME THAT.
I KNEW IT WAS YOU, TRANSIT. YOU WHO TOLD THE FEDERALES WE WERE COMING HERE.
YOU WHO'VE SPIED ON US. RECORDED OUR PLANS AND OUR PRIVATE THOUGHTS.
BORNE WITNESS AGAINST US.
AND NOW MY USE FOR YOU IS AT AN END.
SO WE'VE COME TO THE HOUR OF RECKONING.

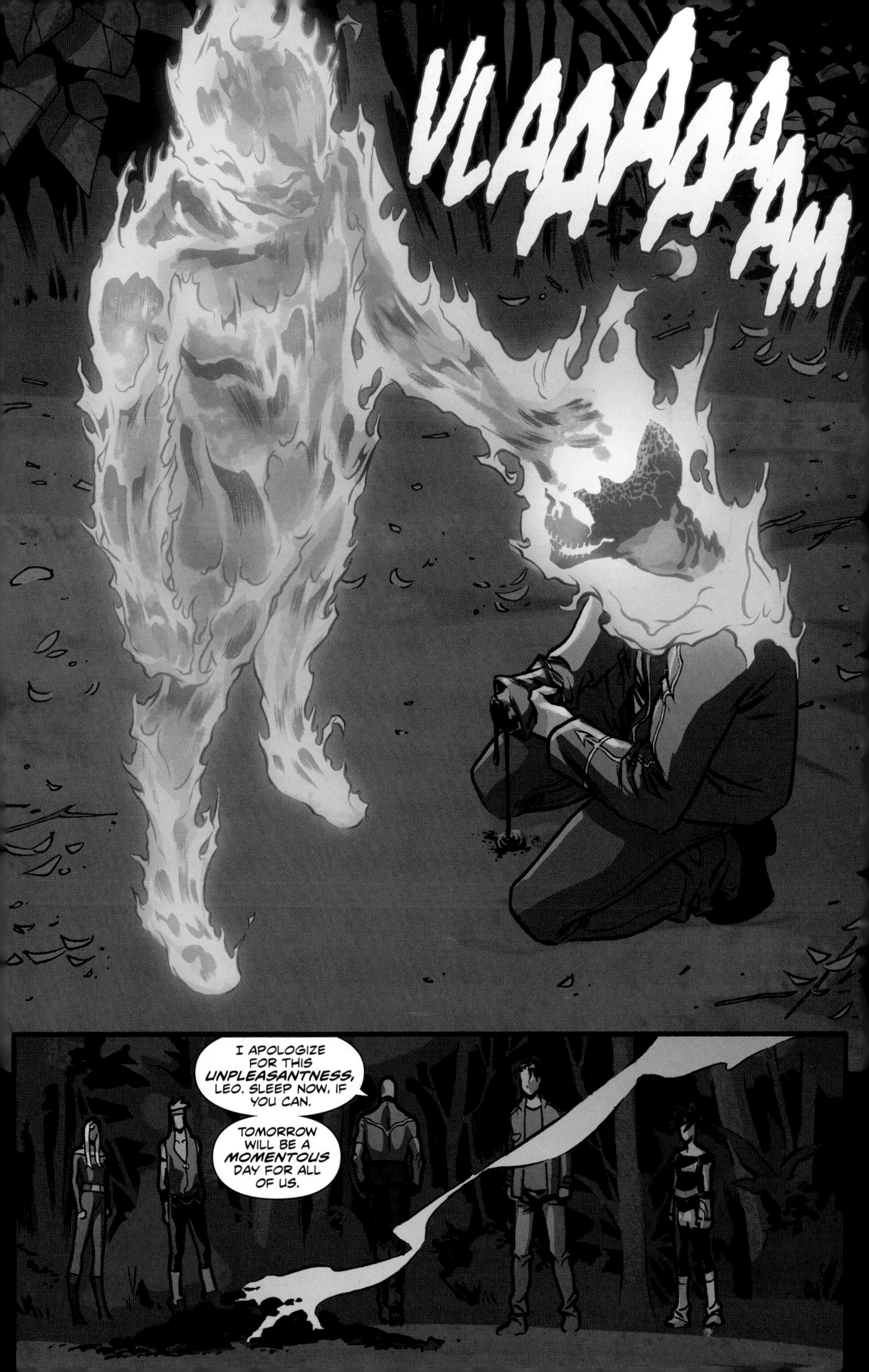
VLAAAAAAM
I APOLOGIZE FOR THIS UNPLEASANTNESS, LEO. SLEEP NOW, IF YOU CAN.
TOMORROW WILL BE A MOMENTOUS DAY FOR ALL OF US.

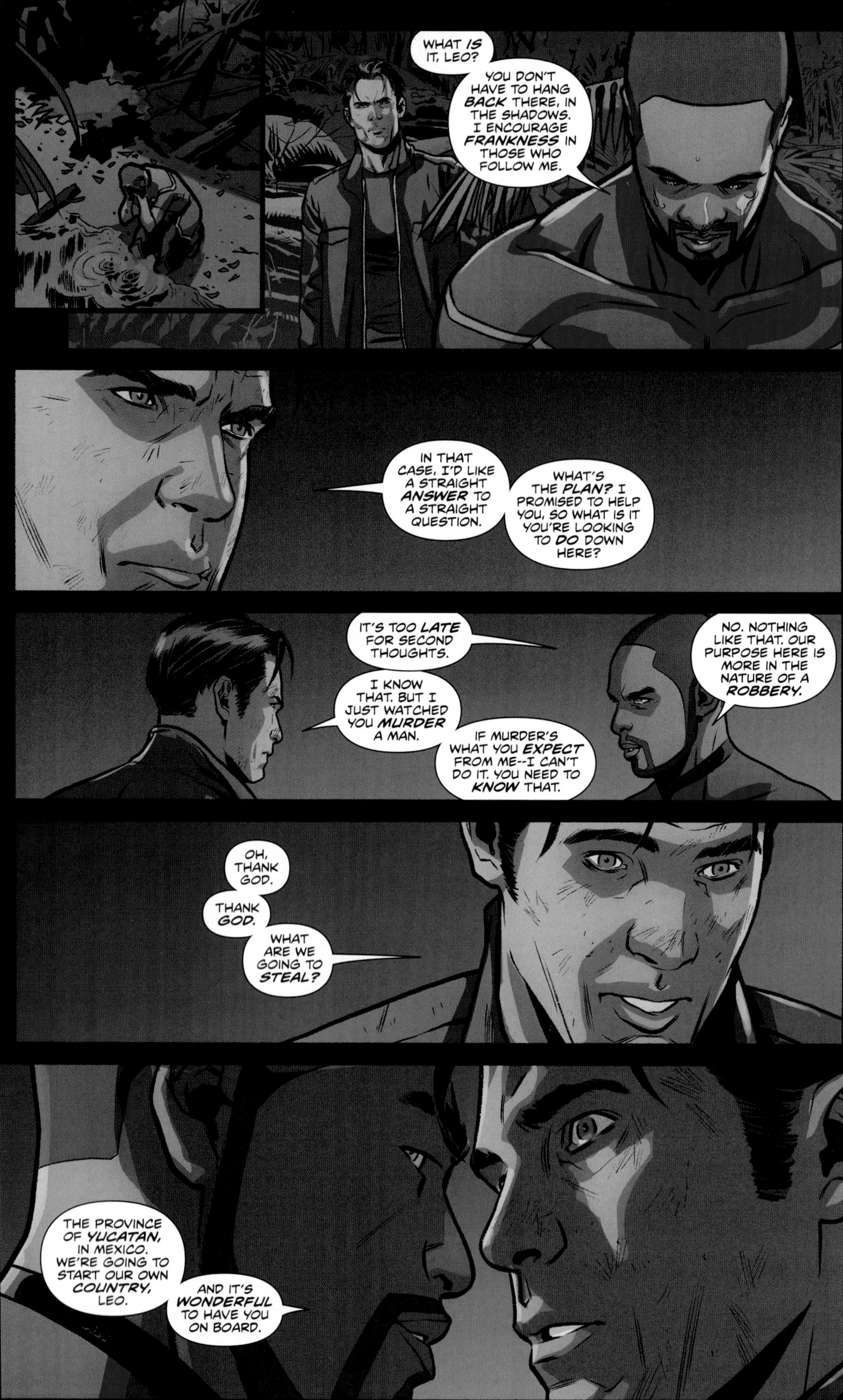
WHAT IS IT, LEO?
YOU DON'T HAVE TO HANG BACK THERE, IN THE SHADOWS. I ENCOURAGE FRANKNESS IN THOSE WHO FOLLOW ME.
IN THAT CASE, I'D LIKE A STRAIGHT ANSWER TO A STRAIGHT QUESTION.
WHAT'S THE PLAN? I PROMISED TO HELP YOU, SO WHAT IS IT YOU'RE LOOKING TO DO DOWN HERE?
IT'S TOO LATE FOR SECOND THOUGHTS.
I KNOW THAT. BUT I JUST WATCHED YOU MURDER A MAN.
IF MURDER'S WHAT YOU EXPECT FROM ME--I CAN'T DO IT. YOU NEED TO KNOW THAT.
NO. NOTHING LIKE THAT. OUR PURPOSE HERE IS MORE IN THE NATURE OF A ROBBERY.
OH, THANK GOD.
THANK GOD.
WHAT ARE WE GOING TO STEAL?
THE PROVINCE OF YUCATAN, IN MEXICO. WE'RE GOING TO START OUR OWN COUNTRY, LEO.
AND IT'S WONDERFUL TO HAVE YOU ON BOARD.

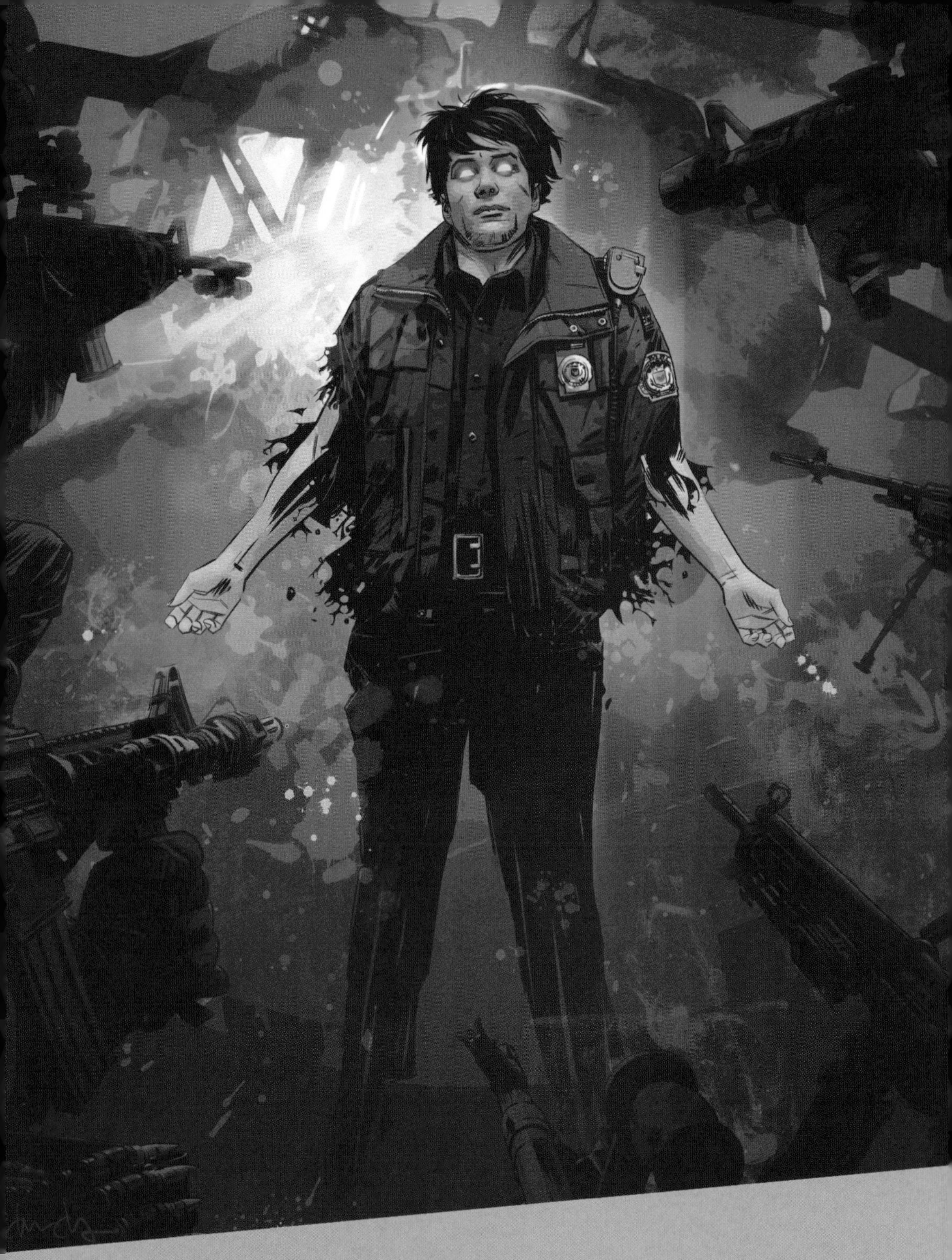

"**VIOLENCE** IS ONLY A MEANS TO AN **END**."
Chapter 7

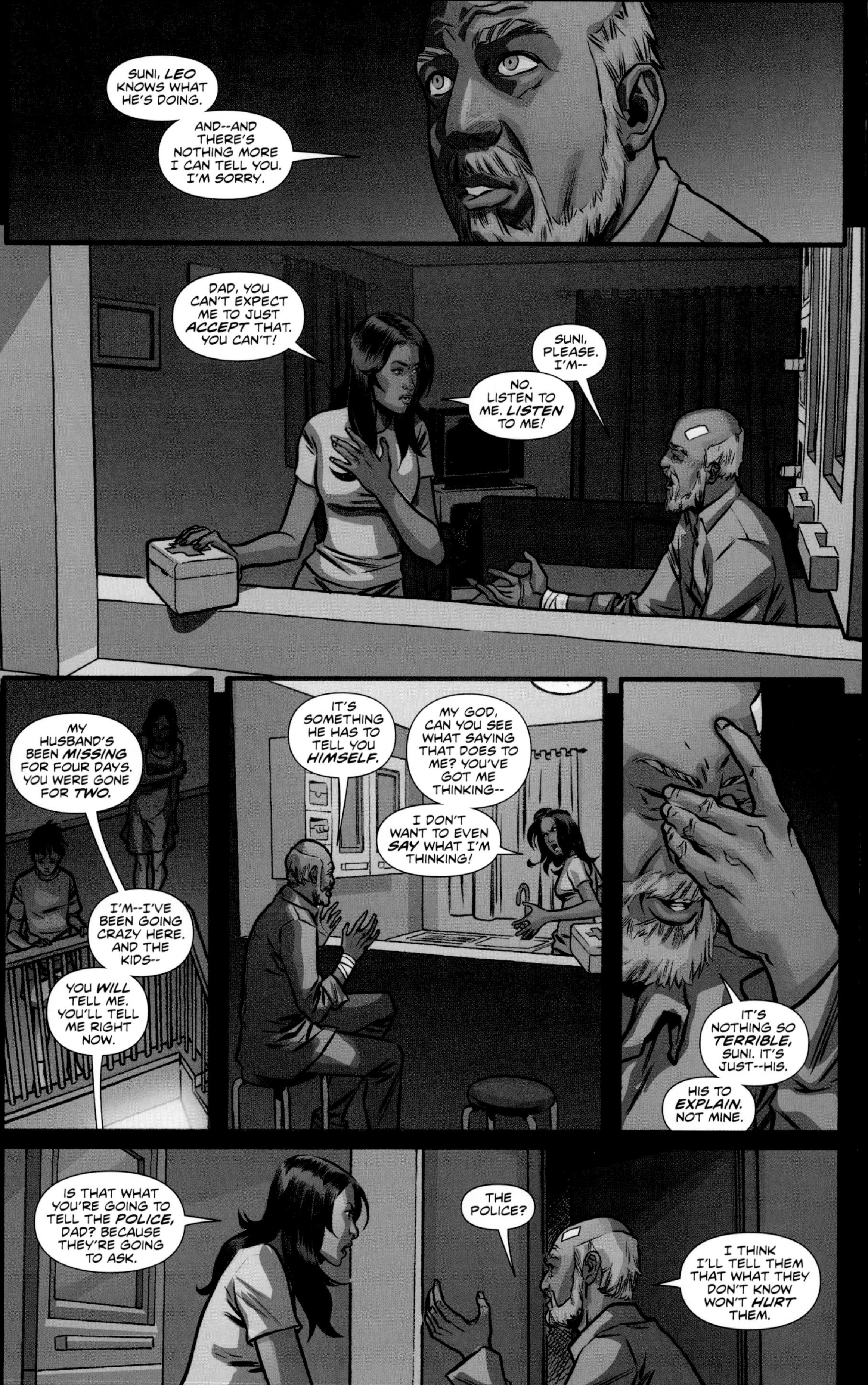
SUNI, LEO KNOWS WHAT HE'S DOING.
AND--AND THERE'S NOTHING MORE I CAN TELL YOU. I'M SORRY.
DAD, YOU CAN'T EXPECT ME TO JUST ACCEPT THAT. YOU CAN'T!
SUNI, PLEASE. I'M--
NO. LISTEN TO ME. LISTEN TO ME!
MY HUSBAND'S BEEN MISSING FOR FOUR DAYS. YOU WERE GONE FOR TWO.
I'M--I'VE BEEN GOING CRAZY HERE. AND THE KIDS--
YOU WILL TELL ME. YOU'LL TELL ME RIGHT NOW.
IT'S SOMETHING HE HAS TO TELL YOU HIMSELF.
MY GOD, CAN YOU SEE WHAT SAYING THAT DOES TO ME? YOU'VE GOT ME THINKING--
I DON'T WANT TO EVEN SAY WHAT I'M THINKING!
IT'S NOTHING SO TERRIBLE, SUNI. IT'S JUST--HIS.
HIS TO EXPLAIN. NOT MINE.
IS THAT WHAT YOU'RE GOING TO TELL THE POLICE, DAD? BECAUSE THEY'RE GOING TO ASK.
THE POLICE?
I THINK I'LL TELL THEM THAT WHAT THEY DON'T KNOW WON'T HURT THEM.

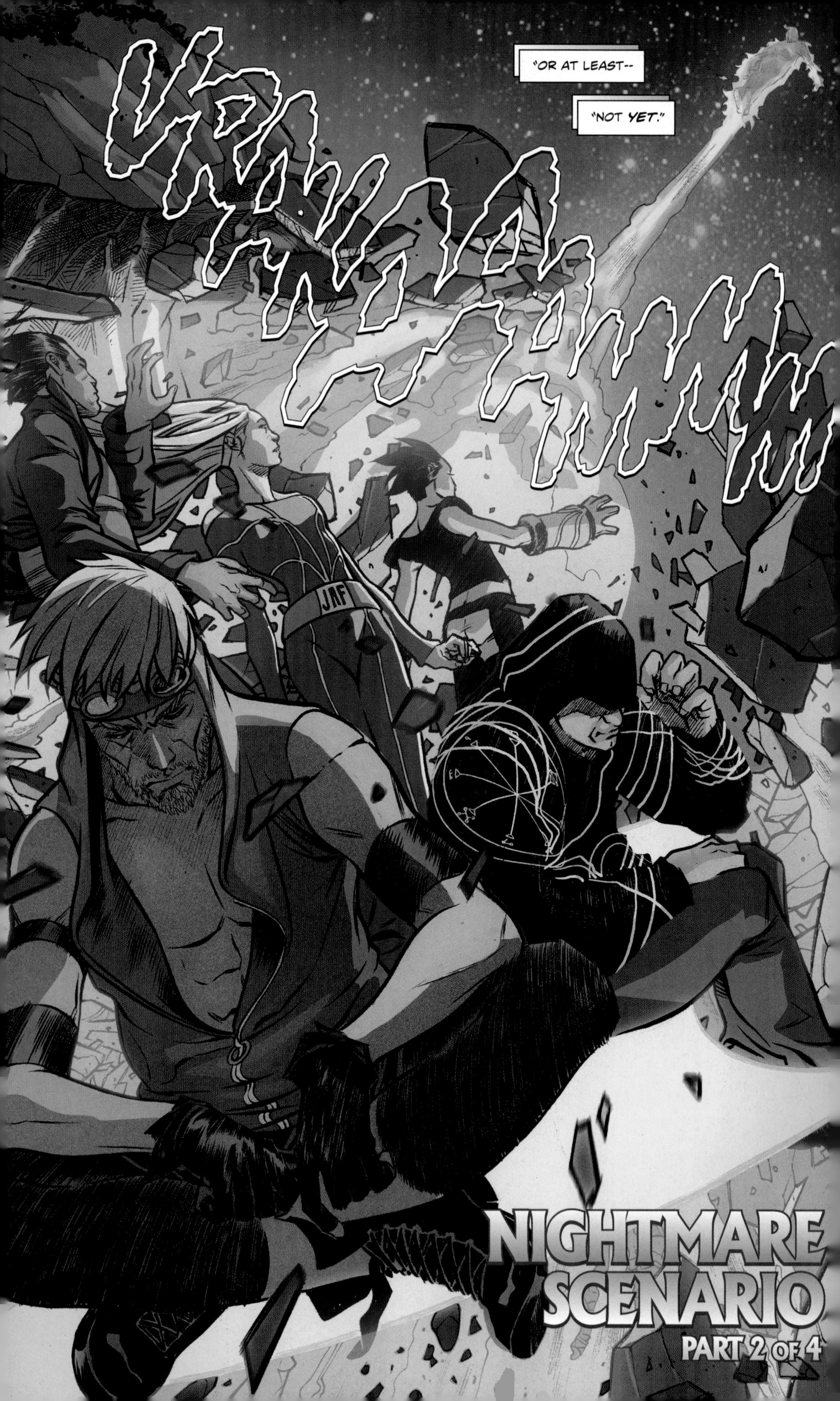
"OR AT LEAST--
"NOT YET."
JAF
NIGHTMARE SCENARIO
PART 2 OF 4

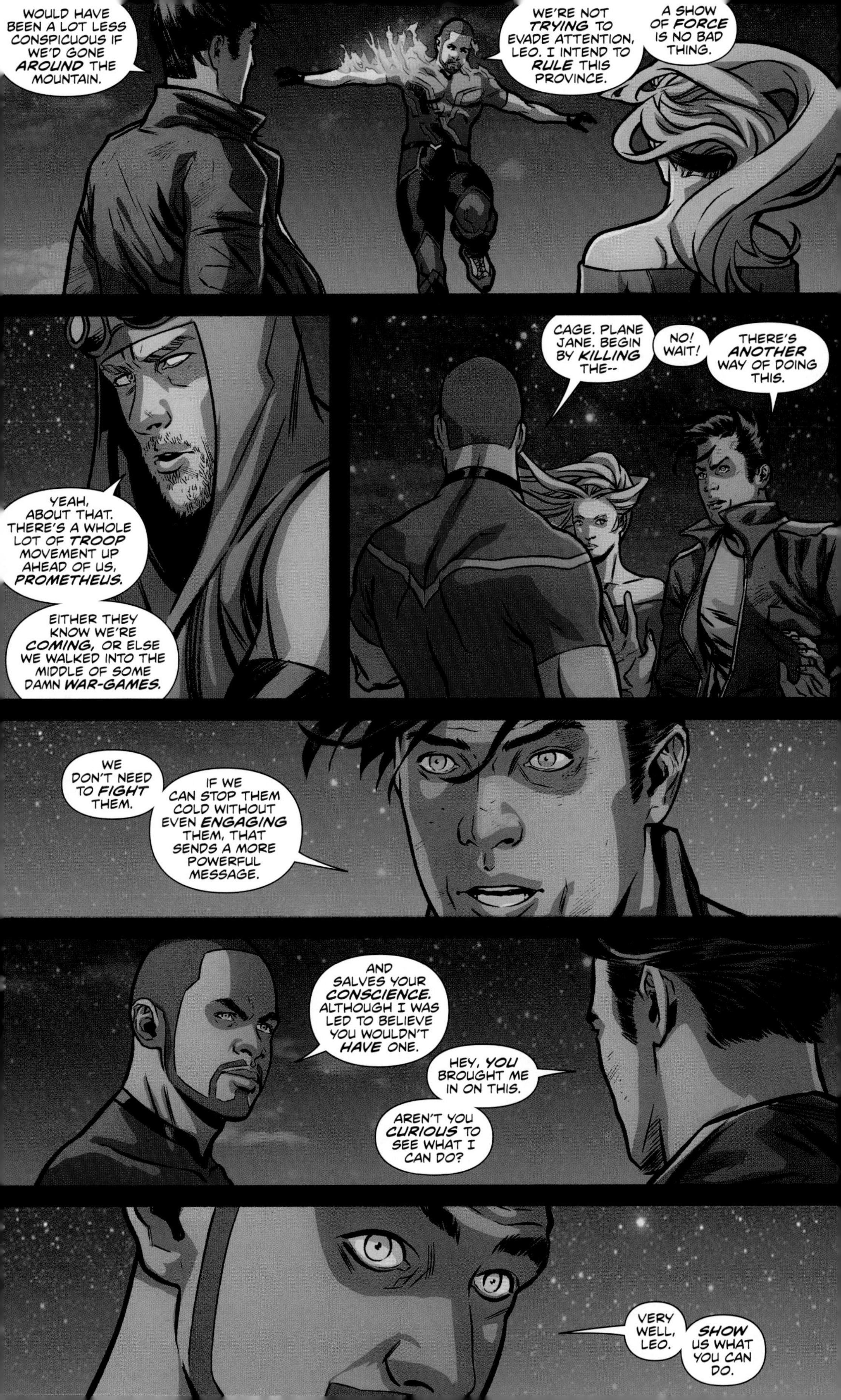
WOULD HAVE BEEN A LOT LESS CONSPICUOUS IF WE'D GONE AROUND THE MOUNTAIN.
WE'RE NOT TRYING TO EVADE ATTENTION, LEO. I INTEND TO RULE THIS PROVINCE.
A SHOW OF FORCE IS NO BAD THING.
YEAH, ABOUT THAT. THERE'S A WHOLE LOT OF TROOP MOVEMENT UP AHEAD OF US, PROMETHEUS.
EITHER THEY KNOW WE'RE COMING, OR ELSE WE WALKED INTO THE MIDDLE OF SOME DAMN WAR-GAMES.
CAGE. PLANE JANE. BEGIN BY KILLING THE--
NO! WAIT!
THERE'S ANOTHER WAY OF DOING THIS.
WE DON'T NEED TO FIGHT THEM.
IF WE CAN STOP THEM COLD WITHOUT EVEN ENGAGING THEM, THAT SENDS A MORE POWERFUL MESSAGE.
AND SALVES YOUR CONSCIENCE. ALTHOUGH I WAS LED TO BELIEVE YOU WOULDN'T HAVE ONE.
HEY, YOU BROUGHT ME IN ON THIS.
AREN'T YOU CURIOUS TO SEE WHAT I CAN DO?
VERY WELL, LEO.
SHOW US WHAT YOU CAN DO.

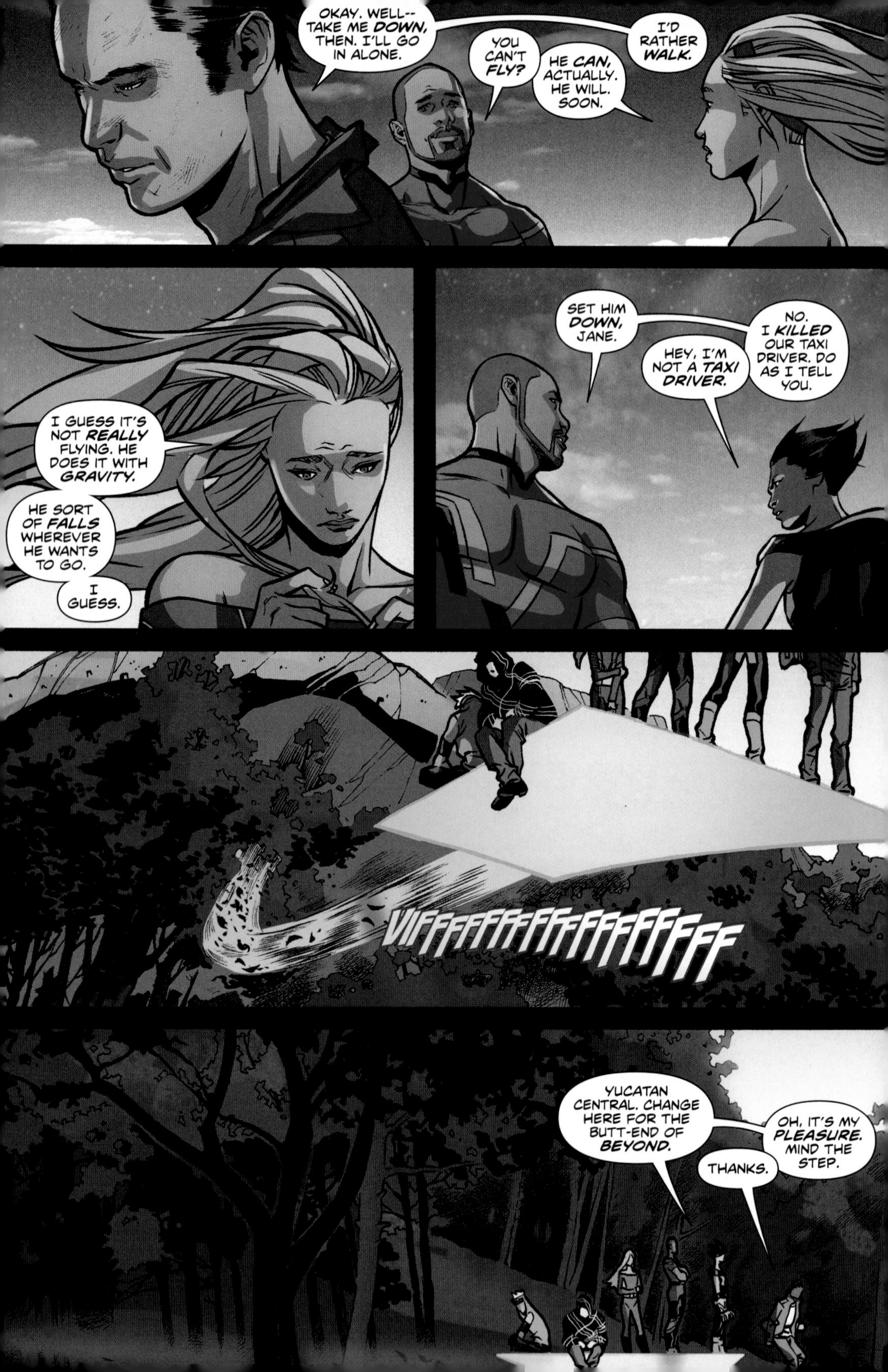
OKAY. WELL-- TAKE ME DOWN, THEN. I'LL GO IN ALONE.
I'D RATHER WALK.
YOU CAN'T FLY?
HE CAN, ACTUALLY. HE WILL. SOON.
I GUESS IT'S NOT REALLY FLYING. HE DOES IT WITH GRAVITY.
HE SORT OF FALLS WHEREVER HE WANTS TO GO.
I GUESS.
SET HIM DOWN, JANE.
NO. I KILLED OUR TAXI DRIVER. DO AS I TELL YOU.
HEY, I'M NOT A TAXI DRIVER.
VIFFFFFFFFFFFFFFFFFFFF
YUCATAN CENTRAL. CHANGE HERE FOR THE BUTT-END OF BEYOND.
OH, IT'S MY PLEASURE. MIND THE STEP.
THANKS.

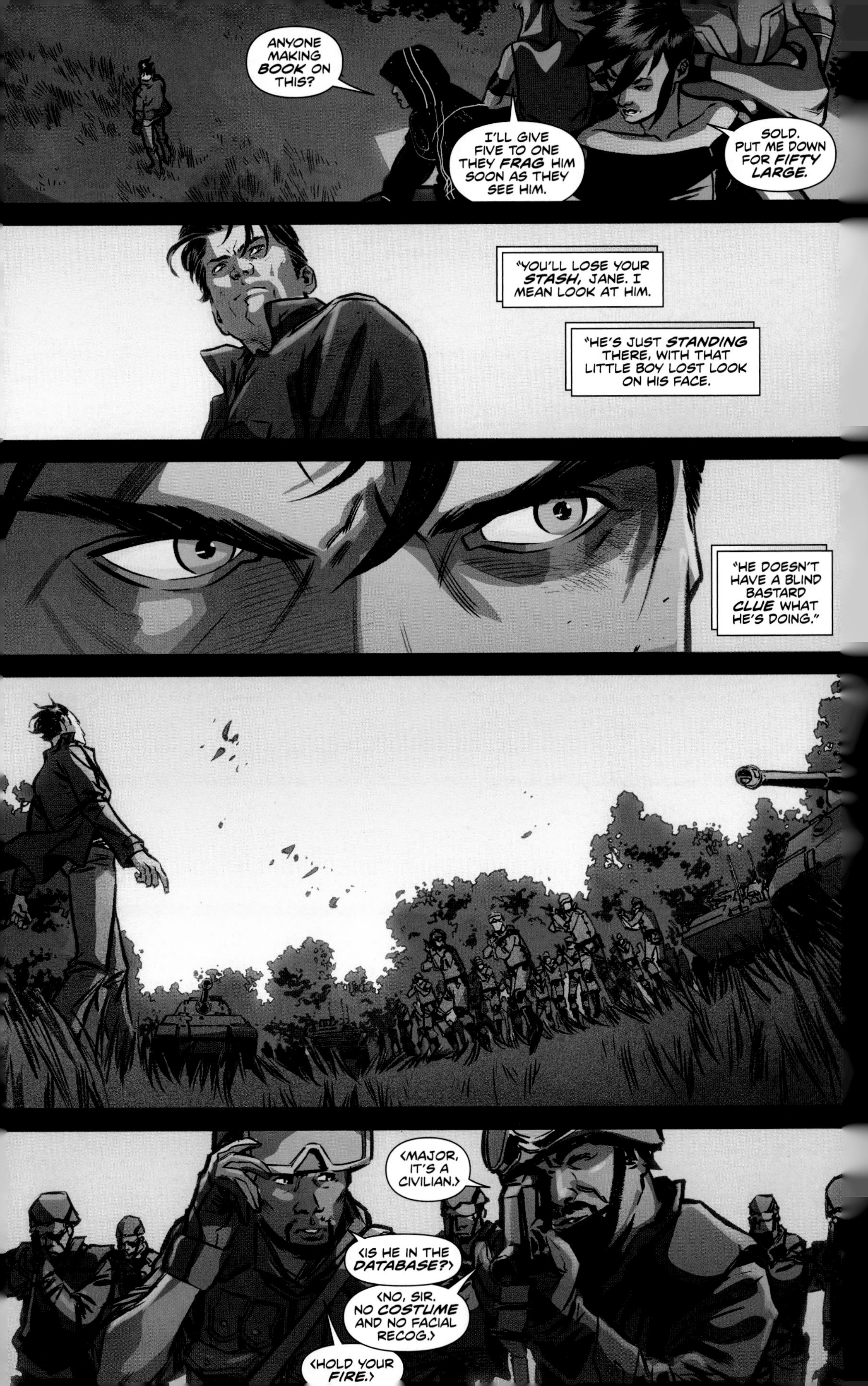

ANYONE MAKING BOOK ON THIS?
I'LL GIVE FIVE TO ONE THEY FRAG HIM SOON AS THEY SEE HIM.
SOLD. PUT ME DOWN FOR FIFTY LARGE.
"YOU'LL LOSE YOUR STASH, JANE. I MEAN LOOK AT HIM.
"HE'S JUST STANDING THERE, WITH THAT LITTLE BOY LOST LOOK ON HIS FACE.
"HE DOESN'T HAVE A BLIND BASTARD CLUE WHAT HE'S DOING."
‹MAJOR, IT'S A CIVILIAN.›
‹IS HE IN THE DATABASE?›
‹NO, SIR. NO COSTUME AND NO FACIAL RECOG.›
‹HOLD YOUR FIRE.›

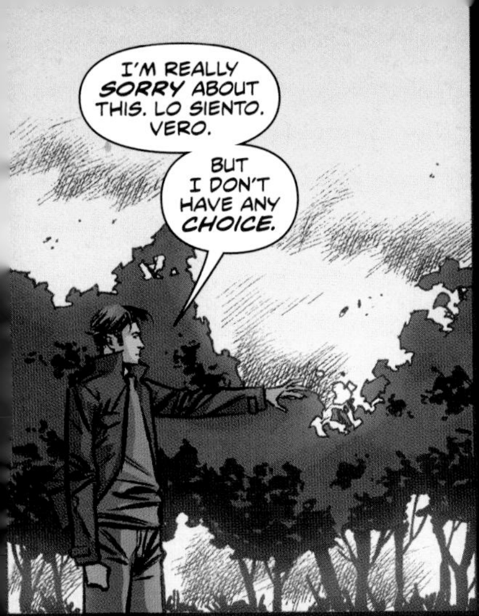
I'M REALLY SORRY ABOUT THIS. LO SIENTO. VERO.
BUT I DON'T HAVE ANY CHOICE.
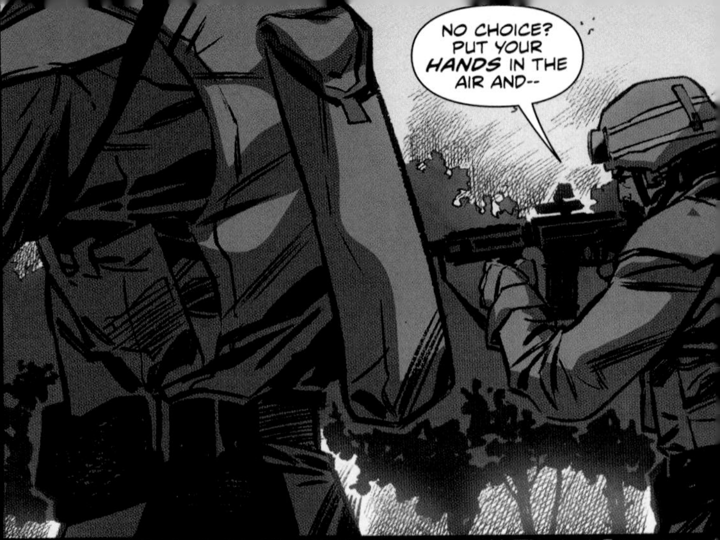
NO CHOICE? PUT YOUR HANDS IN THE AIR AND--
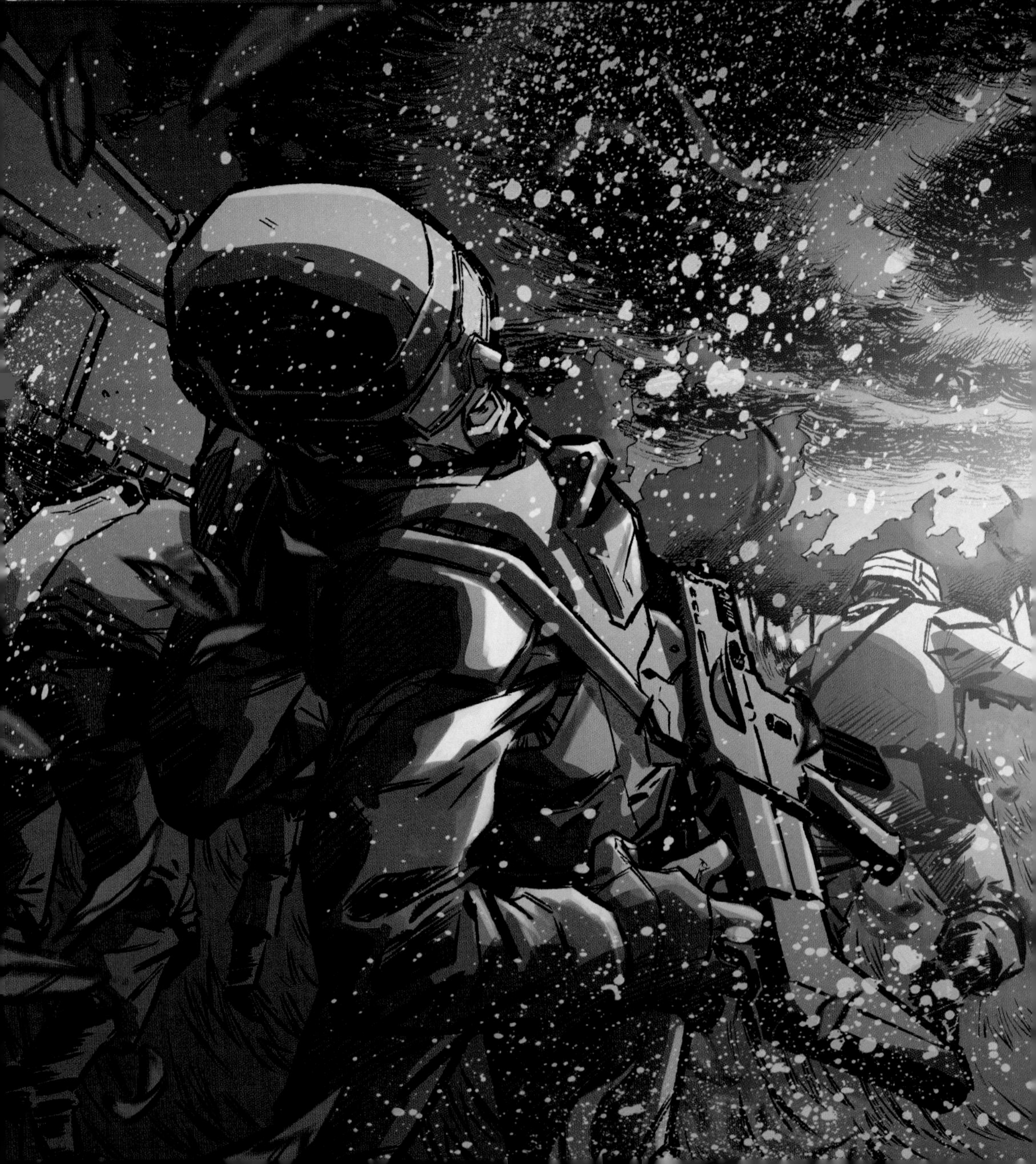

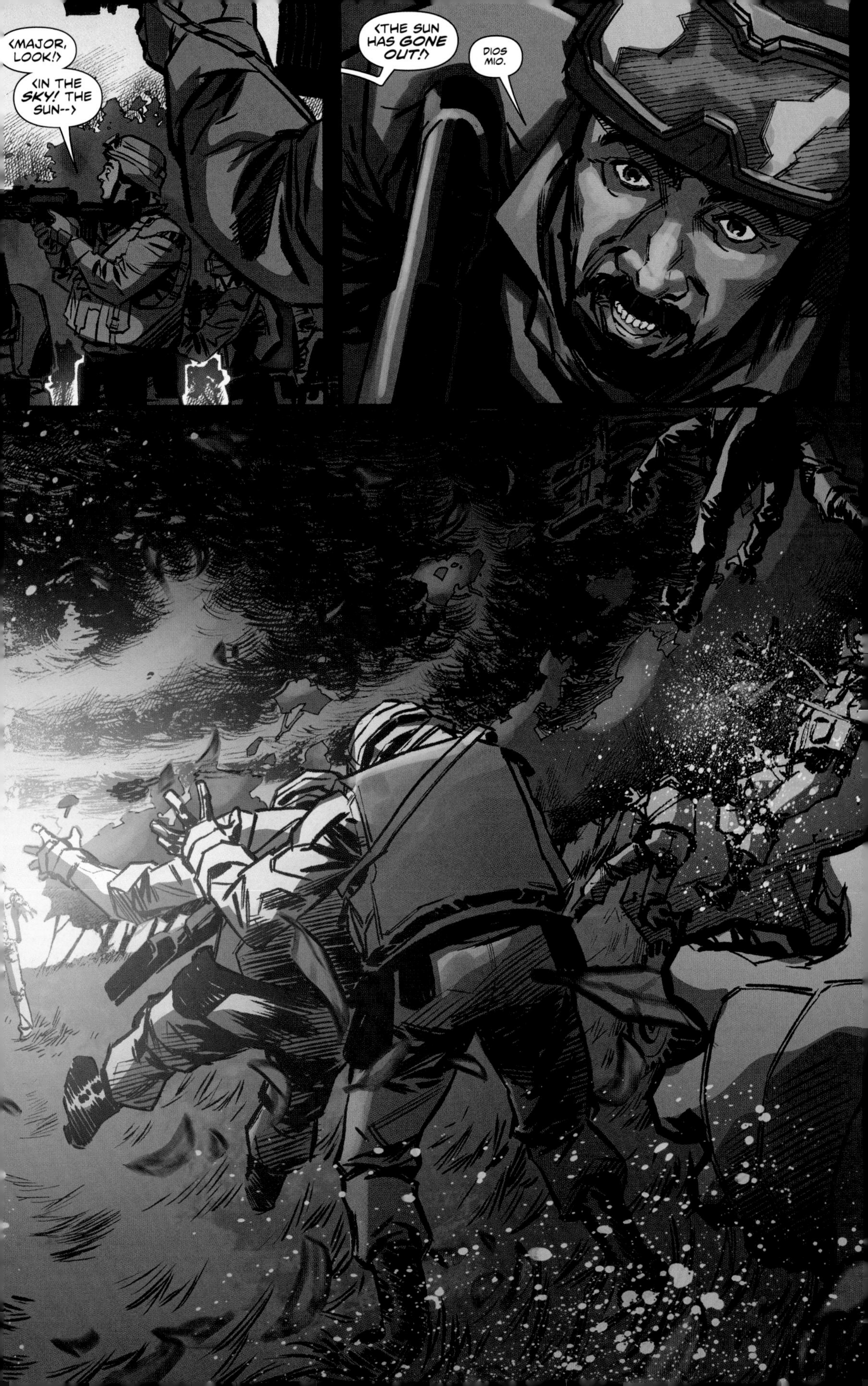

<MAJOR, LOOK!>
<IN THE SKY! THE SUN-->
<THE SUN HAS GONE OUT!>
DIOS MIO.

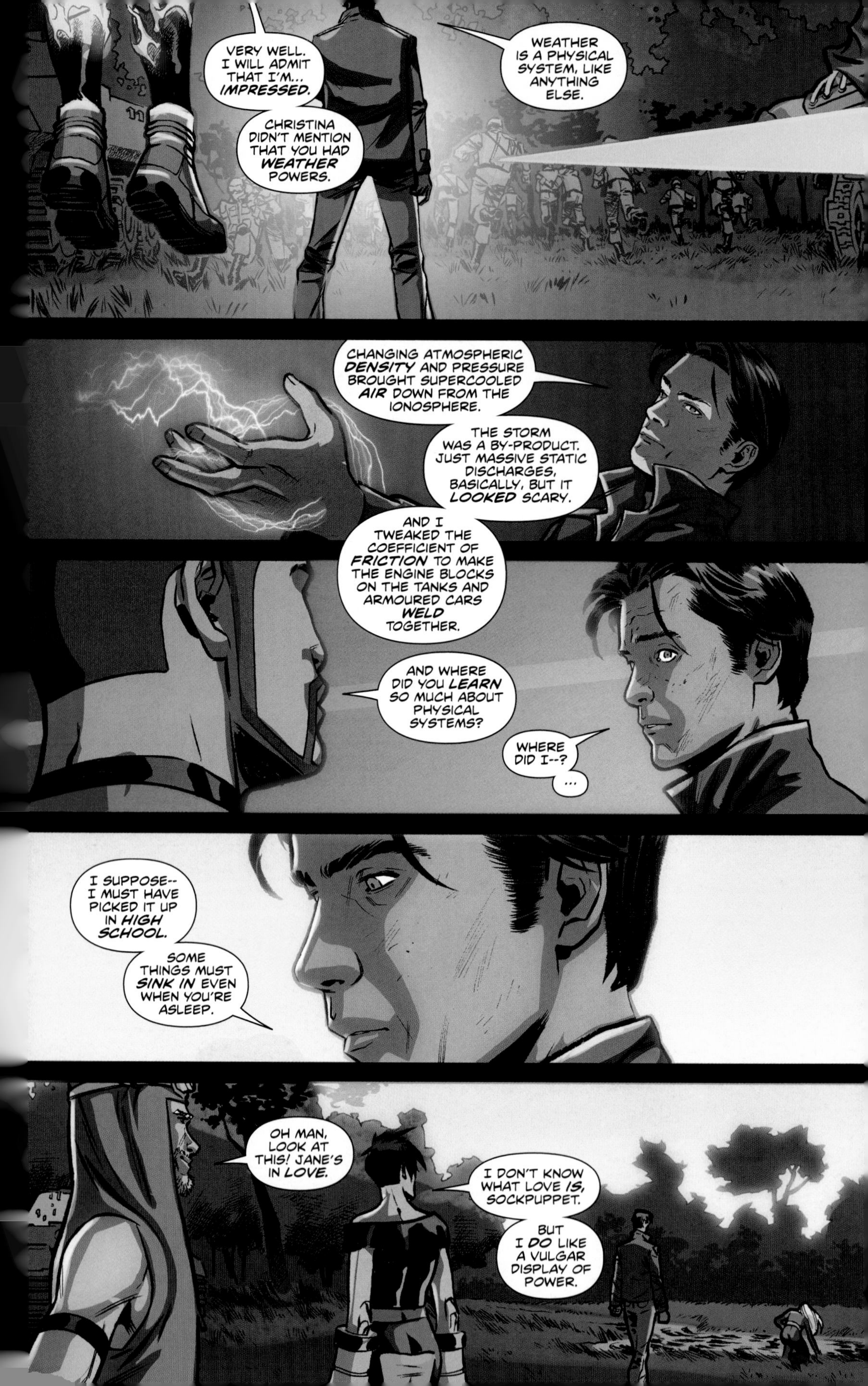
VERY WELL. I WILL ADMIT THAT I'M... IMPRESSED.
CHRISTINA DIDN'T MENTION THAT YOU HAD WEATHER POWERS.
WEATHER IS A PHYSICAL SYSTEM, LIKE ANYTHING ELSE.
CHANGING ATMOSPHERIC DENSITY AND PRESSURE BROUGHT SUPERCOOLED AIR DOWN FROM THE IONOSPHERE.
THE STORM WAS A BY-PRODUCT. JUST MASSIVE STATIC DISCHARGES, BASICALLY, BUT IT LOOKED SCARY.
AND I TWEAKED THE COEFFICIENT OF FRICTION TO MAKE THE ENGINE BLOCKS ON THE TANKS AND ARMOURED CARS WELD TOGETHER.
AND WHERE DID YOU LEARN SO MUCH ABOUT PHYSICAL SYSTEMS?
WHERE DID I--?
...
I SUPPOSE-- I MUST HAVE PICKED IT UP IN HIGH SCHOOL.
SOME THINGS MUST SINK IN EVEN WHEN YOU'RE ASLEEP.
OH MAN, LOOK AT THIS! JANE'S IN LOVE.
I DON'T KNOW WHAT LOVE IS, SOCKPUPPET.
BUT I DO LIKE A VULGAR DISPLAY OF POWER.

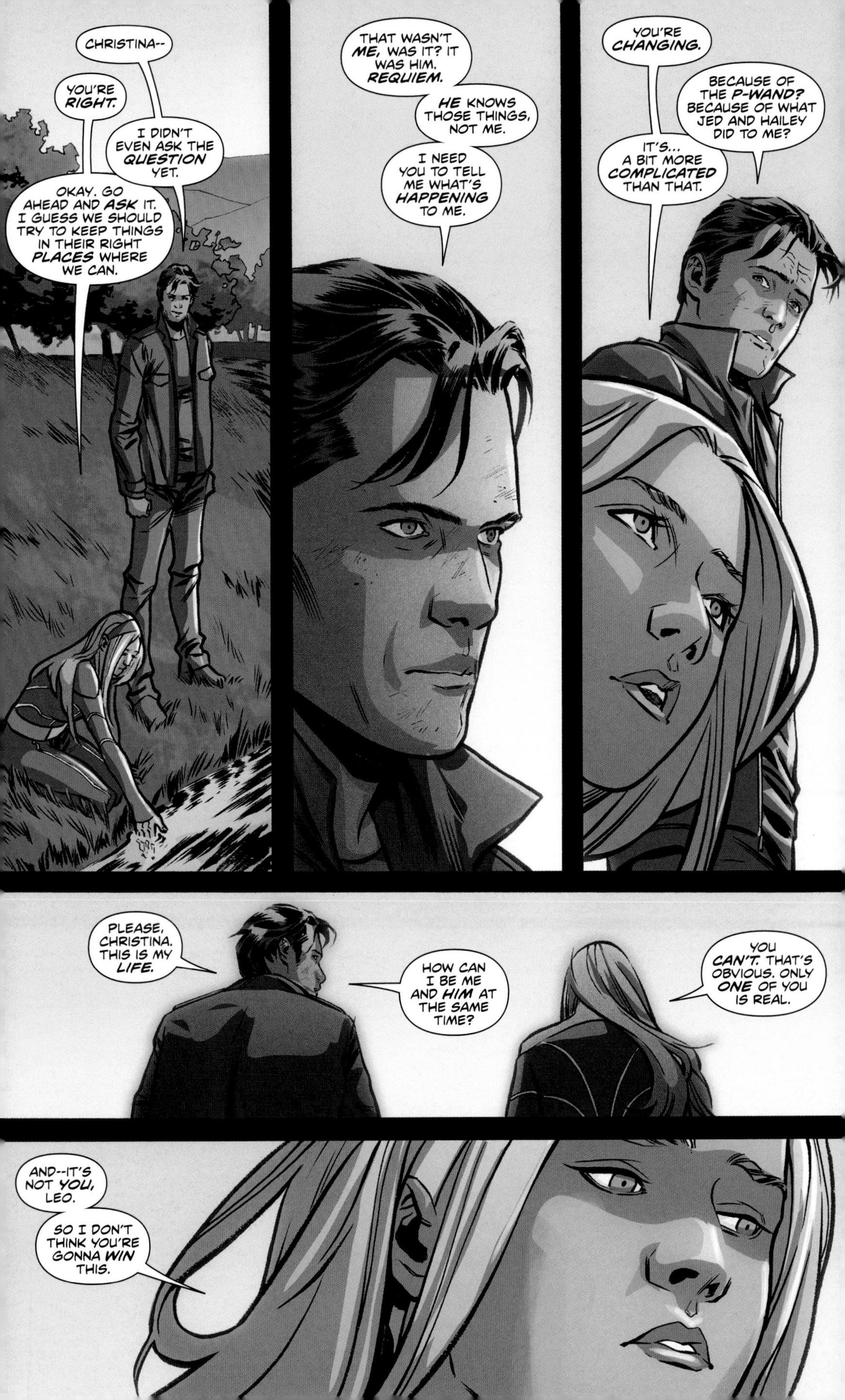
CHRISTINA--
YOU'RE RIGHT.
I DIDN'T EVEN ASK THE QUESTION YET.
OKAY. GO AHEAD AND ASK IT. I GUESS WE SHOULD TRY TO KEEP THINGS IN THEIR RIGHT PLACES WHERE WE CAN.
THAT WASN'T ME, WAS IT? IT WAS HIM. REQUIEM.
HE KNOWS THOSE THINGS, NOT ME.
I NEED YOU TO TELL ME WHAT'S HAPPENING TO ME.
YOU'RE CHANGING.
BECAUSE OF THE P-WAND? BECAUSE OF WHAT JED AND HAILEY DID TO ME?
IT'S... A BIT MORE COMPLICATED THAN THAT.
PLEASE, CHRISTINA. THIS IS MY LIFE.
HOW CAN I BE ME AND HIM AT THE SAME TIME?
YOU CAN'T. THAT'S OBVIOUS. ONLY ONE OF YOU IS REAL.
AND--IT'S NOT YOU, LEO.
SO I DON'T THINK YOU'RE GONNA WIN THIS.

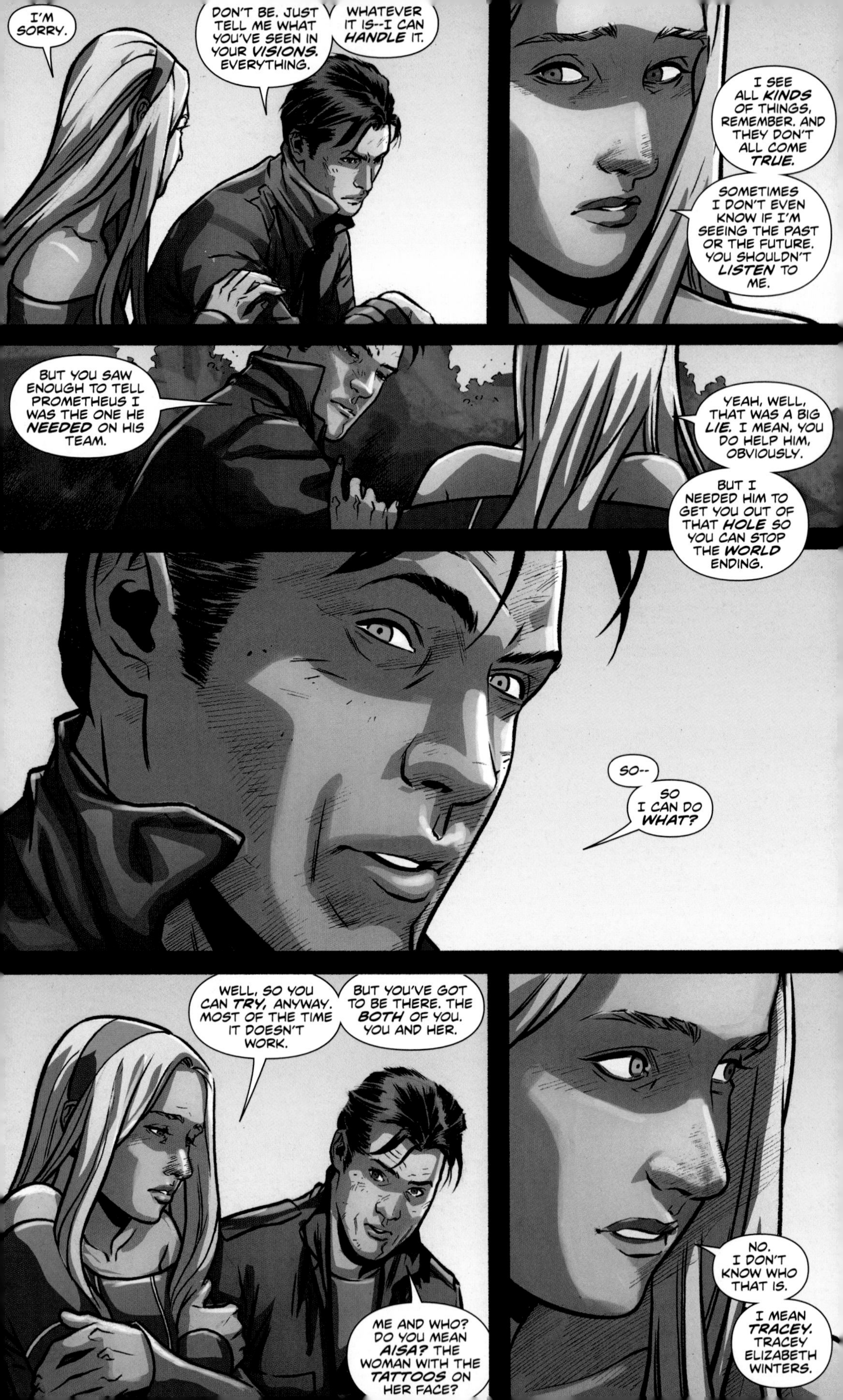
I'M SORRY.
DON'T BE. JUST TELL ME WHAT YOU'VE SEEN IN YOUR VISIONS. EVERYTHING.
WHATEVER IT IS--I CAN HANDLE IT.
I SEE ALL KINDS OF THINGS, REMEMBER. AND THEY DON'T ALL COME TRUE.
SOMETIMES I DON'T EVEN KNOW IF I'M SEEING THE PAST OR THE FUTURE. YOU SHOULDN'T LISTEN TO ME.
BUT YOU SAW ENOUGH TO TELL PROMETHEUS I WAS THE ONE HE NEEDED ON HIS TEAM.
YEAH, WELL, THAT WAS A BIG LIE. I MEAN, YOU DO HELP HIM, OBVIOUSLY.
BUT I NEEDED HIM TO GET YOU OUT OF THAT HOLE SO YOU CAN STOP THE WORLD ENDING.
SO--
SO I CAN DO WHAT?
WELL, SO YOU CAN TRY, ANYWAY. MOST OF THE TIME IT DOESN'T WORK.
BUT YOU'VE GOT TO BE THERE. THE BOTH OF YOU. YOU AND HER.
ME AND WHO? DO YOU MEAN AISA? THE WOMAN WITH THE TATTOOS ON HER FACE?
NO. I DON'T KNOW WHO THAT IS.
I MEAN TRACEY. TRACEY ELIZABETH WINTERS.

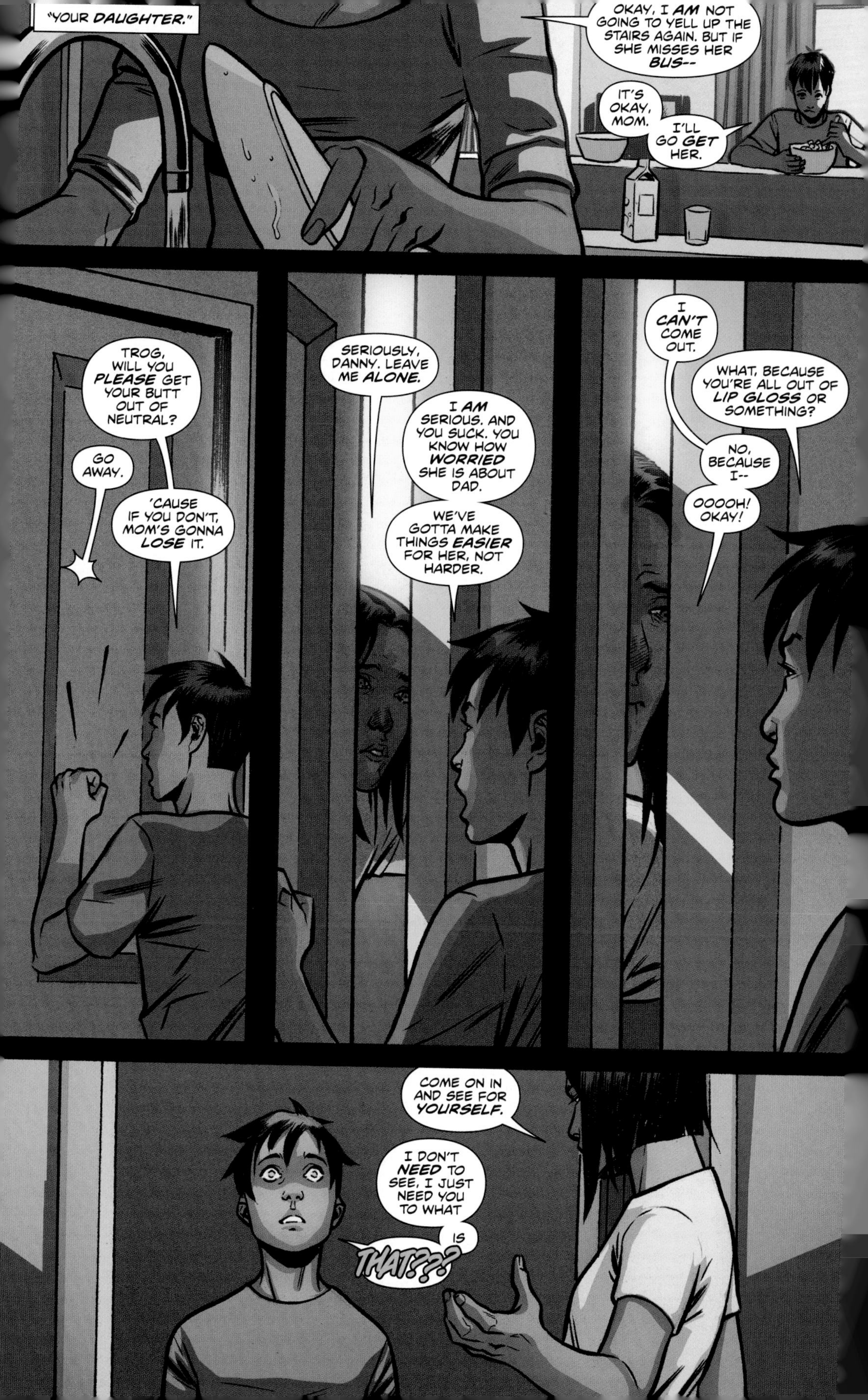
"YOUR DAUGHTER."
OKAY, I AM NOT GOING TO YELL UP THE STAIRS AGAIN. BUT IF SHE MISSES HER BUS--
IT'S OKAY, MOM.
I'LL GO GET HER.
TROG, WILL YOU PLEASE GET YOUR BUTT OUT OF NEUTRAL?
GO AWAY.
'CAUSE IF YOU DON'T, MOM'S GONNA LOSE IT.
SERIOUSLY, DANNY. LEAVE ME ALONE.
I AM SERIOUS. AND YOU SUCK. YOU KNOW HOW WORRIED SHE IS ABOUT DAD.
WE'VE GOTTA MAKE THINGS EASIER FOR HER, NOT HARDER.
I CAN'T COME OUT.
WHAT, BECAUSE YOU'RE ALL OUT OF LIP GLOSS OR SOMETHING?
NO, BECAUSE I--
OOOOH! OKAY!
COME ON IN AND SEE FOR YOURSELF.
I DON'T NEED TO SEE, I JUST NEED YOU TO WHAT
IS
THAT???

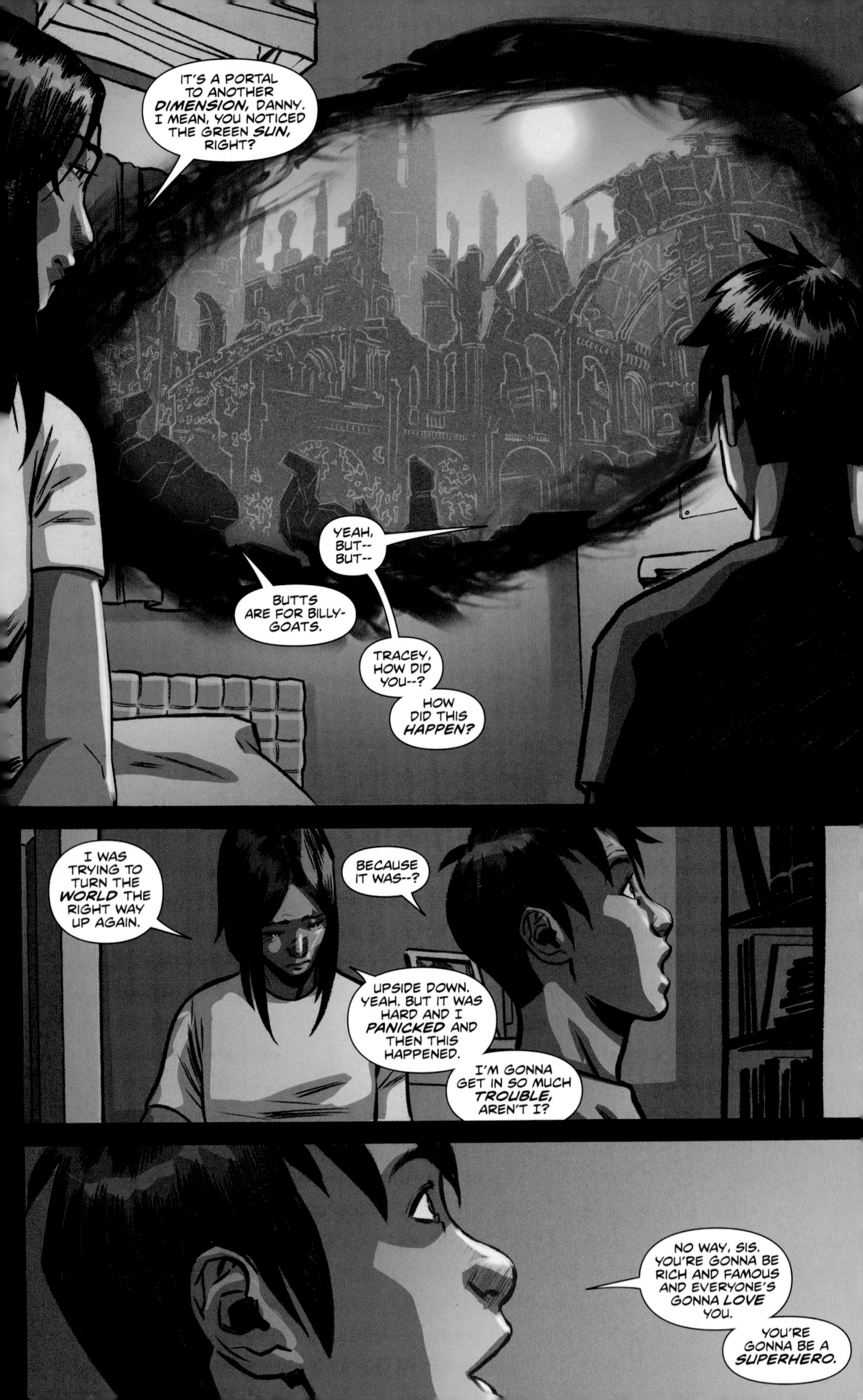
IT'S A PORTAL TO ANOTHER DIMENSION, DANNY. I MEAN, YOU NOTICED THE GREEN SUN, RIGHT?
YEAH, BUT-- BUT--
BUTTS ARE FOR BILLY-GOATS.
TRACEY, HOW DID YOU--?
HOW DID THIS HAPPEN?
I WAS TRYING TO TURN THE WORLD THE RIGHT WAY UP AGAIN.
BECAUSE IT WAS--?
UPSIDE DOWN. YEAH. BUT IT WAS HARD AND I PANICKED AND THEN THIS HAPPENED.
I'M GONNA GET IN SO MUCH TROUBLE, AREN'T I?
NO WAY, SIS. YOU'RE GONNA BE RICH AND FAMOUS AND EVERYONE'S GONNA LOVE YOU.
YOU'RE GONNA BE A SUPERHERO.

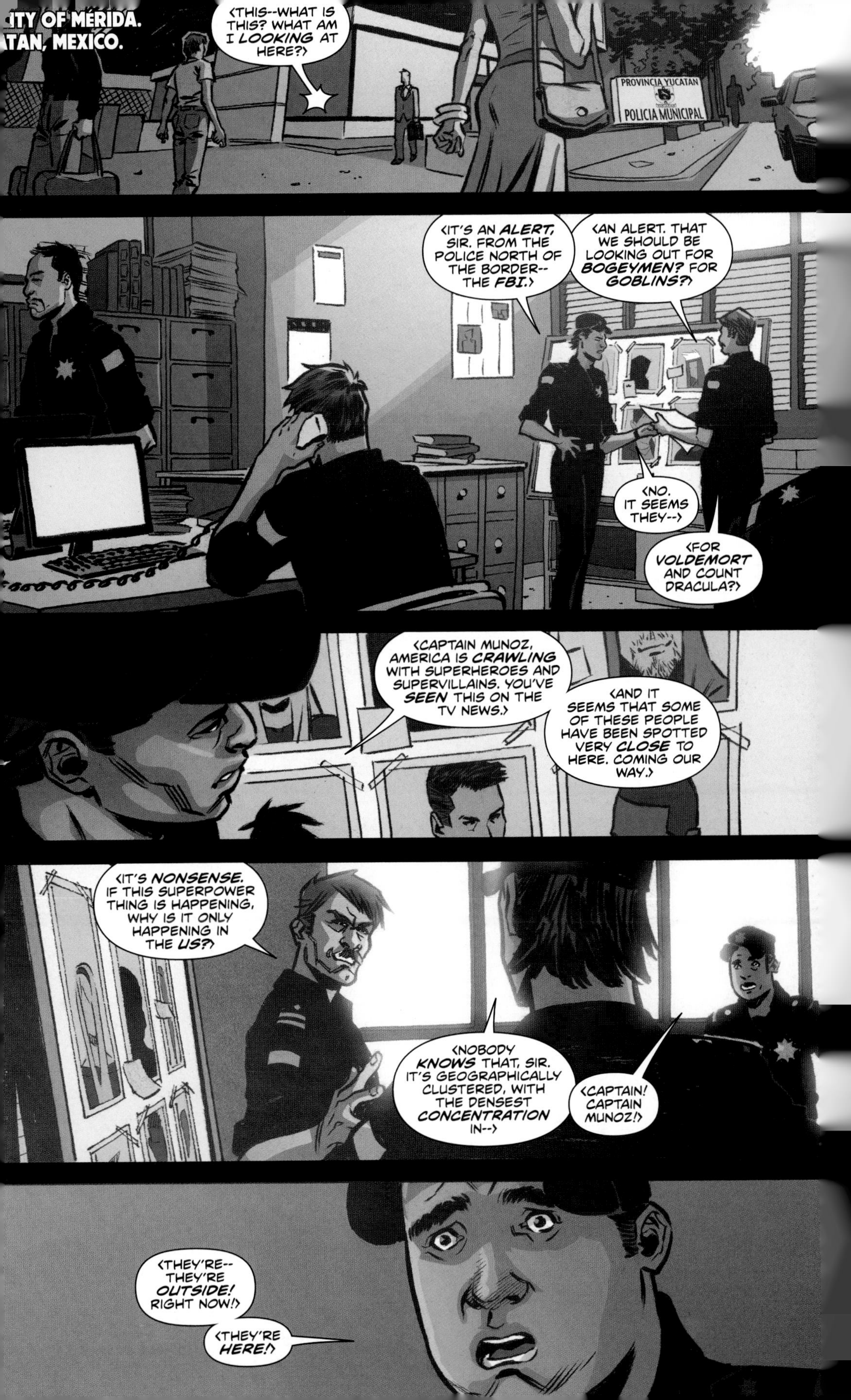
ITY OF MÉRIDA.
TAN, MEXICO.
<THIS--WHAT IS THIS? WHAT AM I LOOKING AT HERE?>
PROVINCIA YUCATAN
POLICIA MUNICIPAL
<IT'S AN ALERT, SIR. FROM THE POLICE NORTH OF THE BORDER-- THE FBI.>
<AN ALERT. THAT WE SHOULD BE LOOKING OUT FOR BOGEYMEN? FOR GOBLINS?>
<NO. IT SEEMS THEY-->
<FOR VOLDEMORT AND COUNT DRACULA?>
<CAPTAIN MUNOZ, AMERICA IS CRAWLING WITH SUPERHEROES AND SUPERVILLAINS. YOU'VE SEEN THIS ON THE TV NEWS.>
<AND IT SEEMS THAT SOME OF THESE PEOPLE HAVE BEEN SPOTTED VERY CLOSE TO HERE. COMING OUR WAY.>
<IT'S NONSENSE. IF THIS SUPERPOWER THING IS HAPPENING, WHY IS IT ONLY HAPPENING IN THE US?>
<NOBODY KNOWS THAT, SIR. IT'S GEOGRAPHICALLY CLUSTERED, WITH THE DENSEST CONCENTRATION IN-->
<CAPTAIN! CAPTAIN MUNOZ!>
<THEY'RE-- THEY'RE OUTSIDE! RIGHT NOW!>
<THEY'RE HERE!>

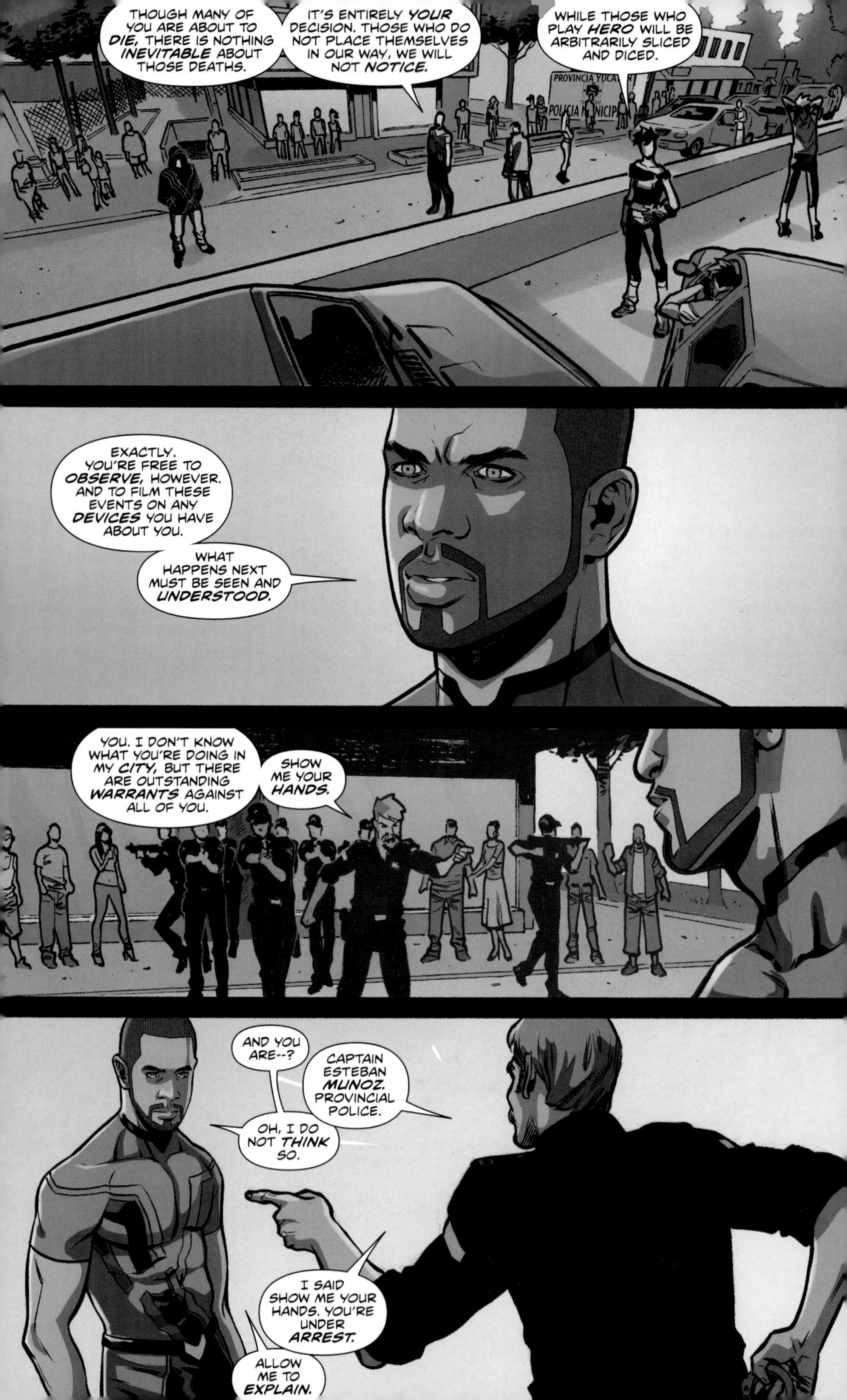
THOUGH MANY OF YOU ARE ABOUT TO DIE, THERE IS NOTHING INEVITABLE ABOUT THOSE DEATHS.
IT'S ENTIRELY YOUR DECISION. THOSE WHO DO NOT PLACE THEMSELVES IN OUR WAY, WE WILL NOT NOTICE.
WHILE THOSE WHO PLAY HERO WILL BE ARBITRARILY SLICED AND DICED.
PROVINCIA YUCA
POLICIA
NICIP
EXACTLY. YOU'RE FREE TO OBSERVE, HOWEVER. AND TO FILM THESE EVENTS ON ANY DEVICES YOU HAVE ABOUT YOU.
WHAT HAPPENS NEXT MUST BE SEEN AND UNDERSTOOD.
YOU. I DON'T KNOW WHAT YOU'RE DOING IN MY CITY, BUT THERE ARE OUTSTANDING WARRANTS AGAINST ALL OF YOU.
SHOW ME YOUR HANDS.
AND YOU ARE--?
CAPTAIN ESTEBAN MUNOZ. PROVINCIAL POLICE.
OH, I DO NOT THINK SO.
I SAID SHOW ME YOUR HANDS. YOU'RE UNDER ARREST.
ALLOW ME TO EXPLAIN.

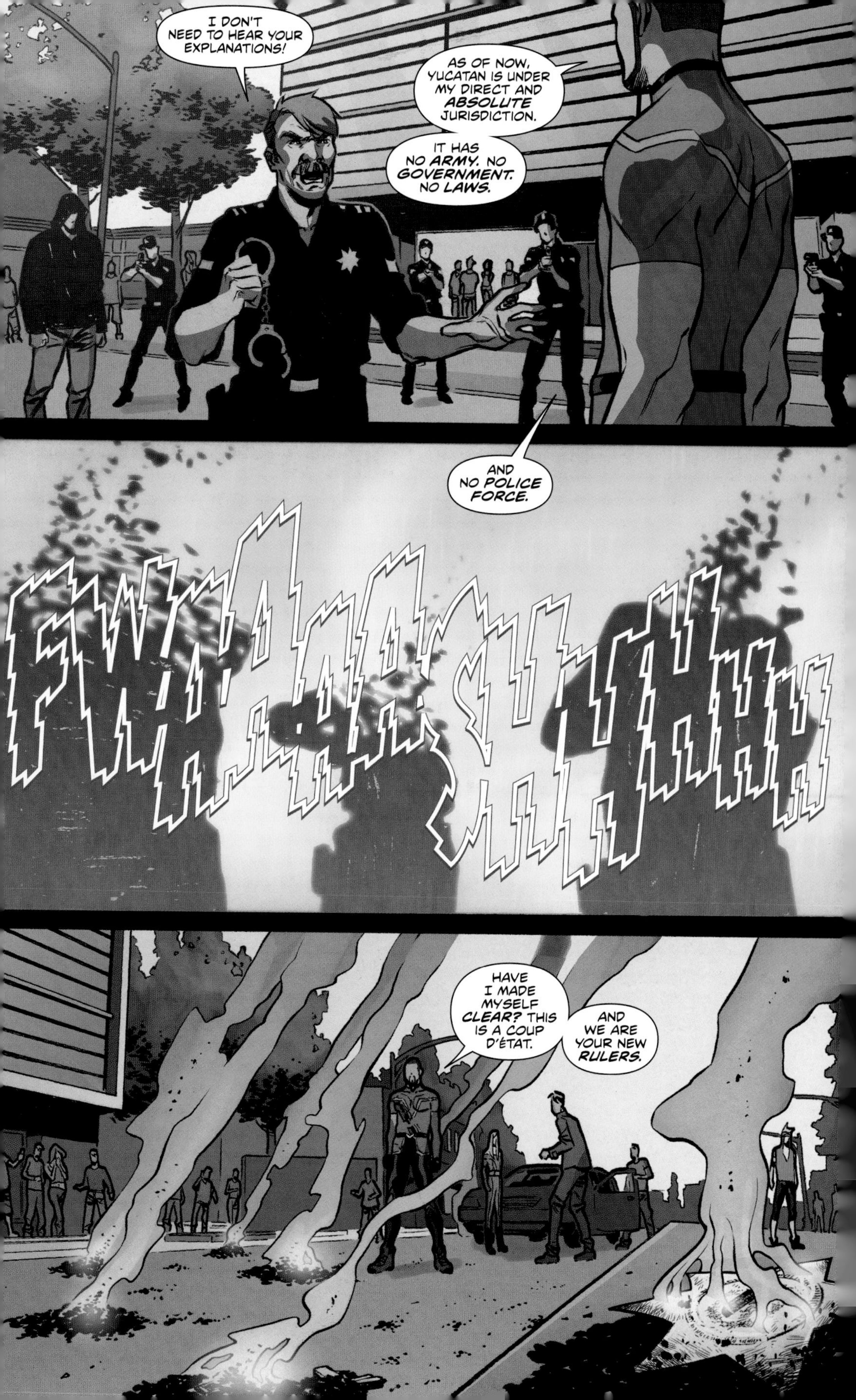
I DON'T NEED TO HEAR YOUR EXPLANATIONS!
AS OF NOW, YUCATAN IS UNDER MY DIRECT AND ABSOLUTE JURISDICTION.
IT HAS NO ARMY. NO GOVERNMENT. NO LAWS.
AND NO POLICE FORCE.
FWAAASHHHK
HAVE I MADE MYSELF CLEAR? THIS IS A COUP D'ÉTAT.
AND WE ARE YOUR NEW RULERS.

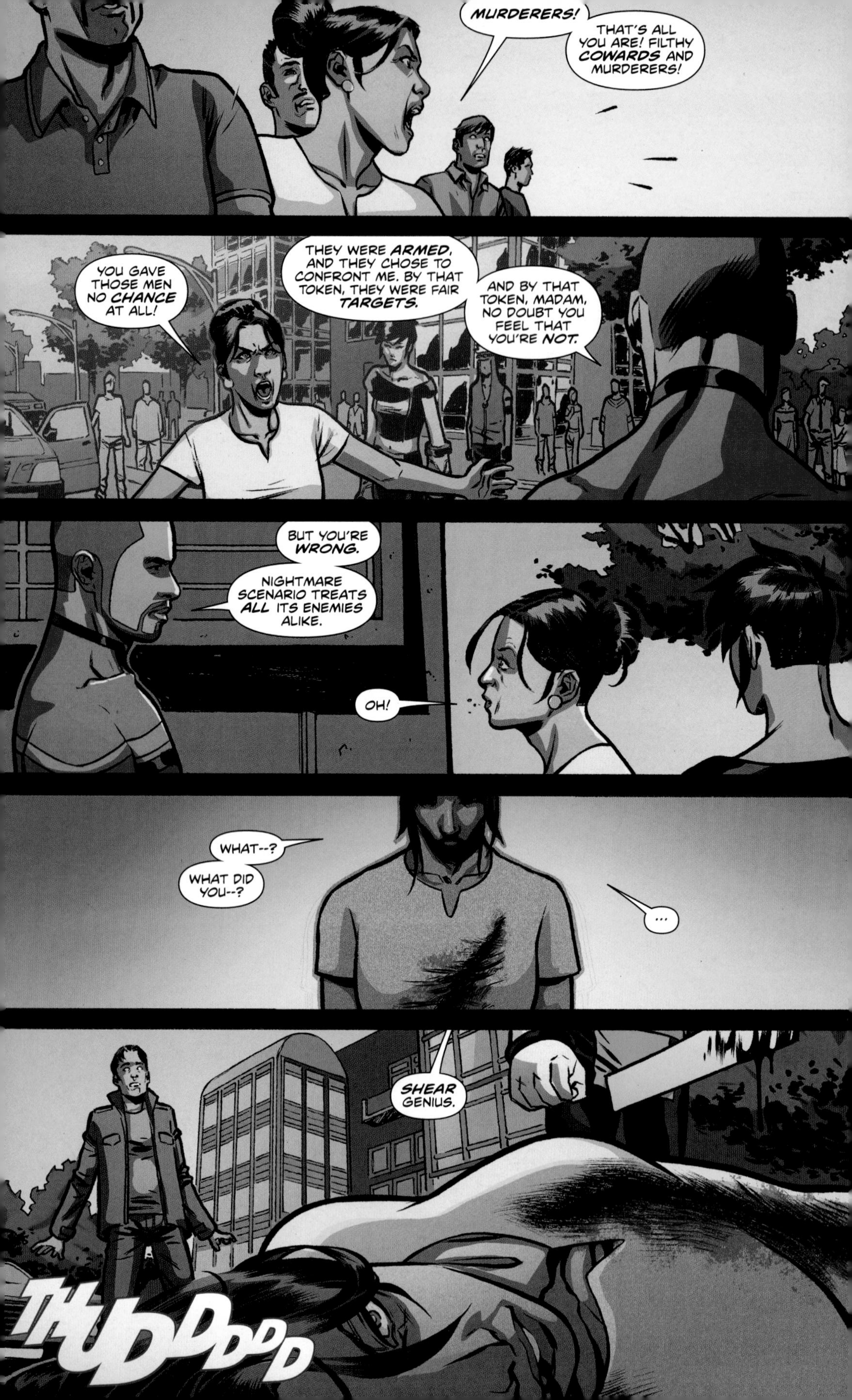
MURDERERS!
THAT'S ALL YOU ARE! FILTHY COWARDS AND MURDERERS!
YOU GAVE THOSE MEN NO CHANCE AT ALL!
THEY WERE ARMED, AND THEY CHOSE TO CONFRONT ME. BY THAT TOKEN, THEY WERE FAIR TARGETS.
AND BY THAT TOKEN, MADAM, NO DOUBT YOU FEEL THAT YOU'RE NOT.
BUT YOU'RE WRONG.
NIGHTMARE SCENARIO TREATS ALL ITS ENEMIES ALIKE.
OH!
WHAT--?
WHAT DID YOU--?
...
SHEAR GENIUS.
THUDDDDD

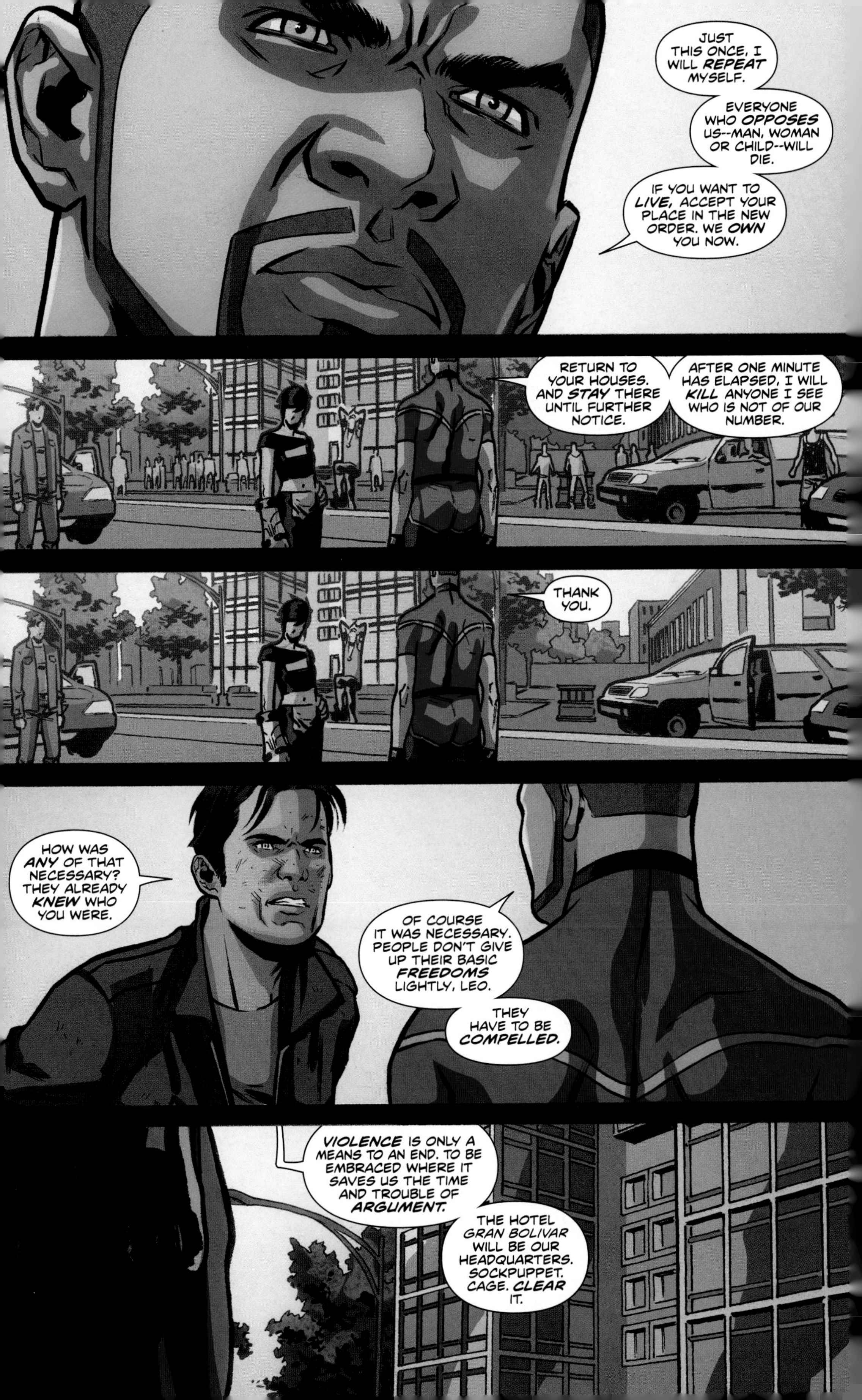
JUST THIS ONCE, I WILL REPEAT MYSELF.
EVERYONE WHO OPPOSES US--MAN, WOMAN OR CHILD--WILL DIE.
IF YOU WANT TO LIVE, ACCEPT YOUR PLACE IN THE NEW ORDER. WE OWN YOU NOW.
RETURN TO YOUR HOUSES. AND STAY THERE UNTIL FURTHER NOTICE.
AFTER ONE MINUTE HAS ELAPSED, I WILL KILL ANYONE I SEE WHO IS NOT OF OUR NUMBER.
THANK YOU.
HOW WAS ANY OF THAT NECESSARY? THEY ALREADY KNEW WHO YOU WERE.
OF COURSE IT WAS NECESSARY. PEOPLE DON'T GIVE UP THEIR BASIC FREEDOMS LIGHTLY, LEO.
THEY HAVE TO BE COMPELLED.
VIOLENCE IS ONLY A MEANS TO AN END. TO BE EMBRACED WHERE IT SAVES US THE TIME AND TROUBLE OF ARGUMENT.
THE HOTEL GRAN BOLIVAR WILL BE OUR HEADQUARTERS. SOCKPUPPET. CAGE. CLEAR IT.

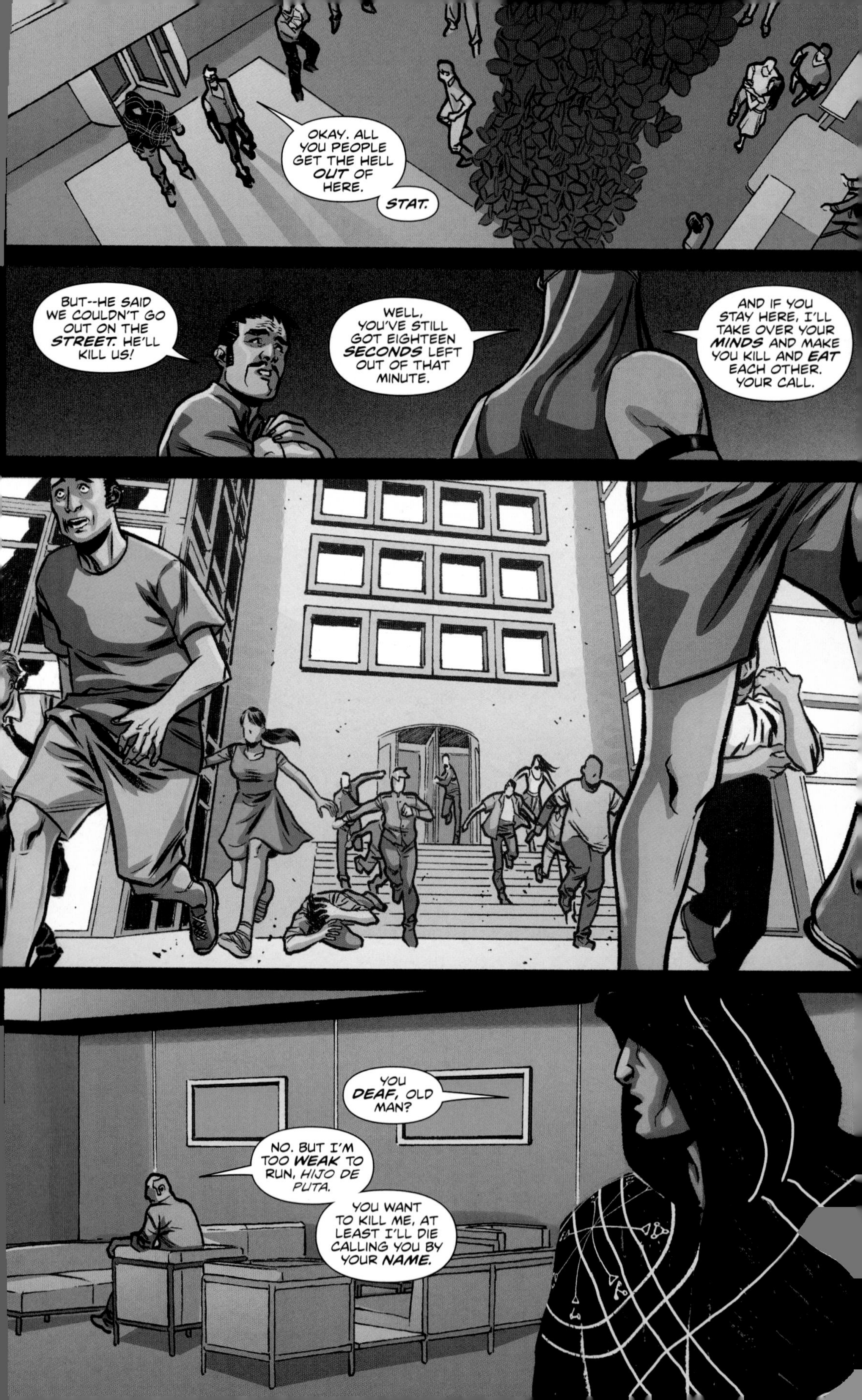
OKAY. ALL YOU PEOPLE GET THE HELL *OUT* OF HERE.
STAT.
BUT--HE SAID WE COULDN'T GO OUT ON THE *STREET.* HE'LL KILL US!
WELL, YOU'VE STILL GOT EIGHTEEN *SECONDS* LEFT OUT OF THAT MINUTE.
AND IF YOU STAY HERE, I'LL TAKE OVER YOUR *MINDS* AND MAKE YOU KILL AND *EAT* EACH OTHER. YOUR CALL.
YOU *DEAF,* OLD MAN?
NO. BUT I'M TOO *WEAK* TO RUN, *HIJO DE PUTA.*
YOU WANT TO KILL ME, AT LEAST I'LL DIE CALLING YOU BY YOUR *NAME.*

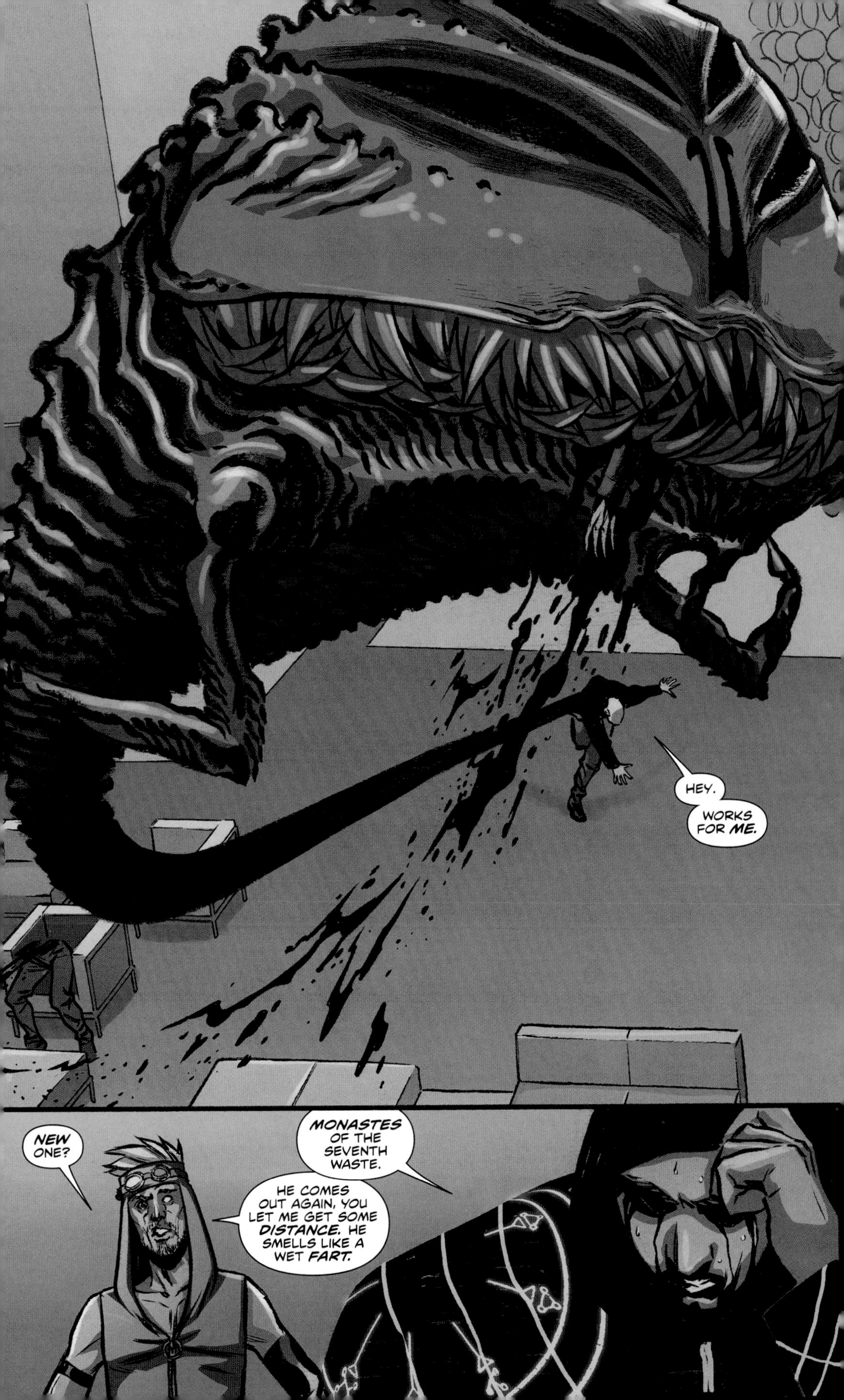
HEY.
WORKS FOR *ME.*
NEW ONE?
MONASTES OF THE SEVENTH WASTE.
HE COMES OUT AGAIN, YOU LET ME GET SOME *DISTANCE.* HE SMELLS LIKE A WET *FART.*

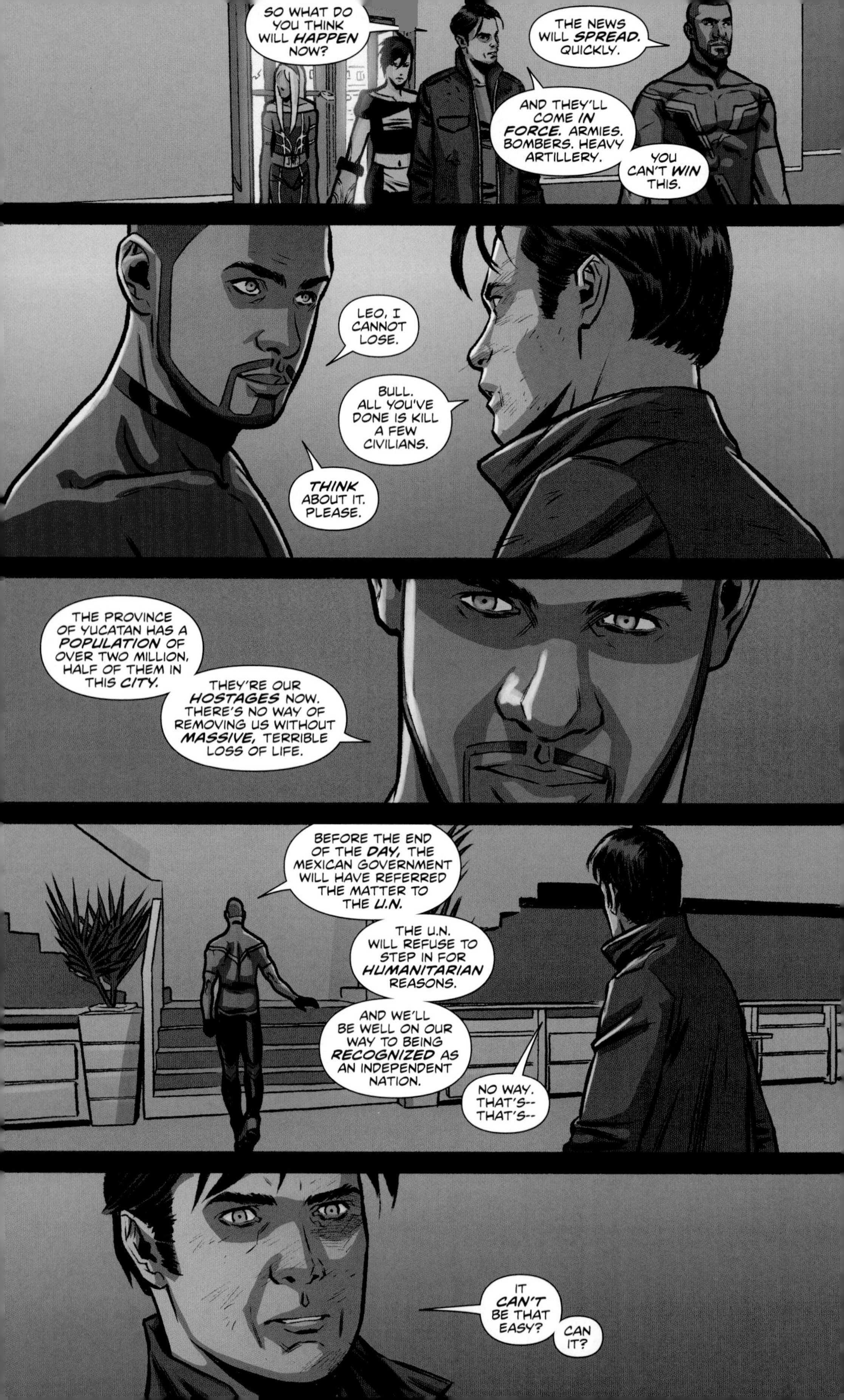
SO WHAT DO YOU THINK WILL HAPPEN NOW?
THE NEWS WILL SPREAD. QUICKLY.
AND THEY'LL COME IN FORCE. ARMIES. BOMBERS. HEAVY ARTILLERY.
YOU CAN'T WIN THIS.
LEO, I CANNOT LOSE.
BULL. ALL YOU'VE DONE IS KILL A FEW CIVILIANS.
THINK ABOUT IT. PLEASE.
THE PROVINCE OF YUCATAN HAS A POPULATION OF OVER TWO MILLION, HALF OF THEM IN THIS CITY.
THEY'RE OUR HOSTAGES NOW. THERE'S NO WAY OF REMOVING US WITHOUT MASSIVE, TERRIBLE LOSS OF LIFE.
BEFORE THE END OF THE DAY, THE MEXICAN GOVERNMENT WILL HAVE REFERRED THE MATTER TO THE U.N.
THE U.N. WILL REFUSE TO STEP IN FOR HUMANITARIAN REASONS.
AND WE'LL BE WELL ON OUR WAY TO BEING RECOGNIZED AS AN INDEPENDENT NATION.
NO WAY. THAT'S-- THAT'S--
IT CAN'T BE THAT EASY?
CAN IT?

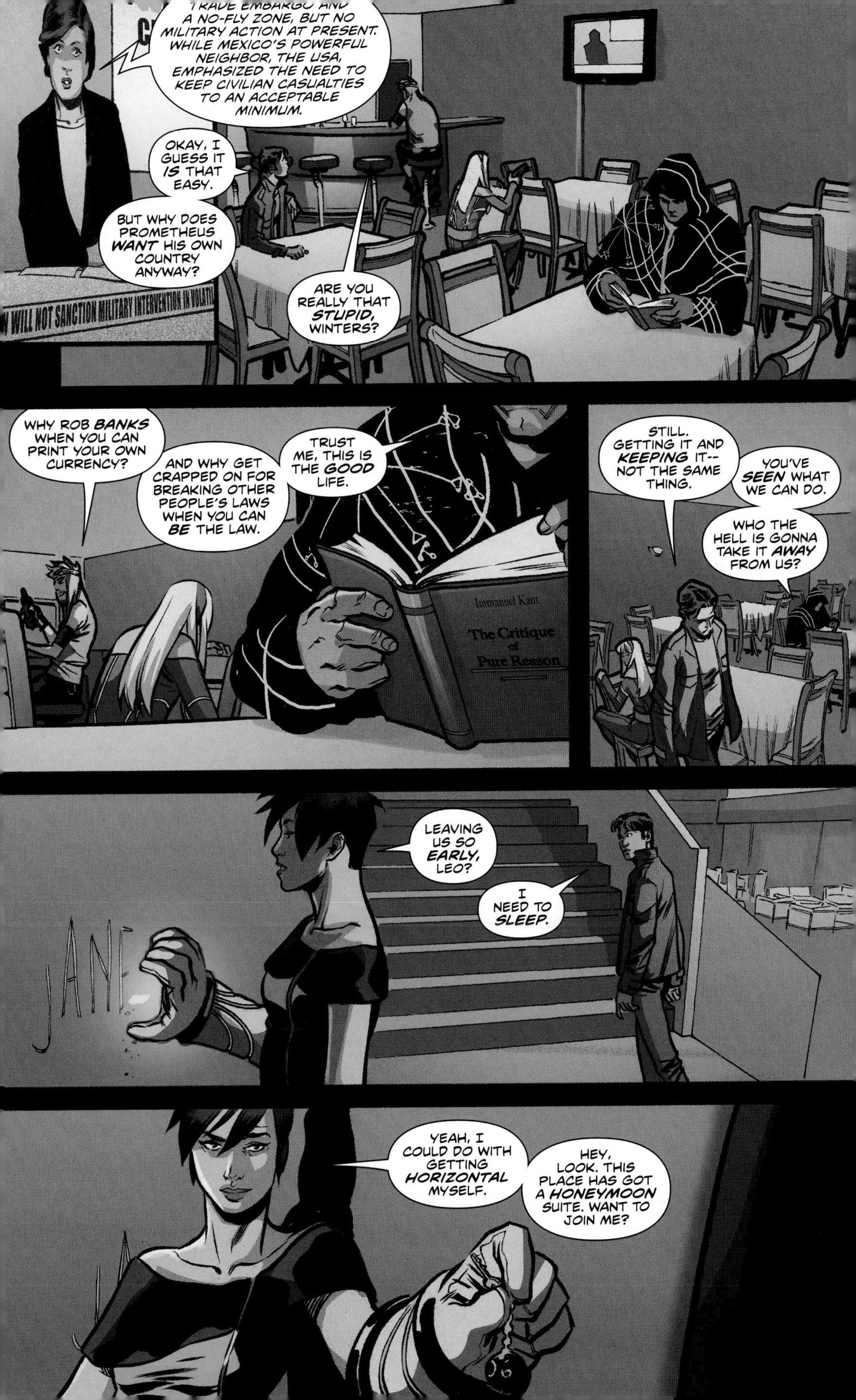
TRADE EMBARGO AND A NO-FLY ZONE, BUT NO MILITARY ACTION AT PRESENT. WHILE MEXICO'S POWERFUL NEIGHBOR, THE USA, EMPHASIZED THE NEED TO KEEP CIVILIAN CASUALTIES TO AN ACCEPTABLE MINIMUM.
WILL NOT SANCTION MILITARY INTERVENTION IN VOLATI
OKAY, I GUESS IT IS THAT EASY.
BUT WHY DOES PROMETHEUS WANT HIS OWN COUNTRY ANYWAY?
ARE YOU REALLY THAT STUPID, WINTERS?
WHY ROB BANKS WHEN YOU CAN PRINT YOUR OWN CURRENCY?
AND WHY GET CRAPPED ON FOR BREAKING OTHER PEOPLE'S LAWS WHEN YOU CAN BE THE LAW.
TRUST ME, THIS IS THE GOOD LIFE.
Immanuel Kant
The Critique of Pure Reason
STILL. GETTING IT AND KEEPING IT-- NOT THE SAME THING.
YOU'VE SEEN WHAT WE CAN DO.
WHO THE HELL IS GONNA TAKE IT AWAY FROM US?
JANE
LEAVING US SO EARLY, LEO?
I NEED TO SLEEP.
YEAH, I COULD DO WITH GETTING HORIZONTAL MYSELF.
HEY, LOOK. THIS PLACE HAS GOT A HONEYMOON SUITE. WANT TO JOIN ME?

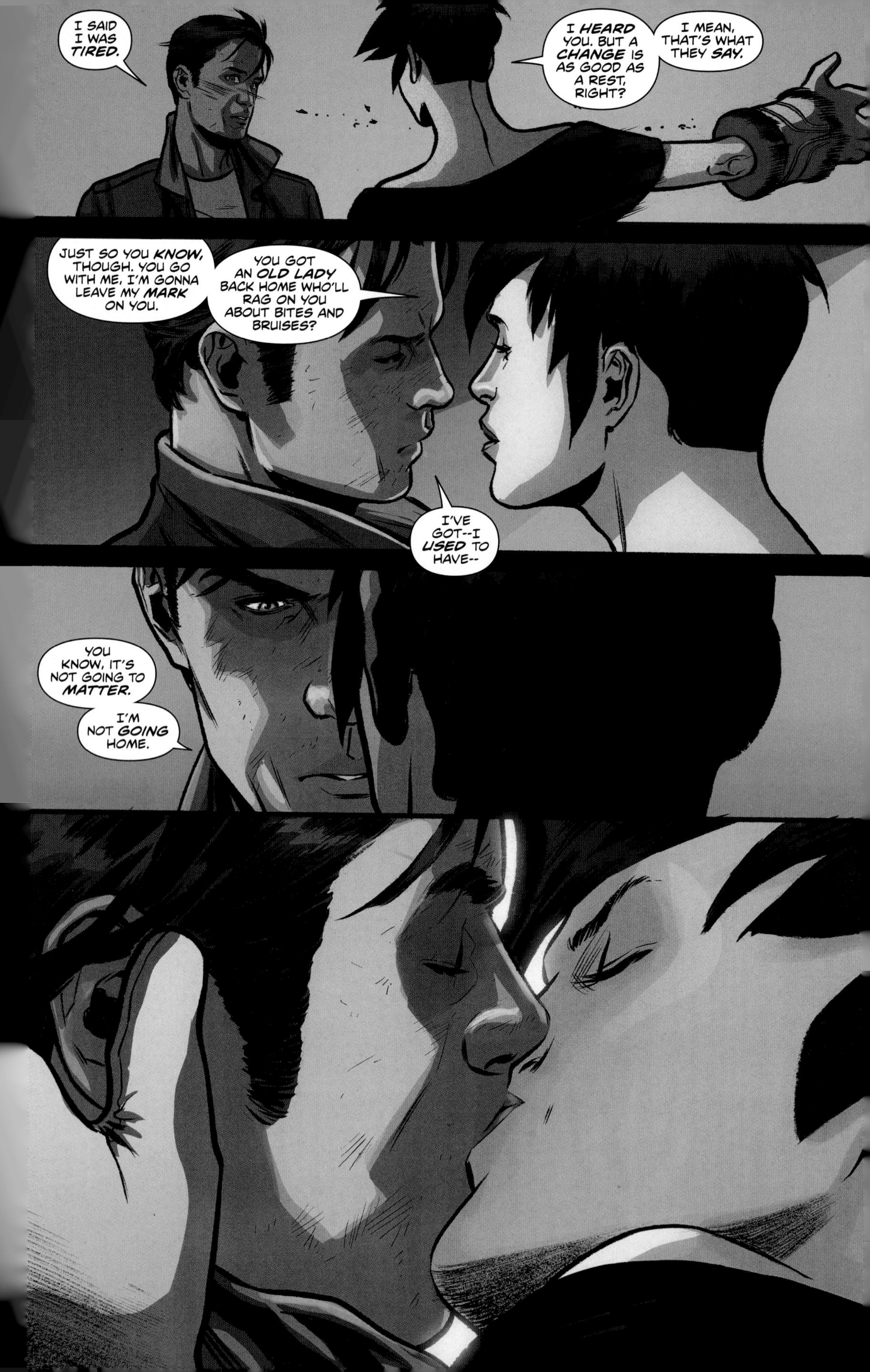
I SAID I WAS *TIRED.*
I *HEARD* YOU. BUT A *CHANGE* IS AS GOOD AS A REST, RIGHT?
I MEAN, THAT'S WHAT THEY *SAY.*
JUST SO YOU *KNOW,* THOUGH. YOU GO WITH ME, I'M GONNA LEAVE MY *MARK* ON YOU.
YOU GOT AN *OLD LADY* BACK HOME WHO'LL RAG ON YOU ABOUT BITES AND BRUISES?
I'VE GOT--I *USED* TO HAVE--
YOU KNOW, IT'S NOT GOING TO *MATTER.*
I'M NOT *GOING* HOME.

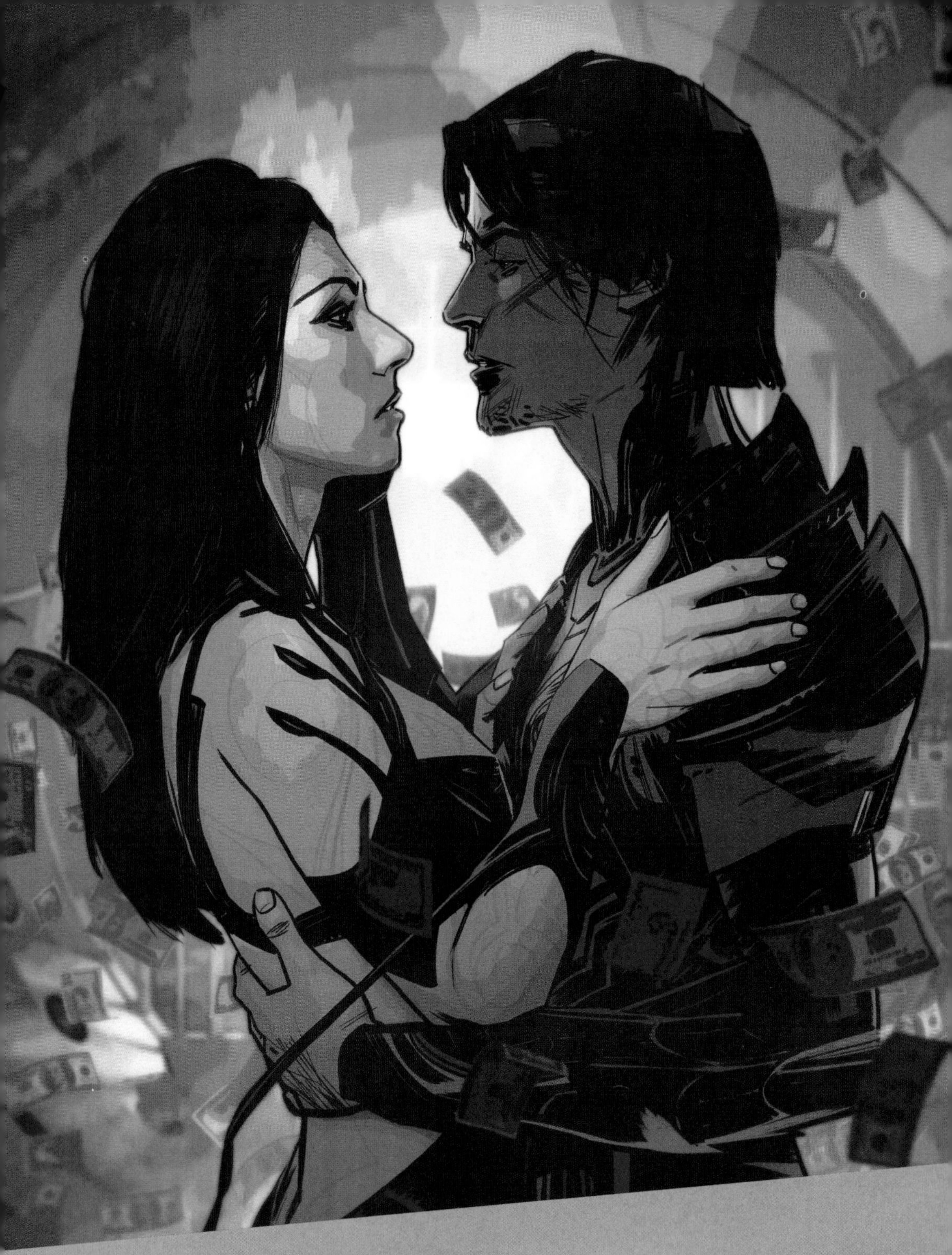

"A HANDFUL OF **SUPERVILLAINS.** WHEN OUR ARMY TOOK THEM ON, THEY DIDN'T LAST A **HEARTBEAT.**"
Chapter 8

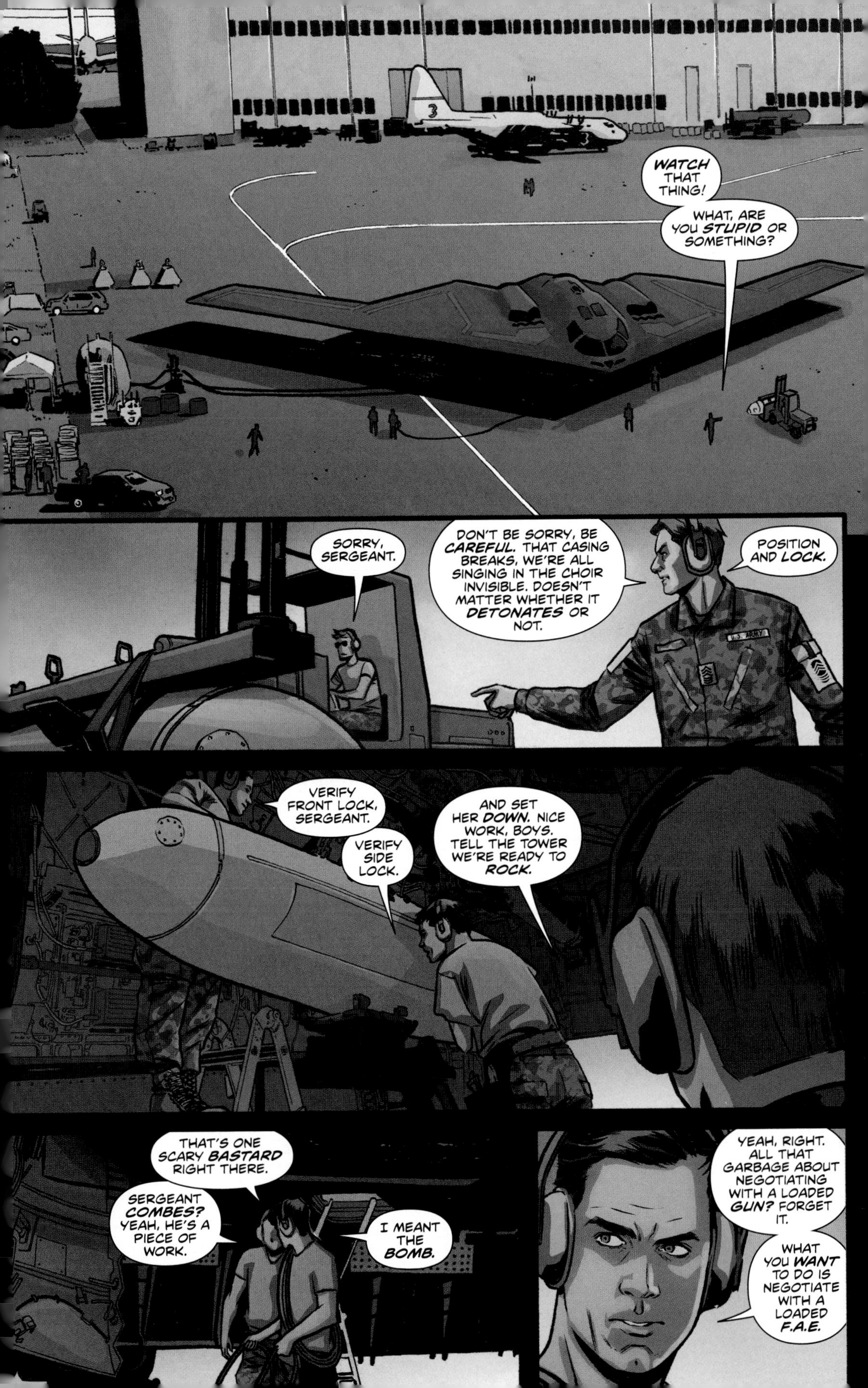
WATCH THAT THING!
WHAT, ARE YOU STUPID OR SOMETHING?
SORRY, SERGEANT.
DON'T BE SORRY, BE CAREFUL. THAT CASING BREAKS, WE'RE ALL SINGING IN THE CHOIR INVISIBLE. DOESN'T MATTER WHETHER IT DETONATES OR NOT.
POSITION AND LOCK.
U.S. ARMY
VERIFY FRONT LOCK, SERGEANT.
VERIFY SIDE LOCK.
AND SET HER DOWN. NICE WORK, BOYS. TELL THE TOWER WE'RE READY TO ROCK.
THAT'S ONE SCARY BASTARD RIGHT THERE.
SERGEANT COMBES? YEAH, HE'S A PIECE OF WORK.
I MEANT THE BOMB.
YEAH, RIGHT. ALL THAT GARBAGE ABOUT NEGOTIATING WITH A LOADED GUN? FORGET IT.
WHAT YOU WANT TO DO IS NEGOTIATE WITH A LOADED F.A.E.

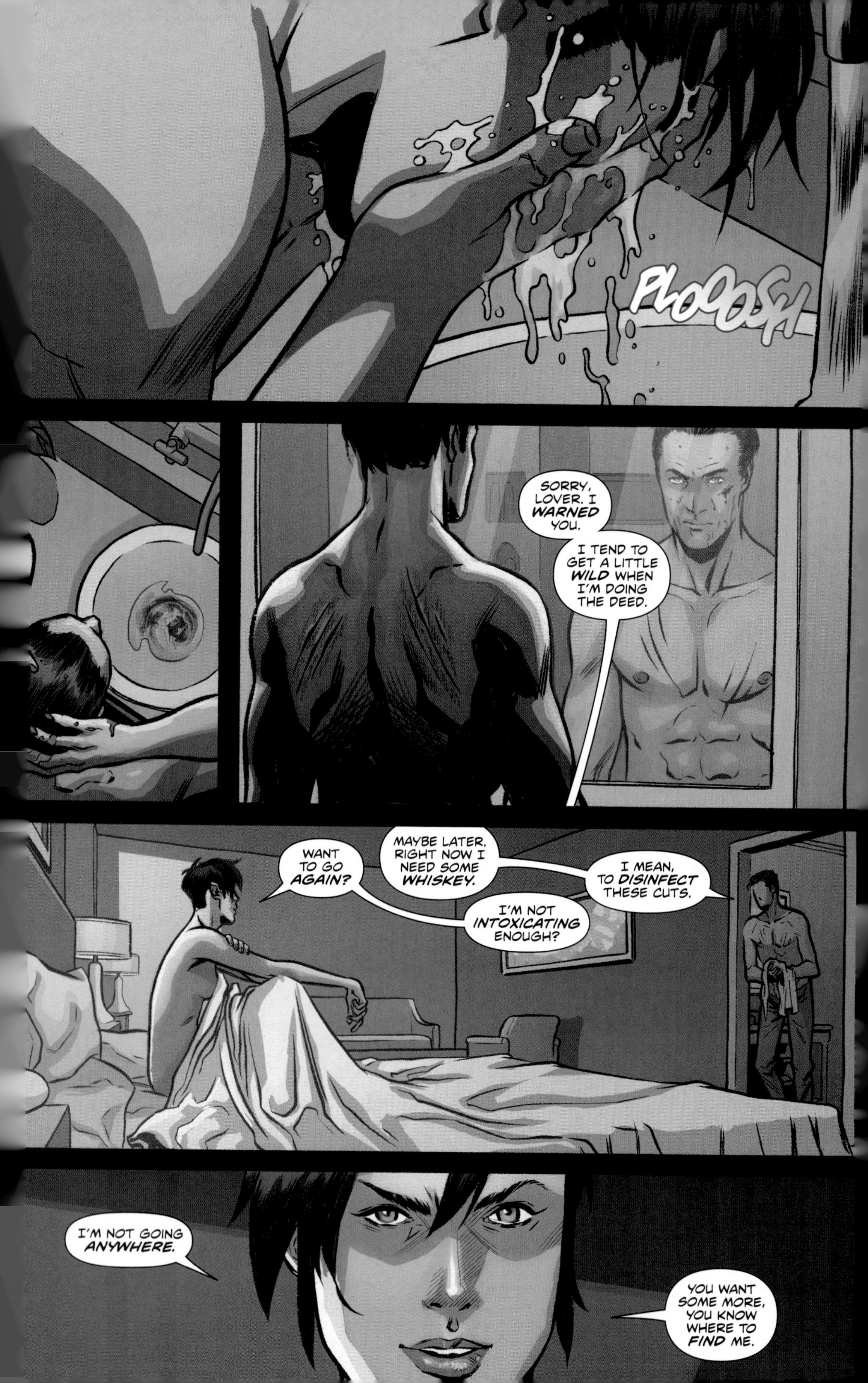
PLOOOOSH
SORRY, LOVER. I WARNED YOU.
I TEND TO GET A LITTLE WILD WHEN I'M DOING THE DEED.
WANT TO GO AGAIN?
MAYBE LATER. RIGHT NOW I NEED SOME WHISKEY.
I'M NOT INTOXICATING ENOUGH?
I MEAN, TO DISINFECT THESE CUTS.
I'M NOT GOING ANYWHERE.
YOU WANT SOME MORE, YOU KNOW WHERE TO FIND ME.

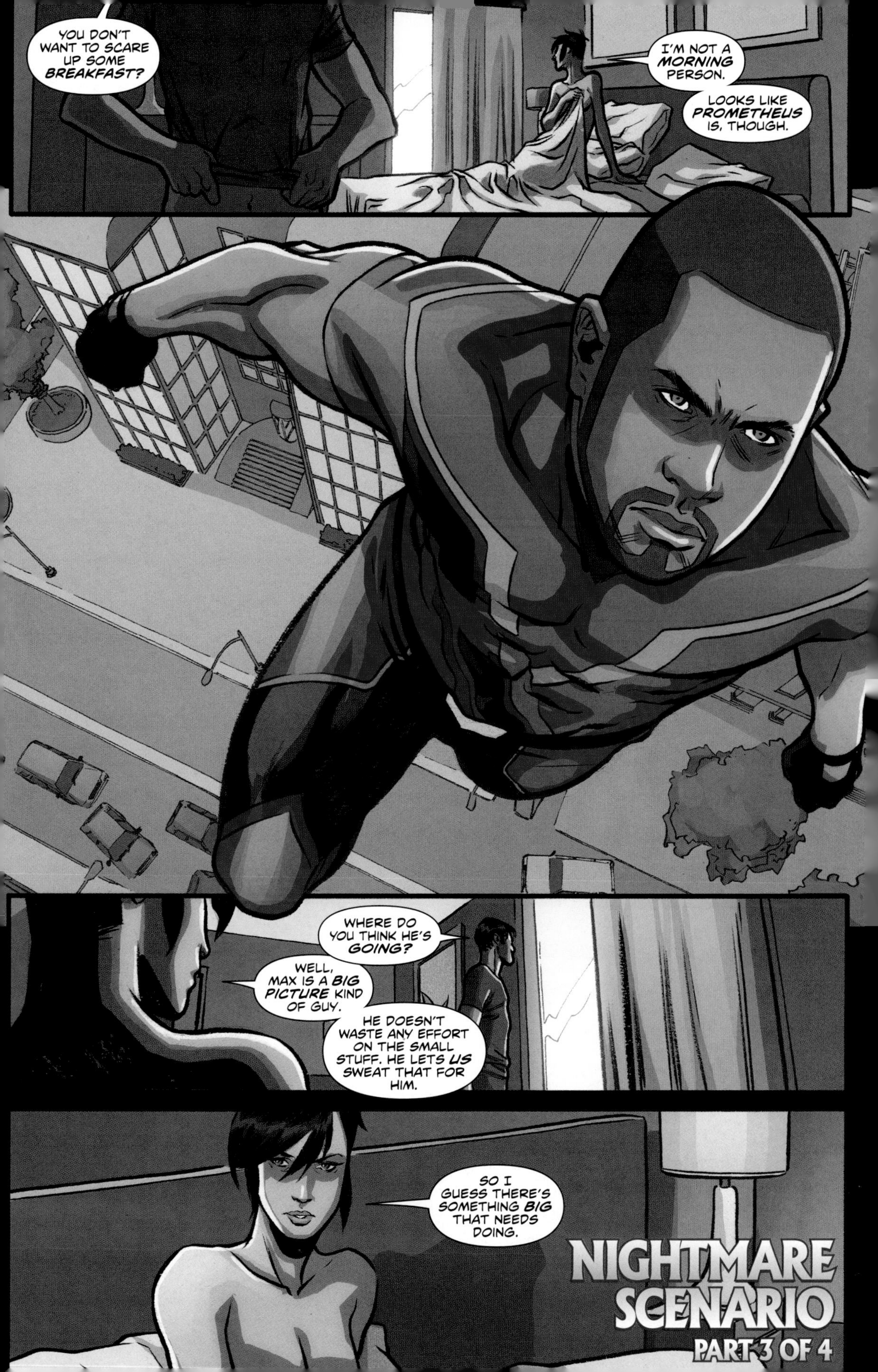

YOU DON'T WANT TO SCARE UP SOME BREAKFAST?
I'M NOT A MORNING PERSON.
LOOKS LIKE PROMETHEUS IS, THOUGH.
WHERE DO YOU THINK HE'S GOING?
WELL, MAX IS A BIG PICTURE KIND OF GUY.
HE DOESN'T WASTE ANY EFFORT ON THE SMALL STUFF. HE LETS US SWEAT THAT FOR HIM.
SO I GUESS THERE'S SOMETHING BIG THAT NEEDS DOING.
NIGHTMARE SCENARIO
PART 3 OF 4

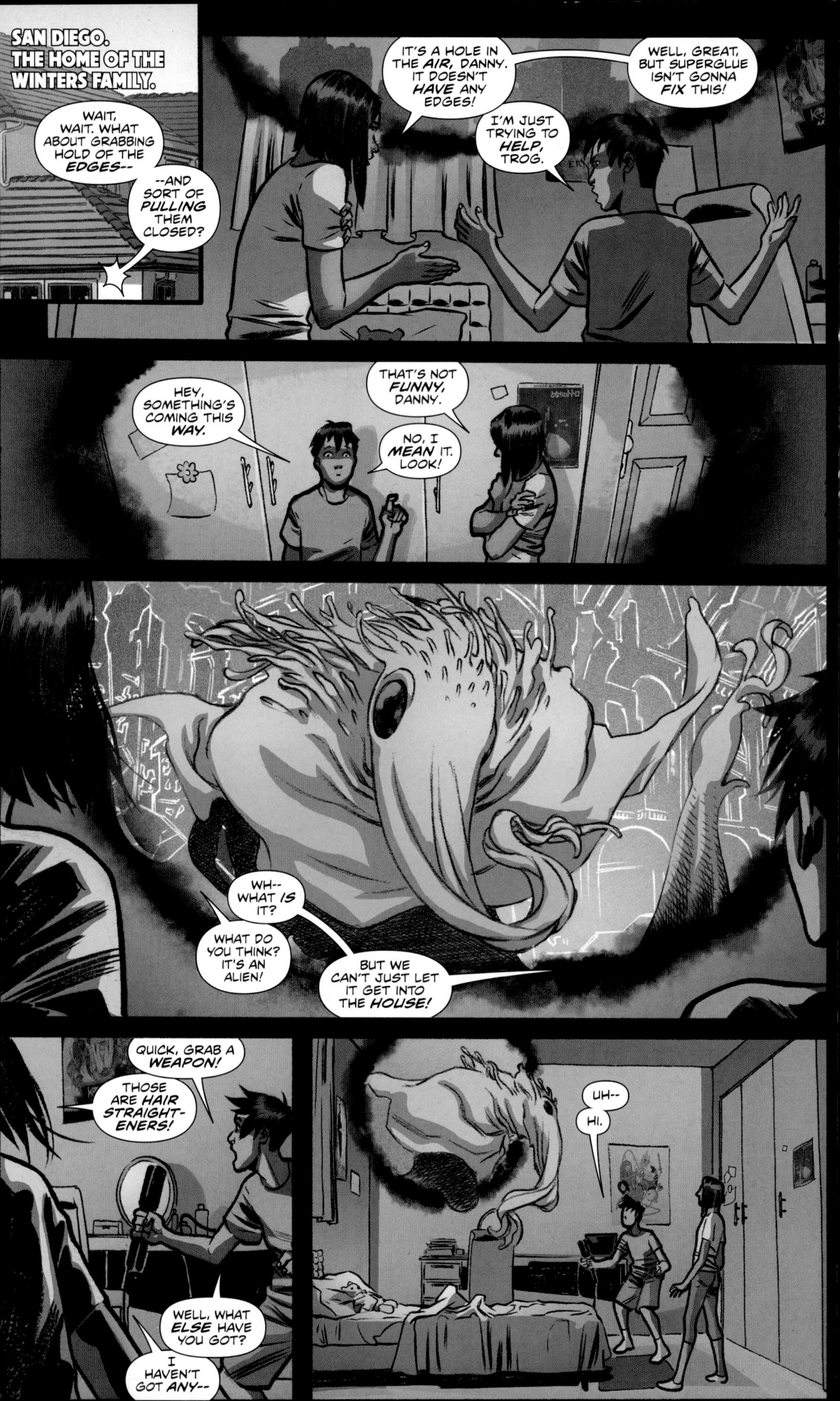
SAN DIEGO. THE HOME OF THE WINTERS FAMILY.
WAIT, WAIT. WHAT ABOUT GRABBING HOLD OF THE EDGES--
--AND SORT OF PULLING THEM CLOSED?
IT'S A HOLE IN THE AIR, DANNY. IT DOESN'T HAVE ANY EDGES!
I'M JUST TRYING TO HELP, TROG.
WELL, GREAT, BUT SUPERGLUE ISN'T GONNA FIX THIS!
HEY, SOMETHING'S COMING THIS WAY.
THAT'S NOT FUNNY, DANNY.
NO, I MEAN IT. LOOK!
WH-- WHAT IS IT?
WHAT DO YOU THINK? IT'S AN ALIEN!
BUT WE CAN'T JUST LET IT GET INTO THE HOUSE!
QUICK, GRAB A WEAPON!
THOSE ARE HAIR STRAIGHT-ENERS!
WELL, WHAT ELSE HAVE YOU GOT?
I HAVEN'T GOT ANY--
UH--
HI.

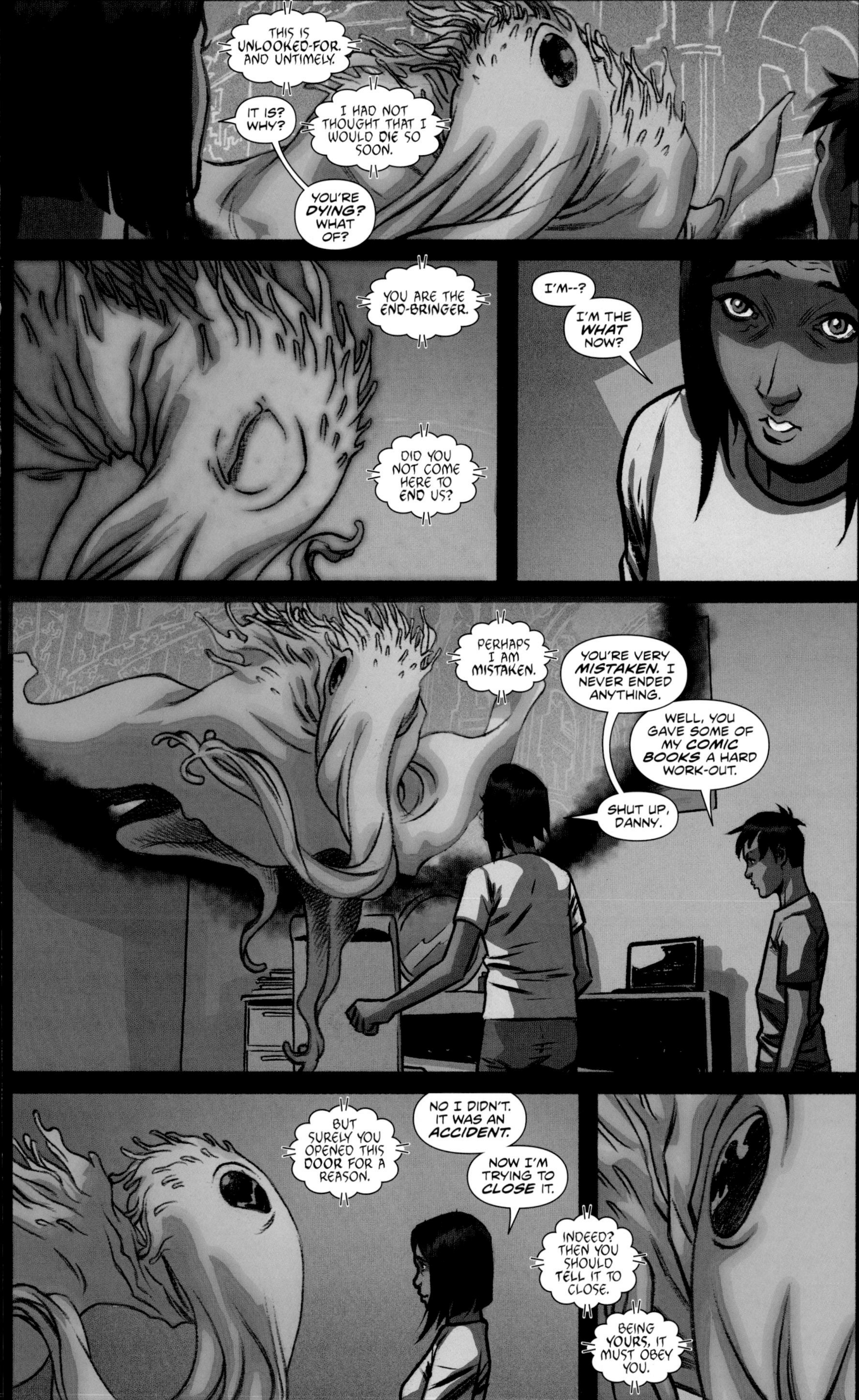
THIS IS UNLOOKED-FOR. AND UNTIMELY.
IT IS? WHY?
I HAD NOT THOUGHT THAT I WOULD DIE SO SOON.
YOU'RE DYING? WHAT OF?
YOU ARE THE END-BRINGER.
DID YOU NOT COME HERE TO END US?
I'M--?
I'M THE WHAT NOW?
PERHAPS I AM MISTAKEN.
YOU'RE VERY MISTAKEN. I NEVER ENDED ANYTHING.
WELL, YOU GAVE SOME OF MY COMIC BOOKS A HARD WORK-OUT.
SHUT UP, DANNY.
BUT SURELY YOU OPENED THIS DOOR FOR A REASON.
NO I DIDN'T. IT WAS AN ACCIDENT.
NOW I'M TRYING TO CLOSE IT.
INDEED? THEN YOU SHOULD TELL IT TO CLOSE.
BEING YOURS, IT MUST OBEY YOU.

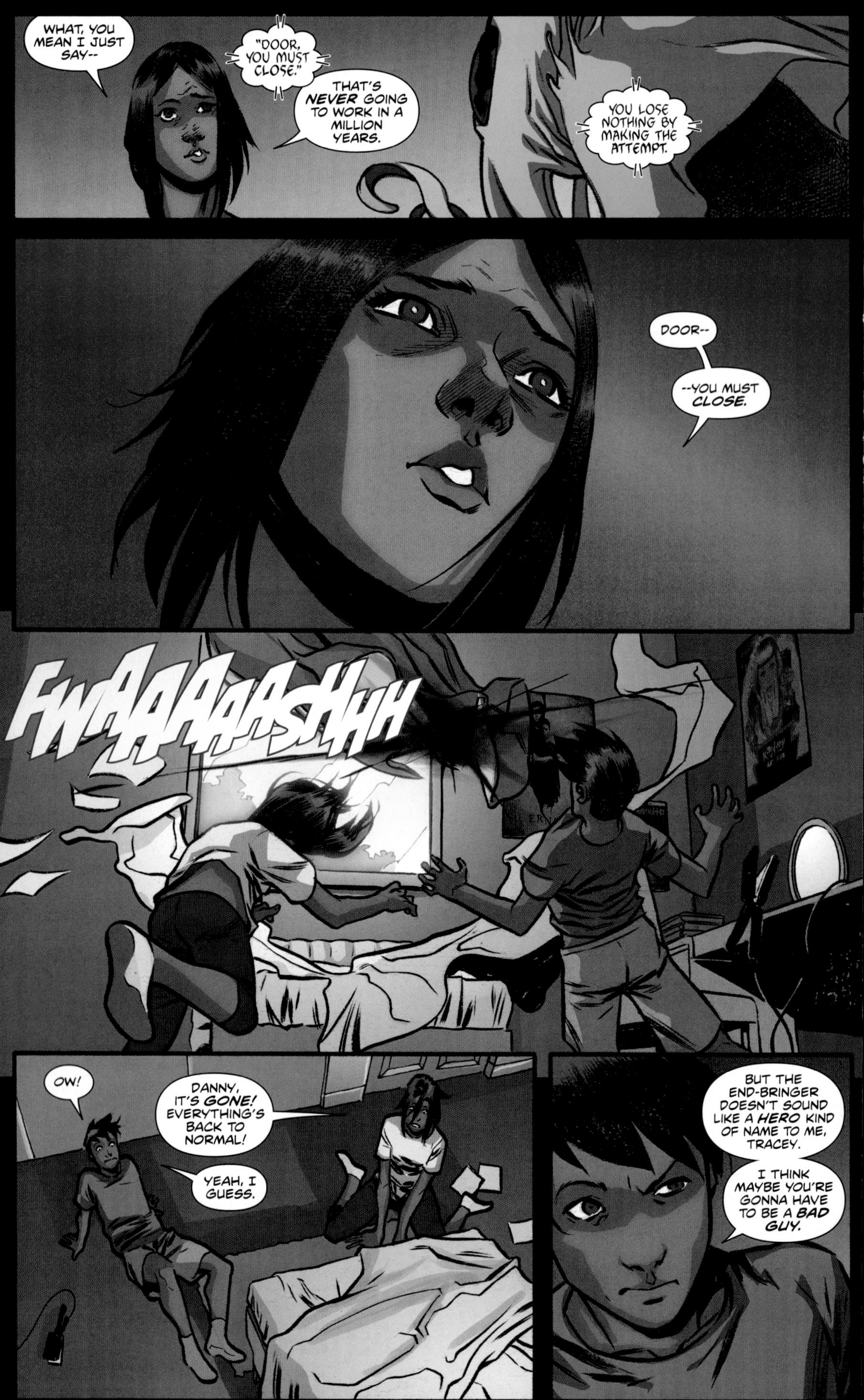
WHAT, YOU MEAN I JUST SAY--
"DOOR, YOU MUST CLOSE."
THAT'S NEVER GOING TO WORK IN A MILLION YEARS.
YOU LOSE NOTHING BY MAKING THE ATTEMPT.
DOOR--
--YOU MUST CLOSE.
FWAAAAAASHHH
OW!
DANNY, IT'S GONE! EVERYTHING'S BACK TO NORMAL!
YEAH, I GUESS.
BUT THE END-BRINGER DOESN'T SOUND LIKE A HERO KIND OF NAME TO ME, TRACEY.
I THINK MAYBE YOU'RE GONNA HAVE TO BE A BAD GUY.

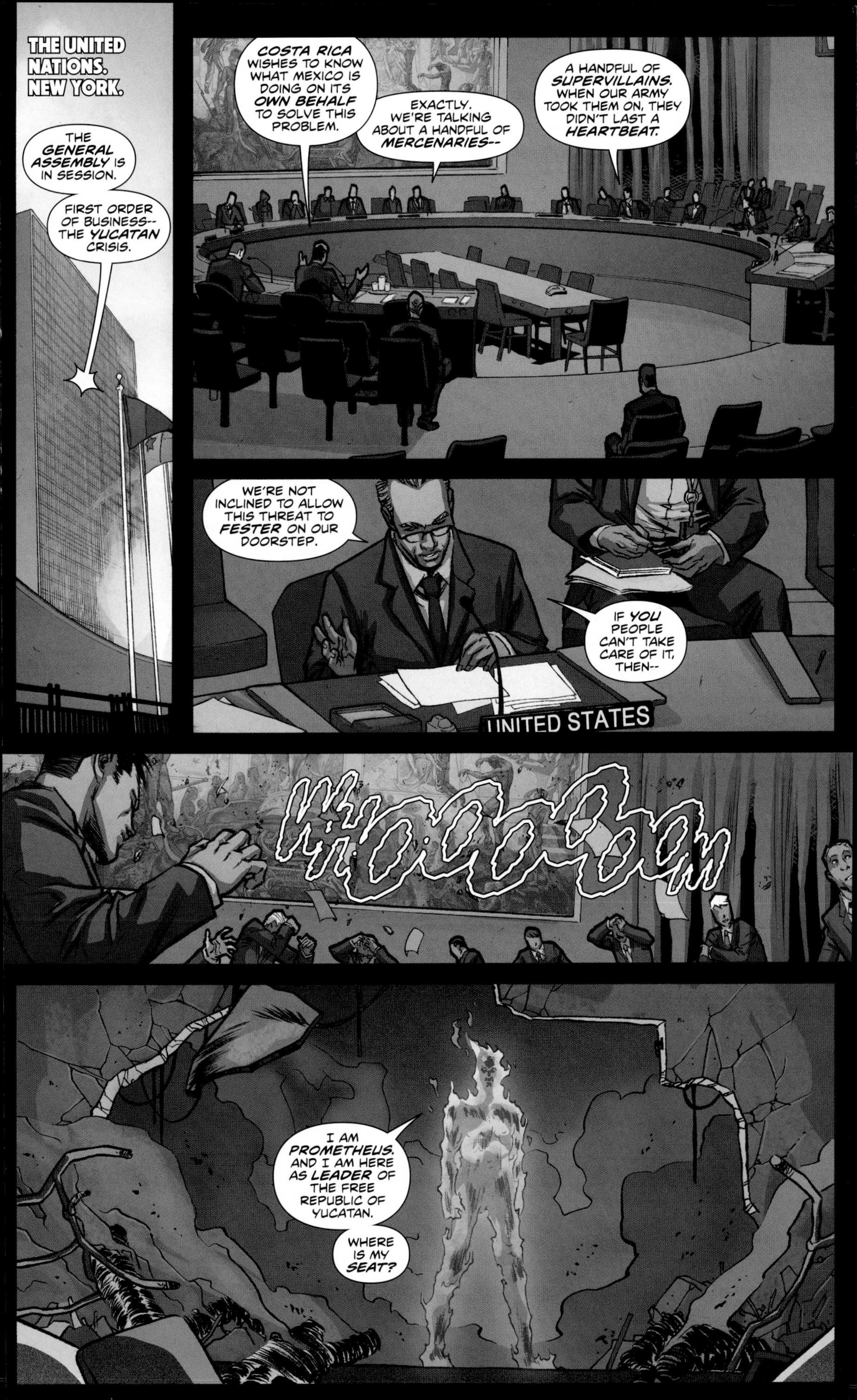
THE UNITED NATIONS. NEW YORK.
THE GENERAL ASSEMBLY IS IN SESSION.
FIRST ORDER OF BUSINESS-- THE YUCATAN CRISIS.
COSTA RICA WISHES TO KNOW WHAT MEXICO IS DOING ON ITS OWN BEHALF TO SOLVE THIS PROBLEM.
EXACTLY. WE'RE TALKING ABOUT A HANDFUL OF MERCENARIES--
A HANDFUL OF SUPERVILLAINS. WHEN OUR ARMY TOOK THEM ON, THEY DIDN'T LAST A HEARTBEAT.
WE'RE NOT INCLINED TO ALLOW THIS THREAT TO FESTER ON OUR DOORSTEP.
IF YOU PEOPLE CAN'T TAKE CARE OF IT, THEN--
UNITED STATES
I AM PROMETHEUS. AND I AM HERE AS LEADER OF THE FREE REPUBLIC OF YUCATAN.
WHERE IS MY SEAT?

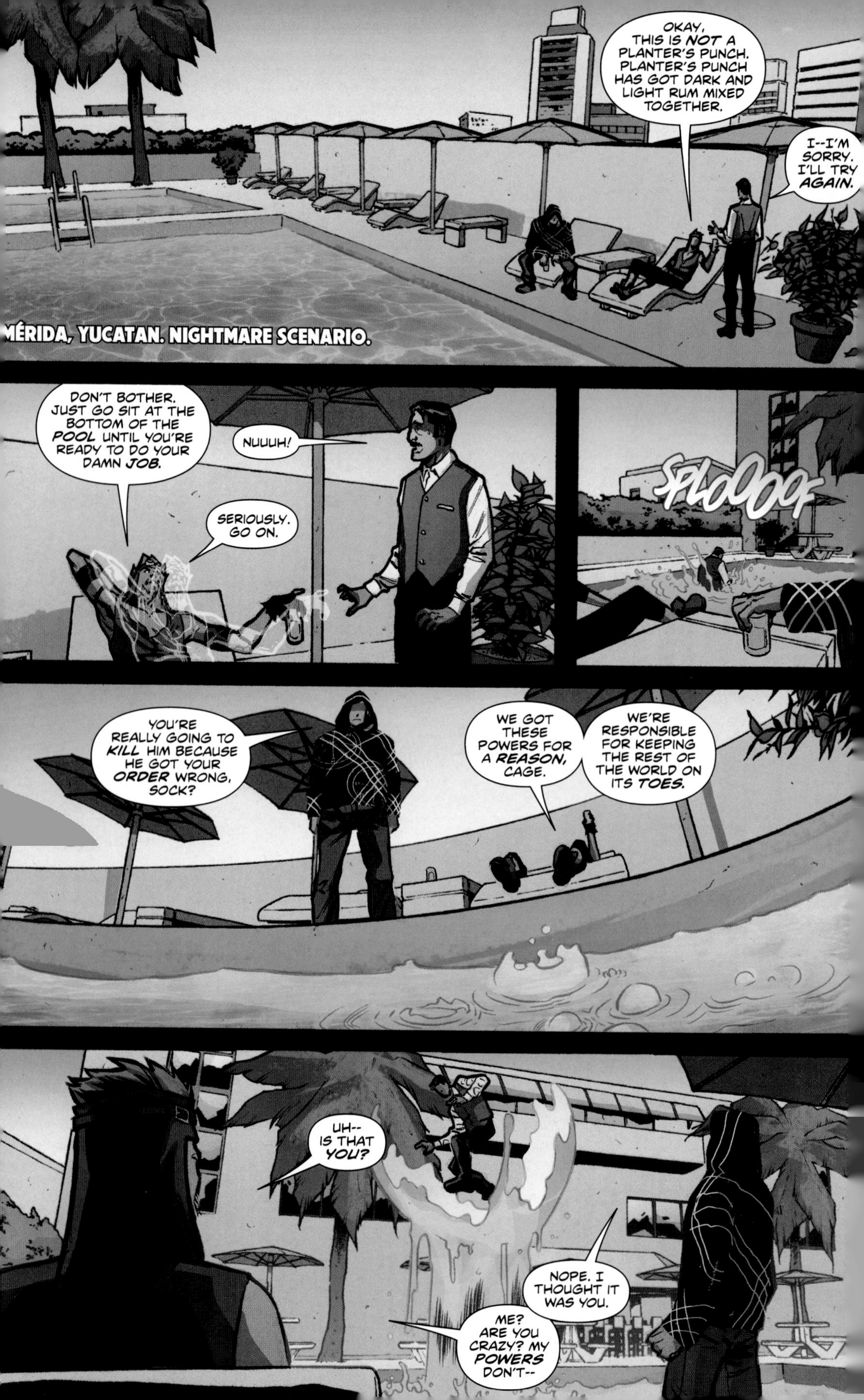
OKAY, THIS IS NOT A PLANTER'S PUNCH. PLANTER'S PUNCH HAS GOT DARK AND LIGHT RUM MIXED TOGETHER.
I--I'M SORRY. I'LL TRY AGAIN.
MÉRIDA, YUCATAN. NIGHTMARE SCENARIO.
DON'T BOTHER. JUST GO SIT AT THE BOTTOM OF THE POOL UNTIL YOU'RE READY TO DO YOUR DAMN JOB.
NUUUH!
SERIOUSLY. GO ON.
SPLOOOOF
YOU'RE REALLY GOING TO KILL HIM BECAUSE HE GOT YOUR ORDER WRONG, SOCK?
WE GOT THESE POWERS FOR A REASON, CAGE.
WE'RE RESPONSIBLE FOR KEEPING THE REST OF THE WORLD ON ITS TOES.
UH-- IS THAT YOU?
NOPE. I THOUGHT IT WAS YOU.
ME? ARE YOU CRAZY? MY POWERS DON'T--

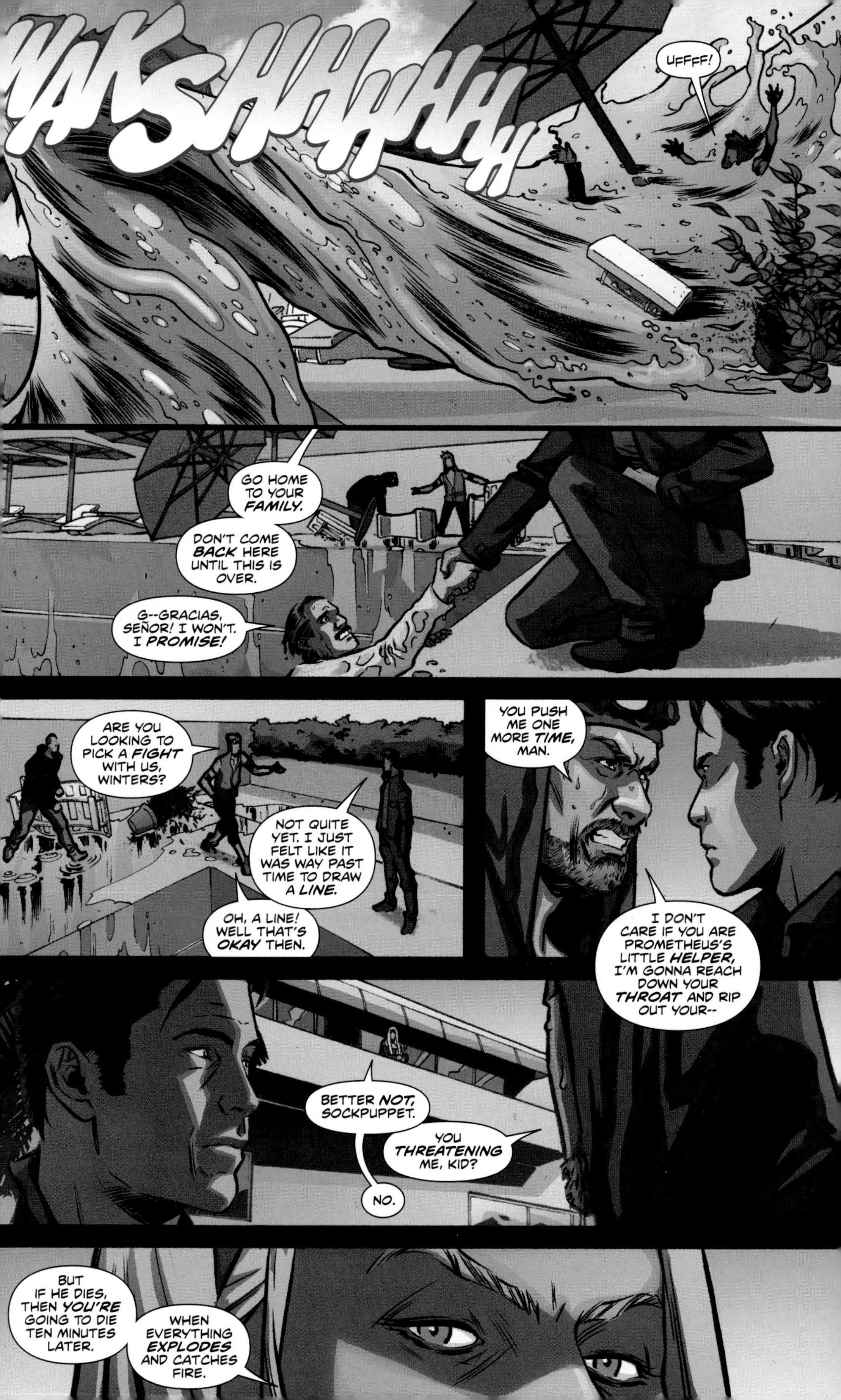

WAKSHHHHHHH
UFFFF!
GO HOME TO YOUR FAMILY.
DON'T COME BACK HERE UNTIL THIS IS OVER.
G--GRACIAS, SEÑOR! I WON'T. I PROMISE!
ARE YOU LOOKING TO PICK A FIGHT WITH US, WINTERS?
NOT QUITE YET. I JUST FELT LIKE IT WAS WAY PAST TIME TO DRAW A LINE.
OH, A LINE! WELL THAT'S OKAY THEN.
YOU PUSH ME ONE MORE TIME, MAN.
I DON'T CARE IF YOU ARE PROMETHEUS'S LITTLE HELPER, I'M GONNA REACH DOWN YOUR THROAT AND RIP OUT YOUR--
BETTER NOT, SOCKPUPPET.
YOU THREATENING ME, KID?
NO.
BUT IF HE DIES, THEN YOU'RE GOING TO DIE TEN MINUTES LATER.
WHEN EVERYTHING EXPLODES AND CATCHES FIRE.

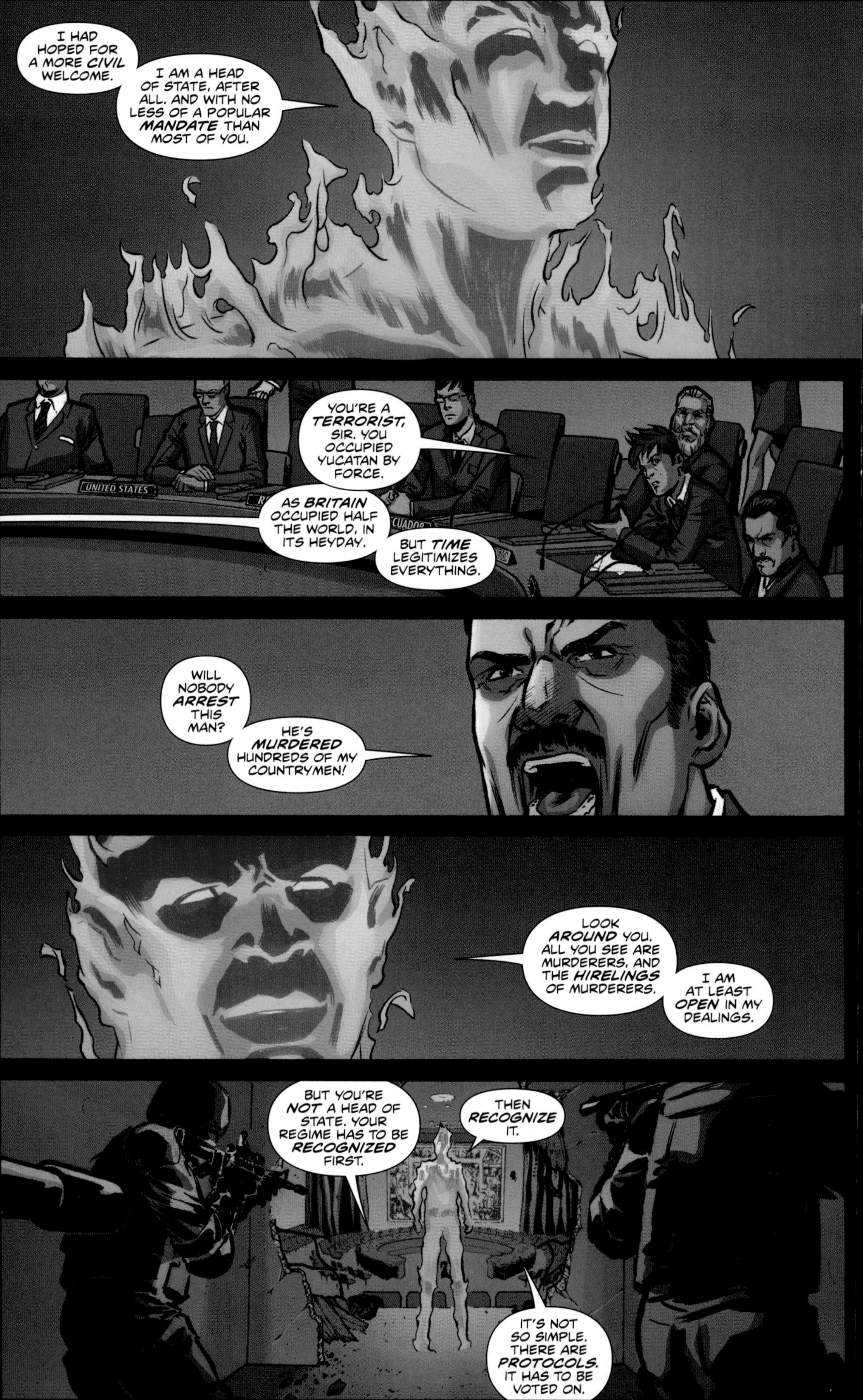
I HAD HOPED FOR A MORE CIVIL WELCOME.
I AM A HEAD OF STATE, AFTER ALL. AND WITH NO LESS OF A POPULAR MANDATE THAN MOST OF YOU.
UNITED STATES
YOU'RE A TERRORIST, SIR. YOU OCCUPIED YUCATAN BY FORCE.
AS BRITAIN OCCUPIED HALF THE WORLD, IN ITS HEYDAY.
BUT TIME LEGITIMIZES EVERYTHING.
WILL NOBODY ARREST THIS MAN?
HE'S MURDERED HUNDREDS OF MY COUNTRYMEN!
LOOK AROUND YOU. ALL YOU SEE ARE MURDERERS, AND THE HIRELINGS OF MURDERERS.
I AM AT LEAST OPEN IN MY DEALINGS.
BUT YOU'RE NOT A HEAD OF STATE. YOUR REGIME HAS TO BE RECOGNIZED FIRST.
THEN RECOGNIZE IT.
IT'S NOT SO SIMPLE. THERE ARE PROTOCOLS. IT HAS TO BE VOTED ON.

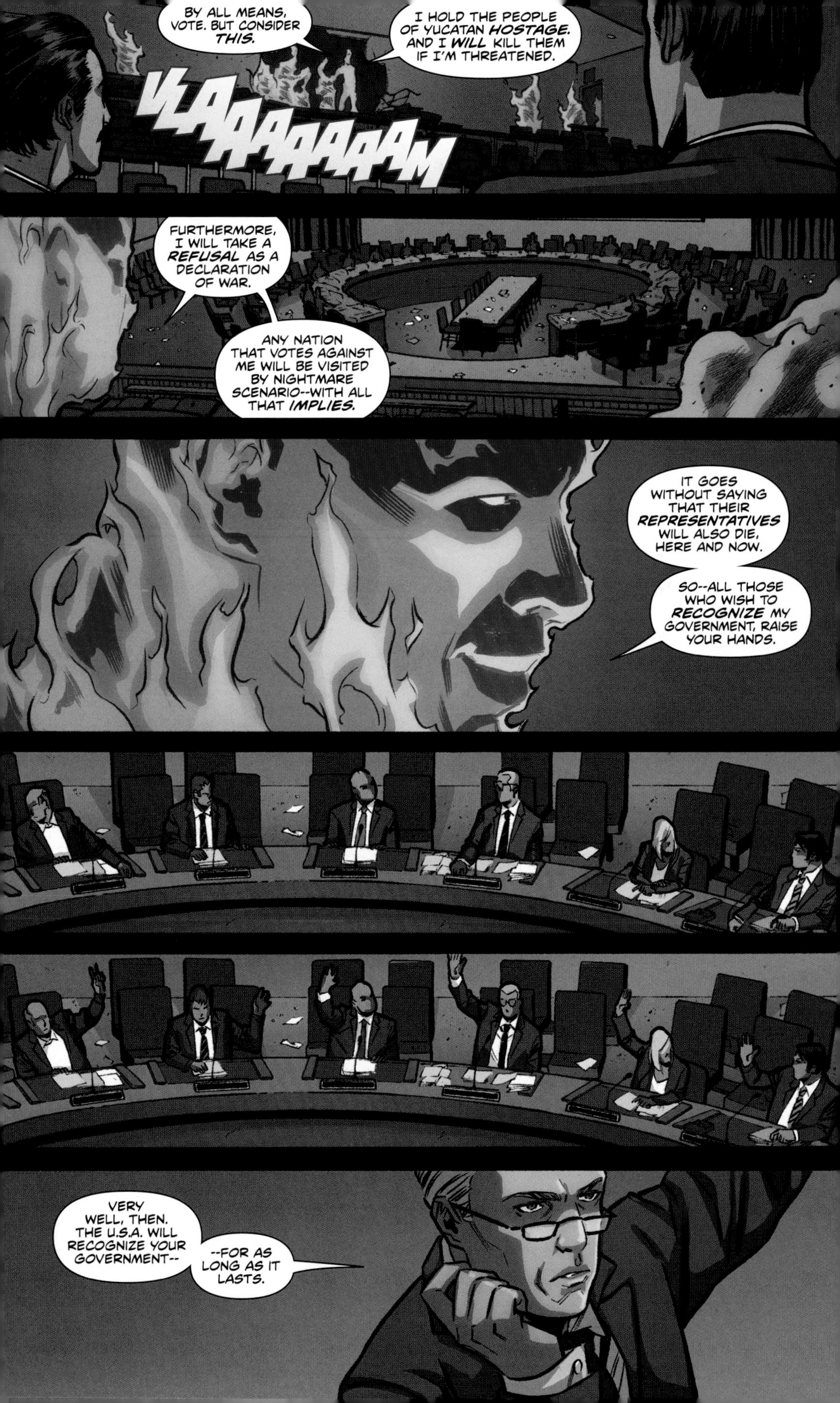
BY ALL MEANS, VOTE. BUT CONSIDER THIS.
I HOLD THE PEOPLE OF YUCATAN HOSTAGE. AND I WILL KILL THEM IF I'M THREATENED.
VLAAAAAAAAM
FURTHERMORE, I WILL TAKE A REFUSAL AS A DECLARATION OF WAR.
ANY NATION THAT VOTES AGAINST ME WILL BE VISITED BY NIGHTMARE SCENARIO--WITH ALL THAT IMPLIES.
IT GOES WITHOUT SAYING THAT THEIR REPRESENTATIVES WILL ALSO DIE, HERE AND NOW.
SO--ALL THOSE WHO WISH TO RECOGNIZE MY GOVERNMENT, RAISE YOUR HANDS.
VERY WELL, THEN. THE U.S.A. WILL RECOGNIZE YOUR GOVERNMENT--
--FOR AS LONG AS IT LASTS.

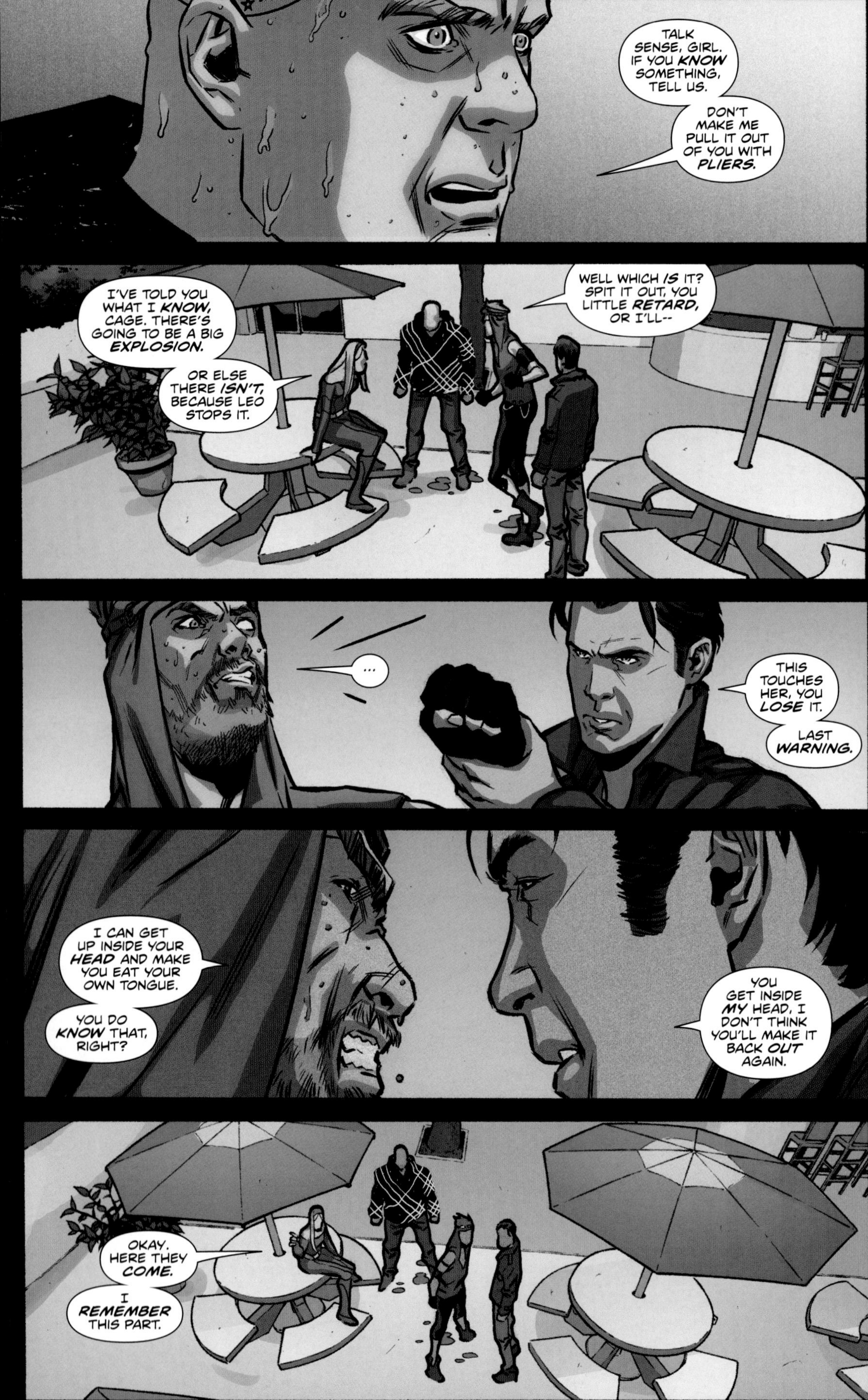

TALK SENSE, GIRL. IF YOU KNOW SOMETHING, TELL US.
DON'T MAKE ME PULL IT OUT OF YOU WITH PLIERS.
I'VE TOLD YOU WHAT I KNOW, CAGE. THERE'S GOING TO BE A BIG EXPLOSION.
OR ELSE THERE ISN'T, BECAUSE LEO STOPS IT.
WELL WHICH IS IT? SPIT IT OUT, YOU LITTLE RETARD, OR I'LL--
...
THIS TOUCHES HER, YOU LOSE IT.
LAST WARNING.
I CAN GET UP INSIDE YOUR HEAD AND MAKE YOU EAT YOUR OWN TONGUE.
YOU DO KNOW THAT, RIGHT?
YOU GET INSIDE MY HEAD, I DON'T THINK YOU'LL MAKE IT BACK OUT AGAIN.
OKAY. HERE THEY COME.
I REMEMBER THIS PART.

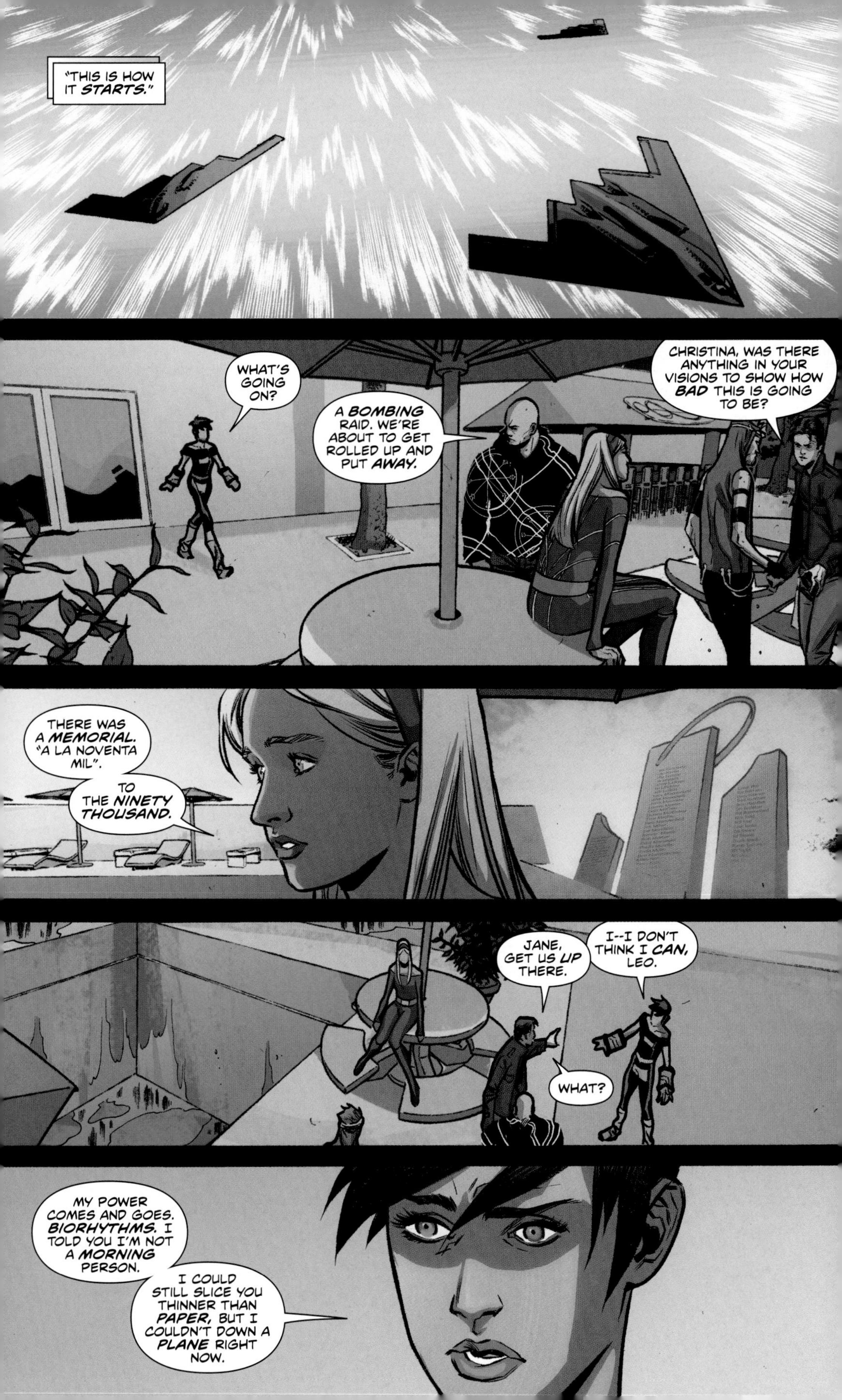
"THIS IS HOW IT STARTS."
WHAT'S GOING ON?
A BOMBING RAID. WE'RE ABOUT TO GET ROLLED UP AND PUT AWAY.
CHRISTINA, WAS THERE ANYTHING IN YOUR VISIONS TO SHOW HOW BAD THIS IS GOING TO BE?
THERE WAS A MEMORIAL. "A LA NOVENTA MIL".
TO THE NINETY THOUSAND.
JANE, GET US UP THERE.
I--I DON'T THINK I CAN, LEO.
WHAT?
MY POWER COMES AND GOES. BIORHYTHMS. I TOLD YOU I'M NOT A MORNING PERSON.
I COULD STILL SLICE YOU THINNER THAN PAPER, BUT I COULDN'T DOWN A PLANE RIGHT NOW.

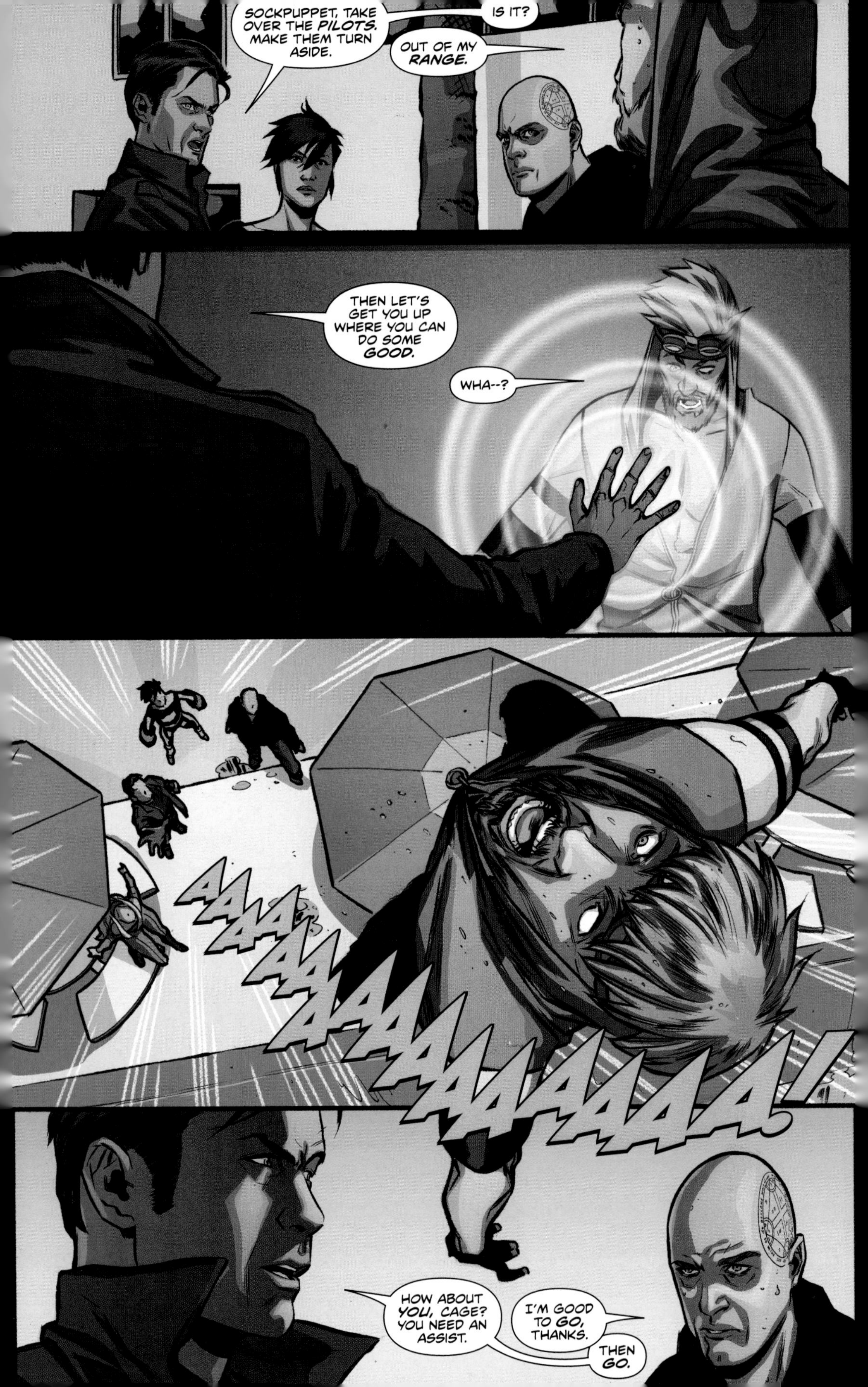
SOCKPUPPET, TAKE OVER THE PILOTS. MAKE THEM TURN ASIDE.
IS IT?
OUT OF MY RANGE.
THEN LET'S GET YOU UP WHERE YOU CAN DO SOME GOOD.
WHA--?
AAAAAAAAAAAAAAAAA!
HOW ABOUT YOU, CAGE? YOU NEED AN ASSIST.
I'M GOOD TO GO, THANKS.
THEN GO.

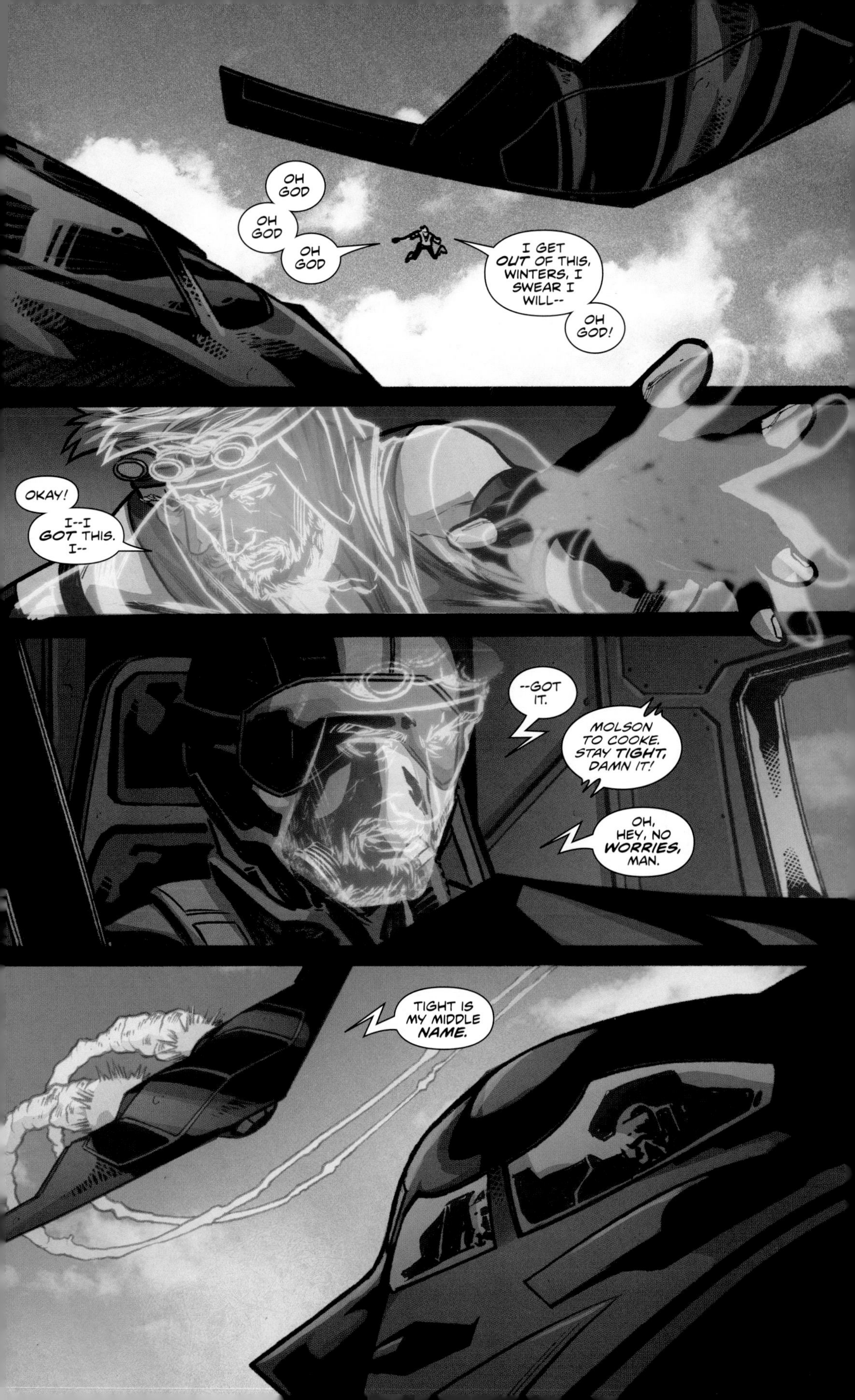
OH GOD
OH GOD
OH GOD
I GET OUT OF THIS, WINTERS, I SWEAR I WILL--
OH GOD!
OKAY!
I--I GOT THIS. I--
--GOT IT.
MOLSON TO COOKE. STAY TIGHT, DAMN IT!
OH, HEY, NO WORRIES, MAN.
TIGHT IS MY MIDDLE NAME.

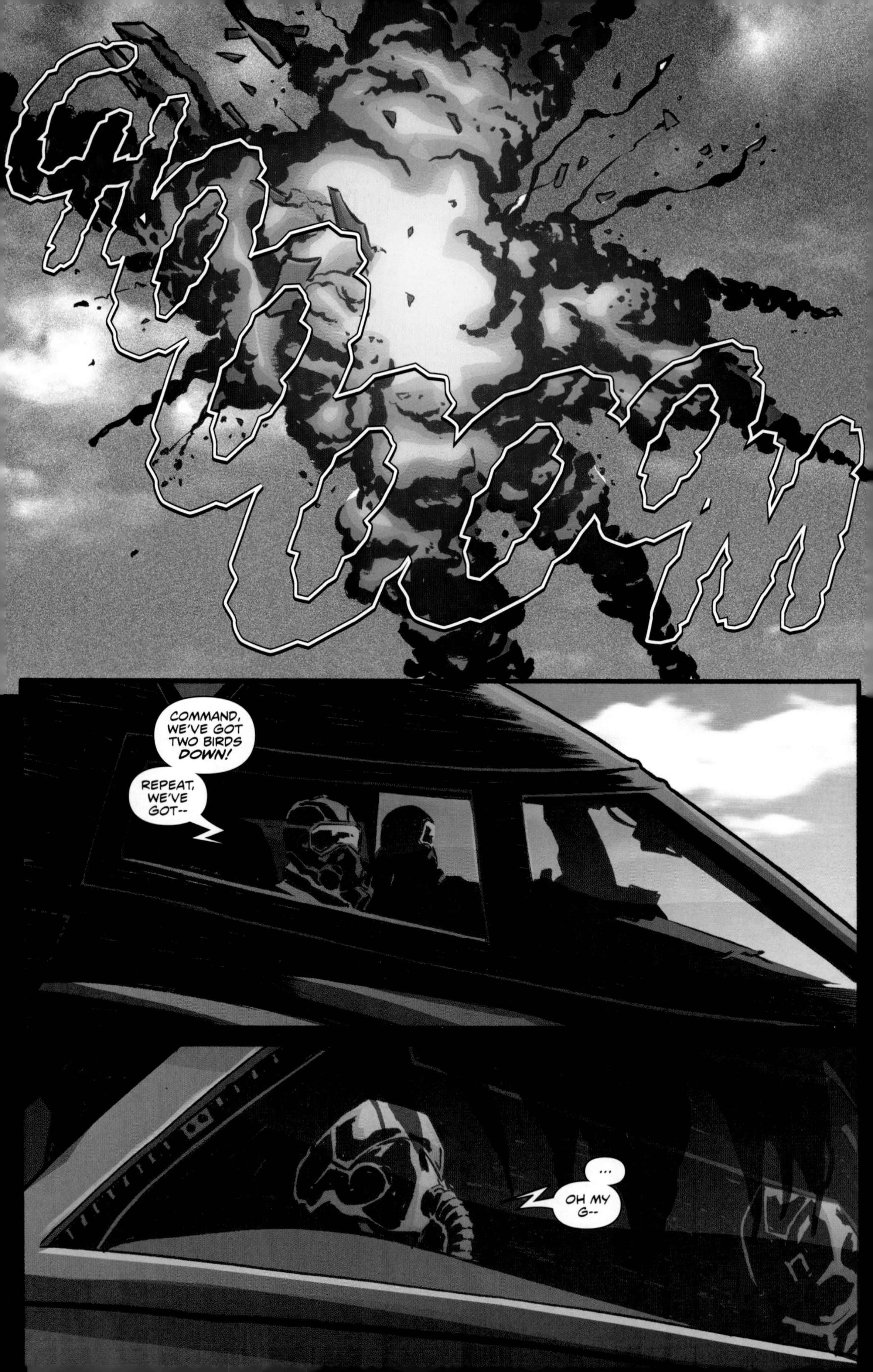
GKRROOM
COMMAND, WE'VE GOT TWO BIRDS DOWN!
REPEAT, WE'VE GOT--
...
OH MY G--

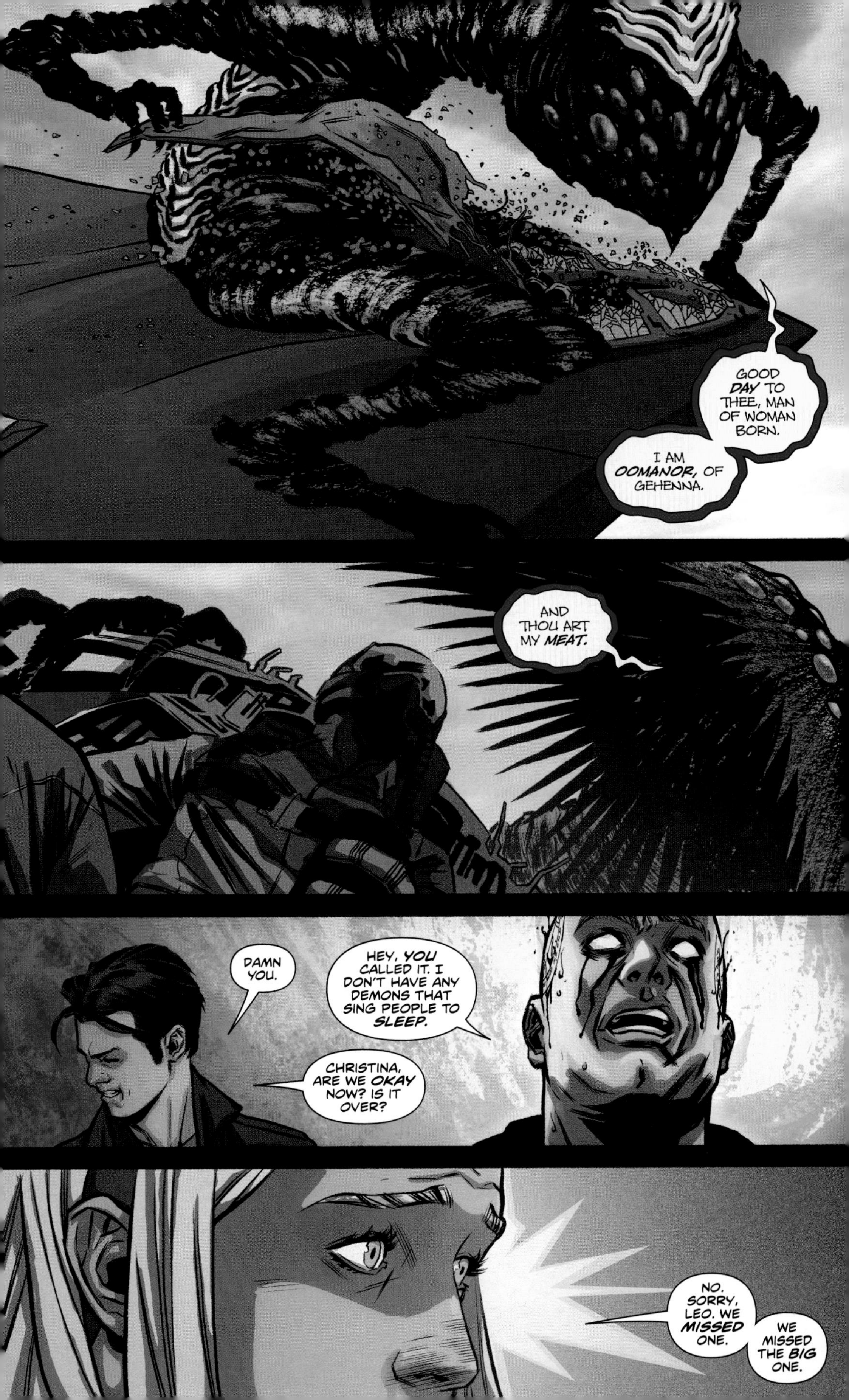
GOOD DAY TO THEE, MAN OF WOMAN BORN.
I AM OOMANOR, OF GEHENNA.
AND THOU ART MY MEAT.
DAMN YOU.
HEY, YOU CALLED IT. I DON'T HAVE ANY DEMONS THAT SING PEOPLE TO SLEEP.
CHRISTINA, ARE WE OKAY NOW? IS IT OVER?
NO. SORRY, LEO. WE MISSED ONE.
WE MISSED THE BIG ONE.

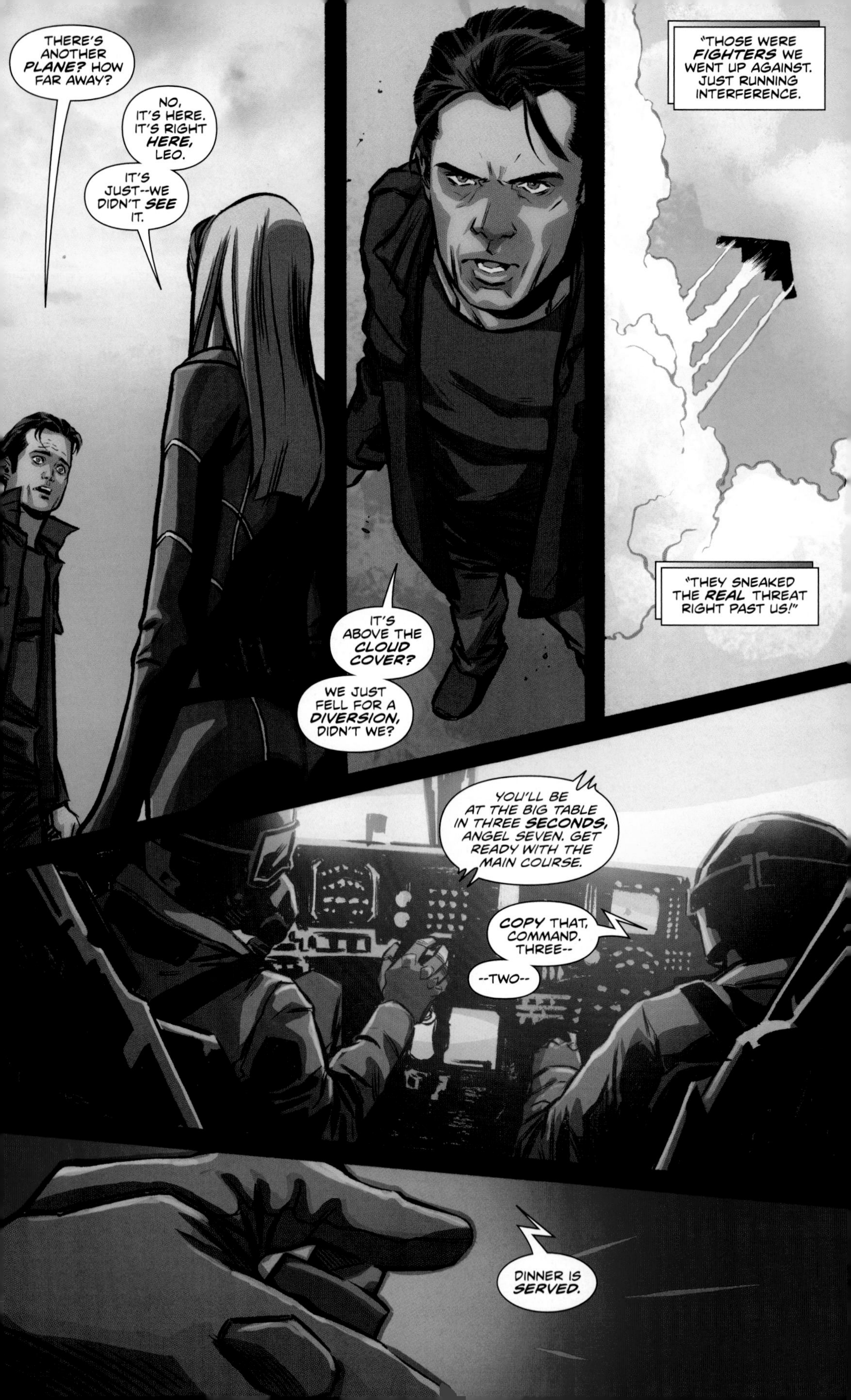

THERE'S ANOTHER PLANE? HOW FAR AWAY?
NO, IT'S HERE. IT'S RIGHT HERE, LEO.
IT'S JUST--WE DIDN'T SEE IT.
IT'S ABOVE THE CLOUD COVER?
WE JUST FELL FOR A DIVERSION, DIDN'T WE?
"THOSE WERE FIGHTERS WE WENT UP AGAINST. JUST RUNNING INTERFERENCE.
"THEY SNEAKED THE REAL THREAT RIGHT PAST US!"
YOU'LL BE AT THE BIG TABLE IN THREE SECONDS, ANGEL SEVEN. GET READY WITH THE MAIN COURSE.
COPY THAT, COMMAND. THREE--
--TWO--
DINNER IS SERVED.

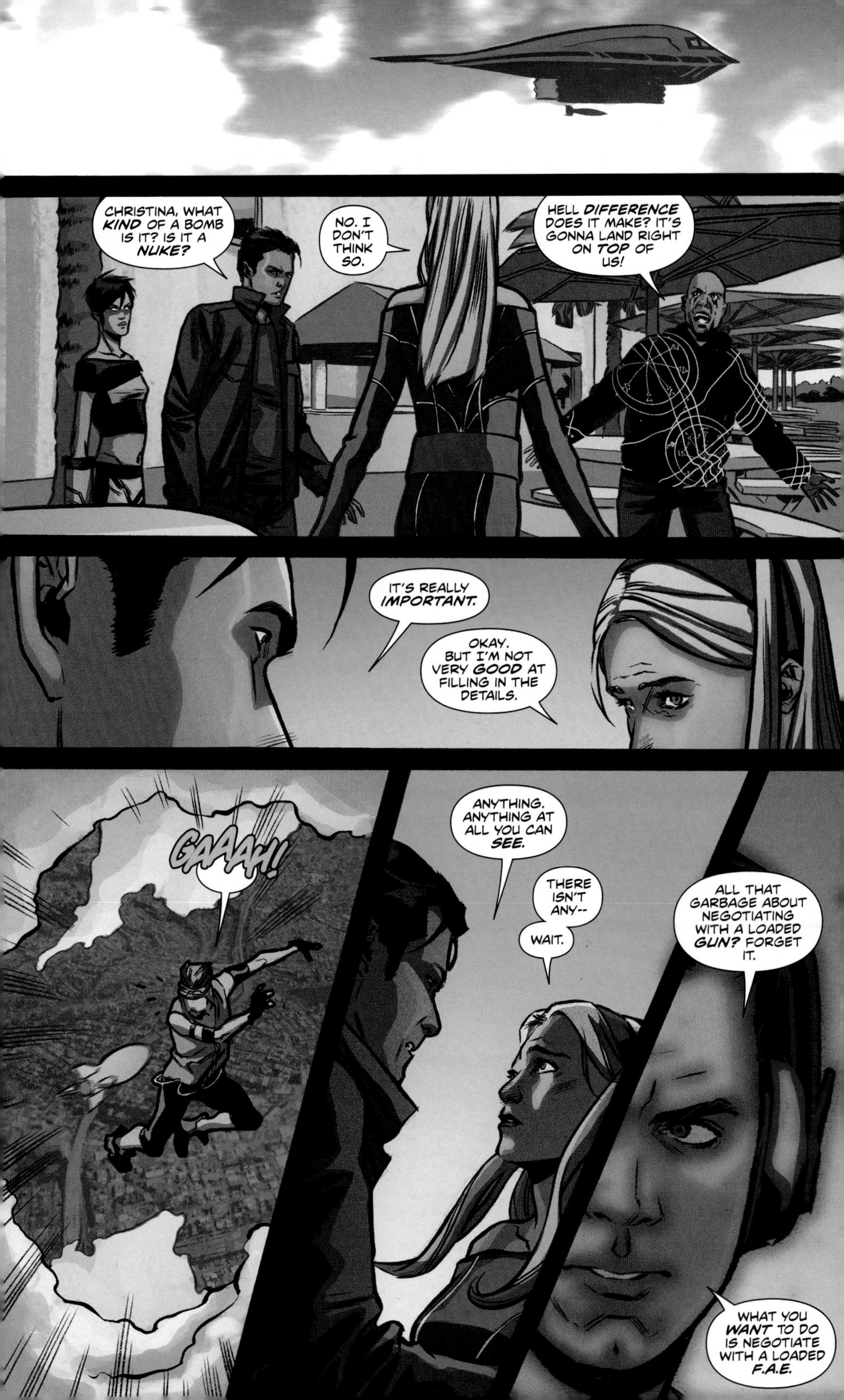

CHRISTINA, WHAT KIND OF A BOMB IS IT? IS IT A NUKE?
NO. I DON'T THINK SO.
HELL DIFFERENCE DOES IT MAKE? IT'S GONNA LAND RIGHT ON TOP OF US!
IT'S REALLY IMPORTANT.
OKAY. BUT I'M NOT VERY GOOD AT FILLING IN THE DETAILS.
GAAAH!
ANYTHING. ANYTHING AT ALL YOU CAN SEE.
THERE ISN'T ANY--
WAIT.
ALL THAT GARBAGE ABOUT NEGOTIATING WITH A LOADED GUN? FORGET IT.
WHAT YOU WANT TO DO IS NEGOTIATE WITH A LOADED F.A.E.

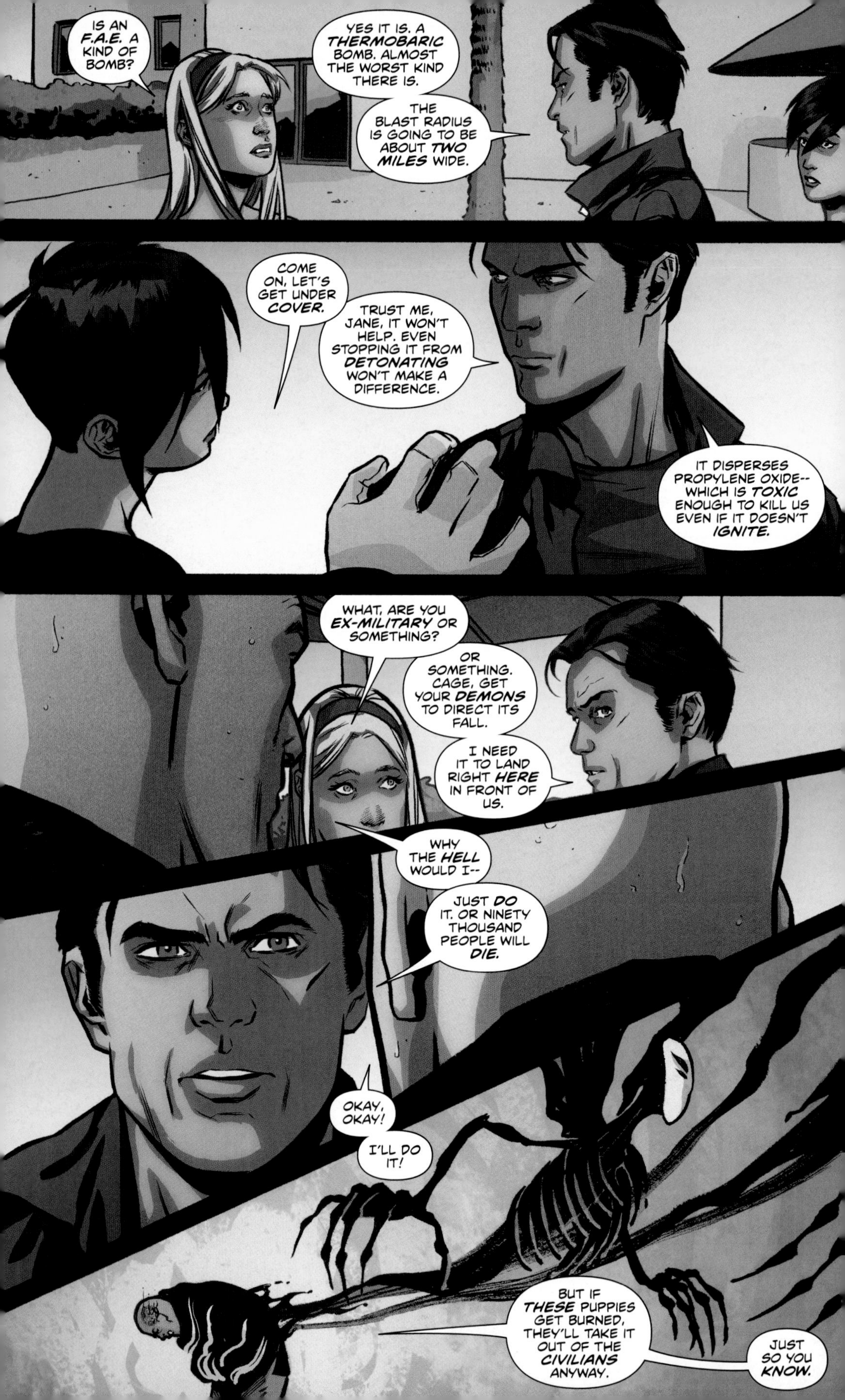

IS AN F.A.E. A KIND OF BOMB?
YES IT IS. A THERMOBARIC BOMB. ALMOST THE WORST KIND THERE IS.
THE BLAST RADIUS IS GOING TO BE ABOUT TWO MILES WIDE.
COME ON, LET'S GET UNDER COVER.
TRUST ME, JANE, IT WON'T HELP. EVEN STOPPING IT FROM DETONATING WON'T MAKE A DIFFERENCE.
IT DISPERSES PROPYLENE OXIDE--WHICH IS TOXIC ENOUGH TO KILL US EVEN IF IT DOESN'T IGNITE.
WHAT, ARE YOU EX-MILITARY OR SOMETHING?
OR SOMETHING. CAGE, GET YOUR DEMONS TO DIRECT ITS FALL.
I NEED IT TO LAND RIGHT HERE IN FRONT OF US.
WHY THE HELL WOULD I--
JUST DO IT. OR NINETY THOUSAND PEOPLE WILL DIE.
OKAY, OKAY!
I'LL DO IT!
BUT IF THESE PUPPIES GET BURNED, THEY'LL TAKE IT OUT OF THE CIVILIANS ANYWAY.
JUST SO YOU KNOW.

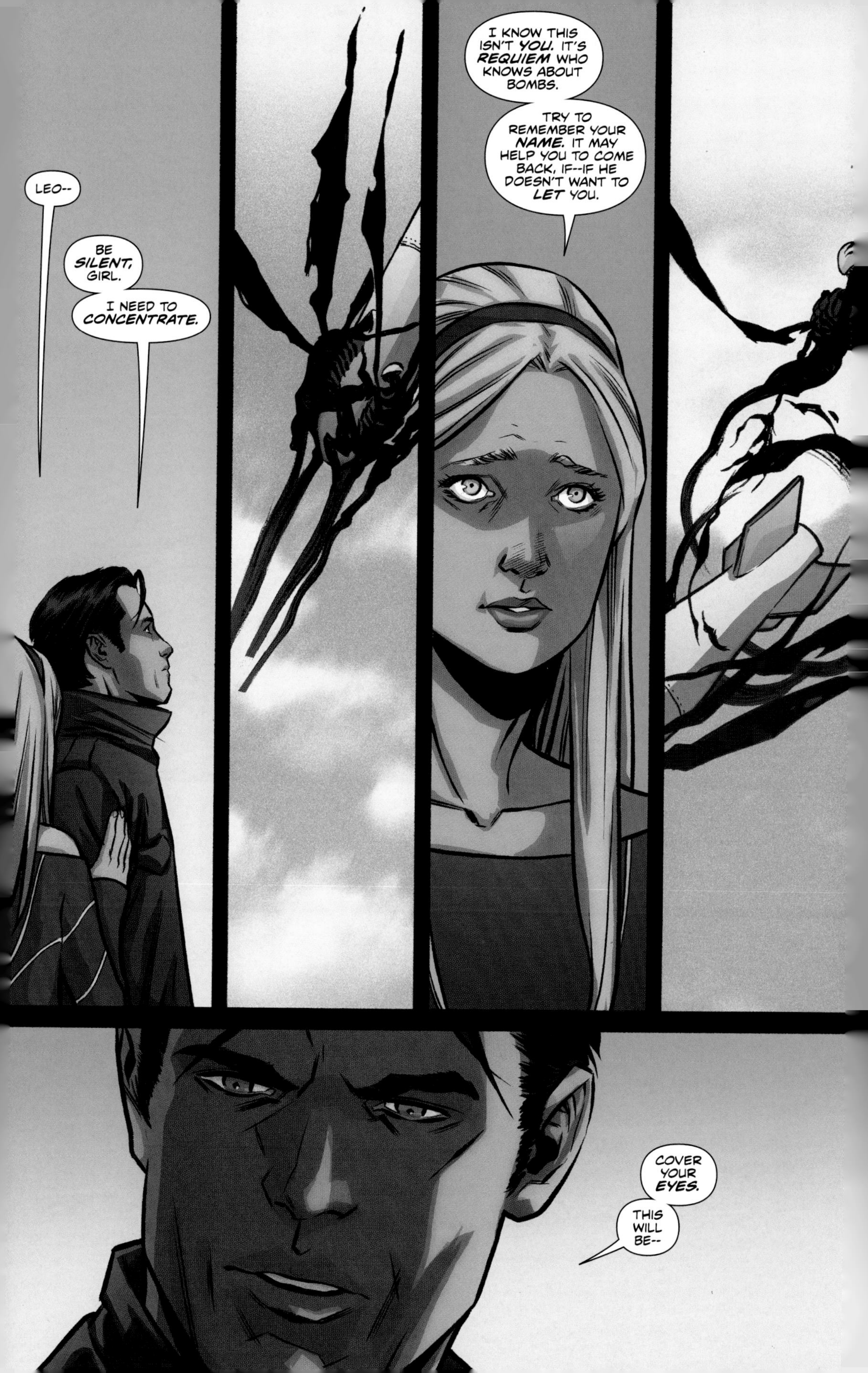
LEO--
BE SILENT, GIRL.
I NEED TO CONCENTRATE.
I KNOW THIS ISN'T YOU. IT'S REQUIEM WHO KNOWS ABOUT BOMBS.
TRY TO REMEMBER YOUR NAME. IT MAY HELP YOU TO COME BACK, IF--IF HE DOESN'T WANT TO LET YOU.
COVER YOUR EYES.
THIS WILL BE--

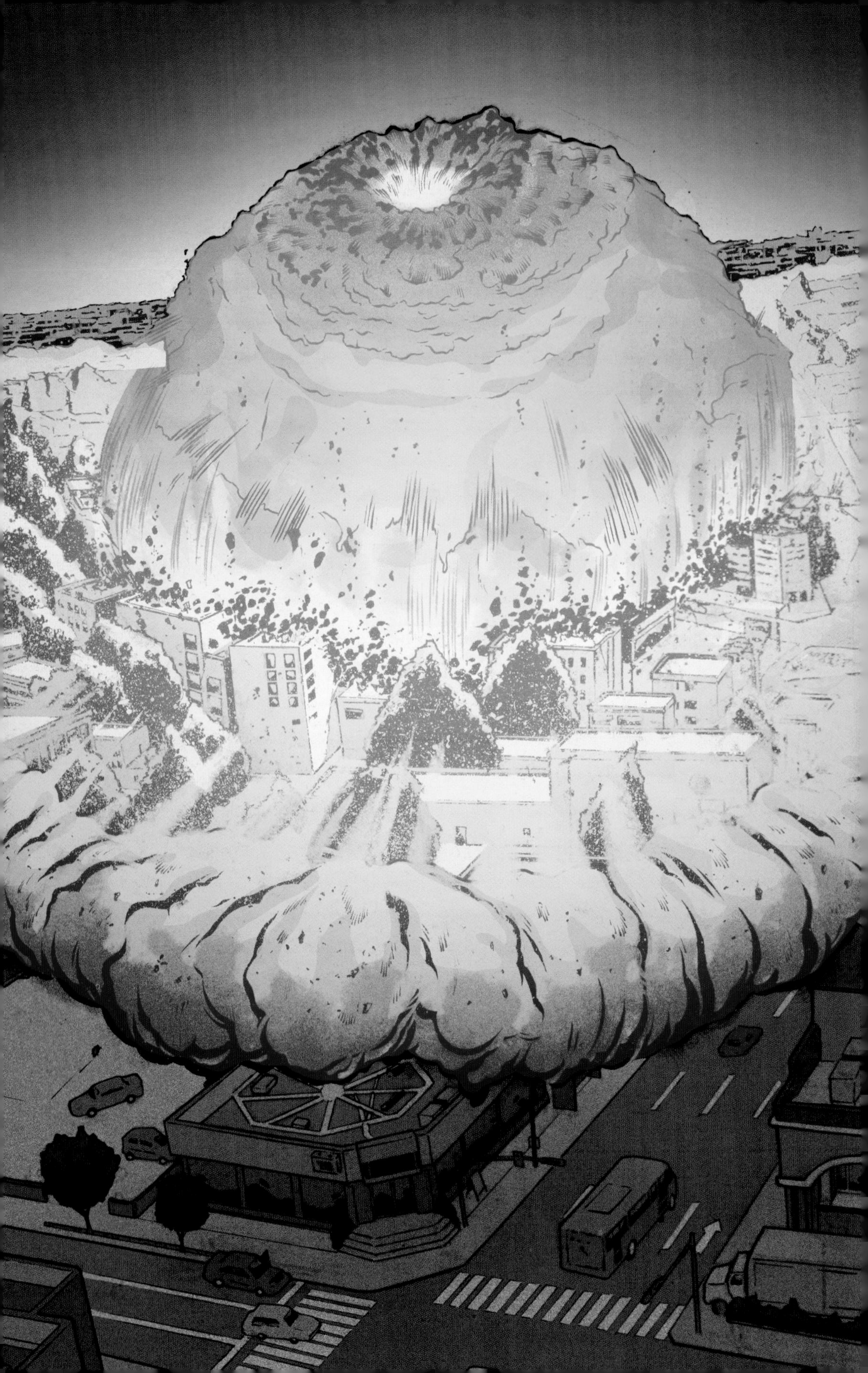

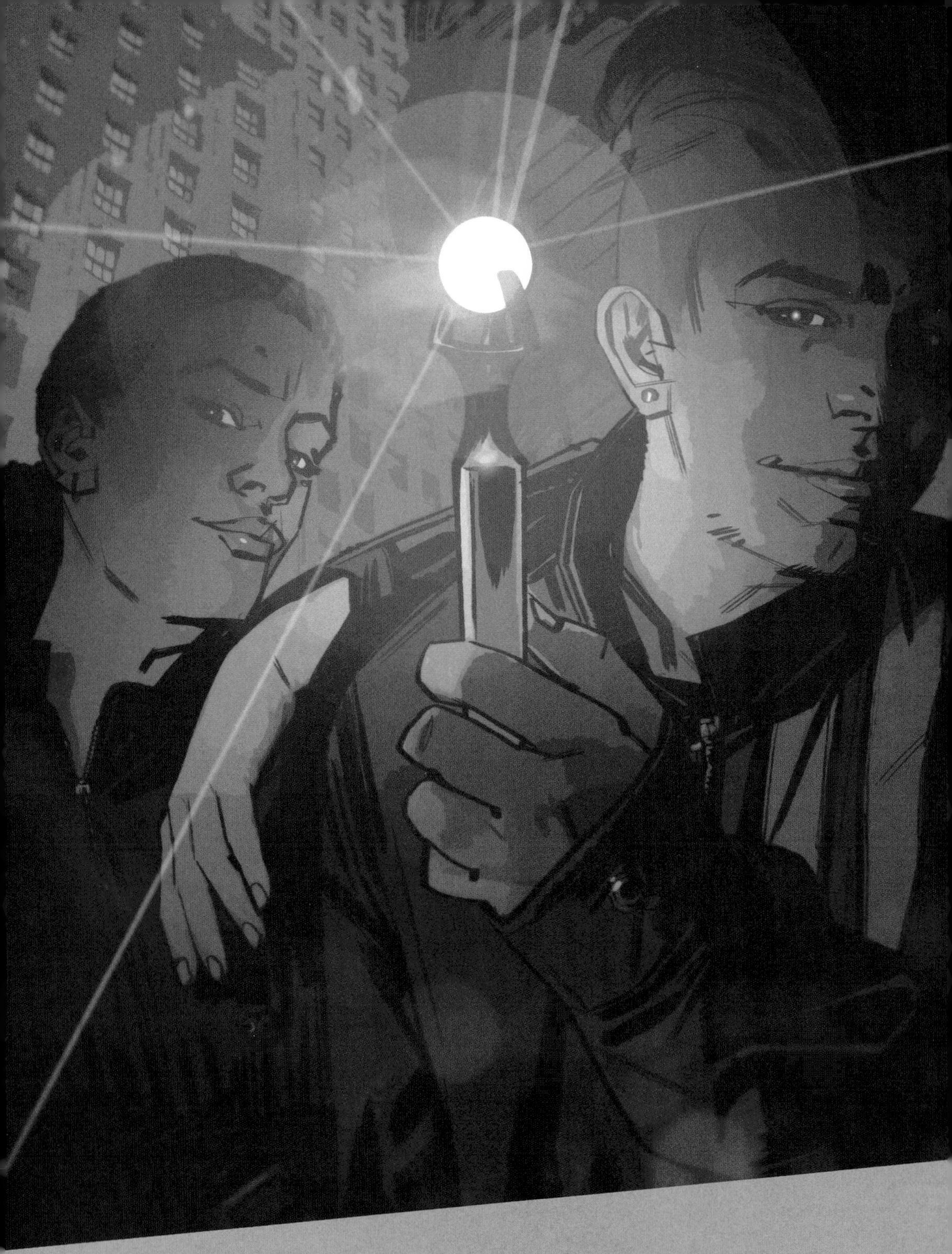

"IT COMES EASY TO ME. **TERRIFYINGLY** EASY. THE HARD PART — THAT COMES LATER."
Chapter 9

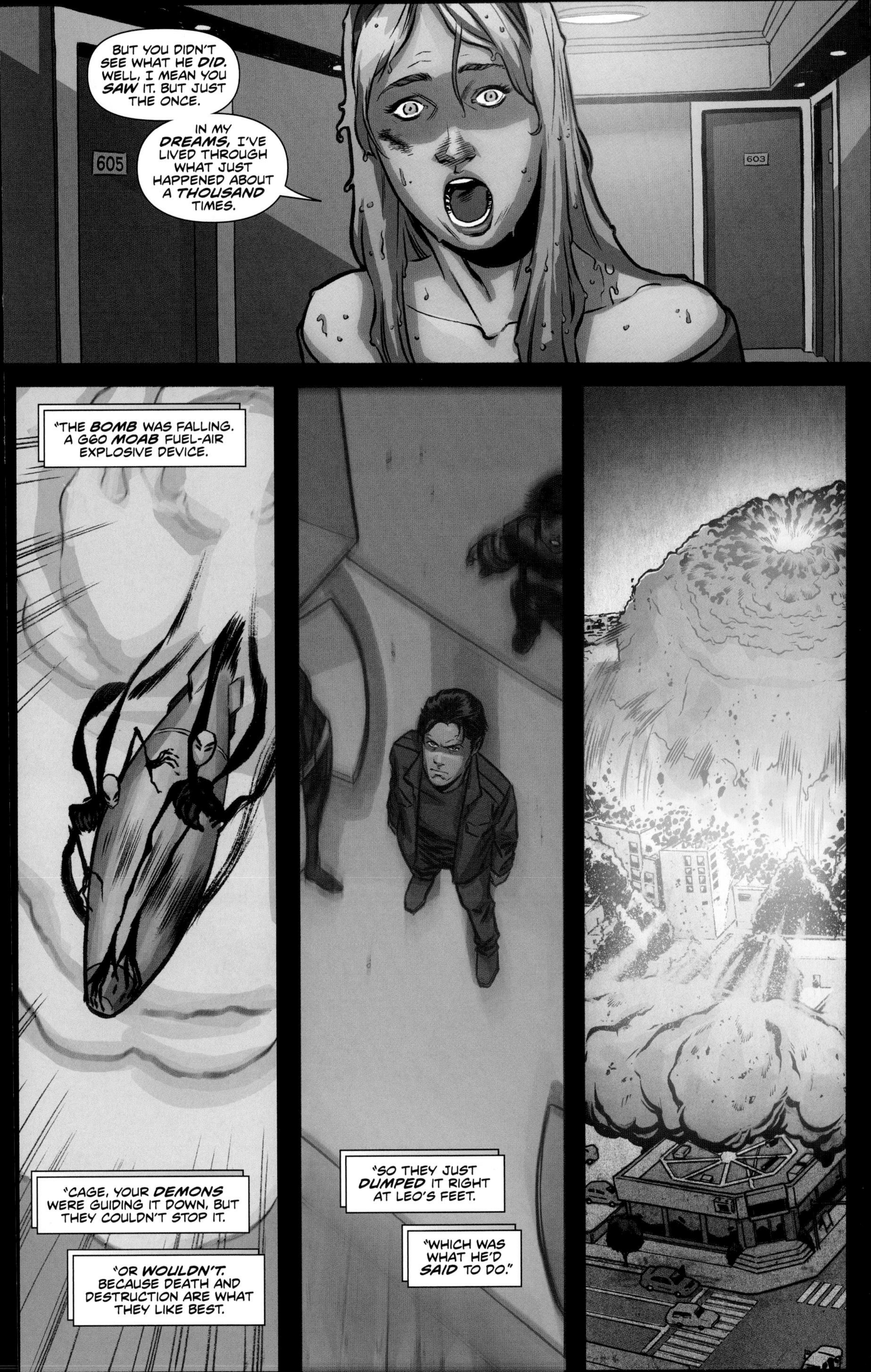
BUT YOU DIDN'T SEE WHAT HE DID. WELL, I MEAN YOU SAW IT. BUT JUST THE ONCE.
IN MY DREAMS, I'VE LIVED THROUGH WHAT JUST HAPPENED ABOUT A THOUSAND TIMES.
605
603
"THE BOMB WAS FALLING. A G60 MOAB FUEL-AIR EXPLOSIVE DEVICE.
"CAGE, YOUR DEMONS WERE GUIDING IT DOWN, BUT THEY COULDN'T STOP IT.
"OR WOULDN'T. BECAUSE DEATH AND DESTRUCTION ARE WHAT THEY LIKE BEST.
"SO THEY JUST DUMPED IT RIGHT AT LEO'S FEET.
"WHICH WAS WHAT HE'D SAID TO DO."

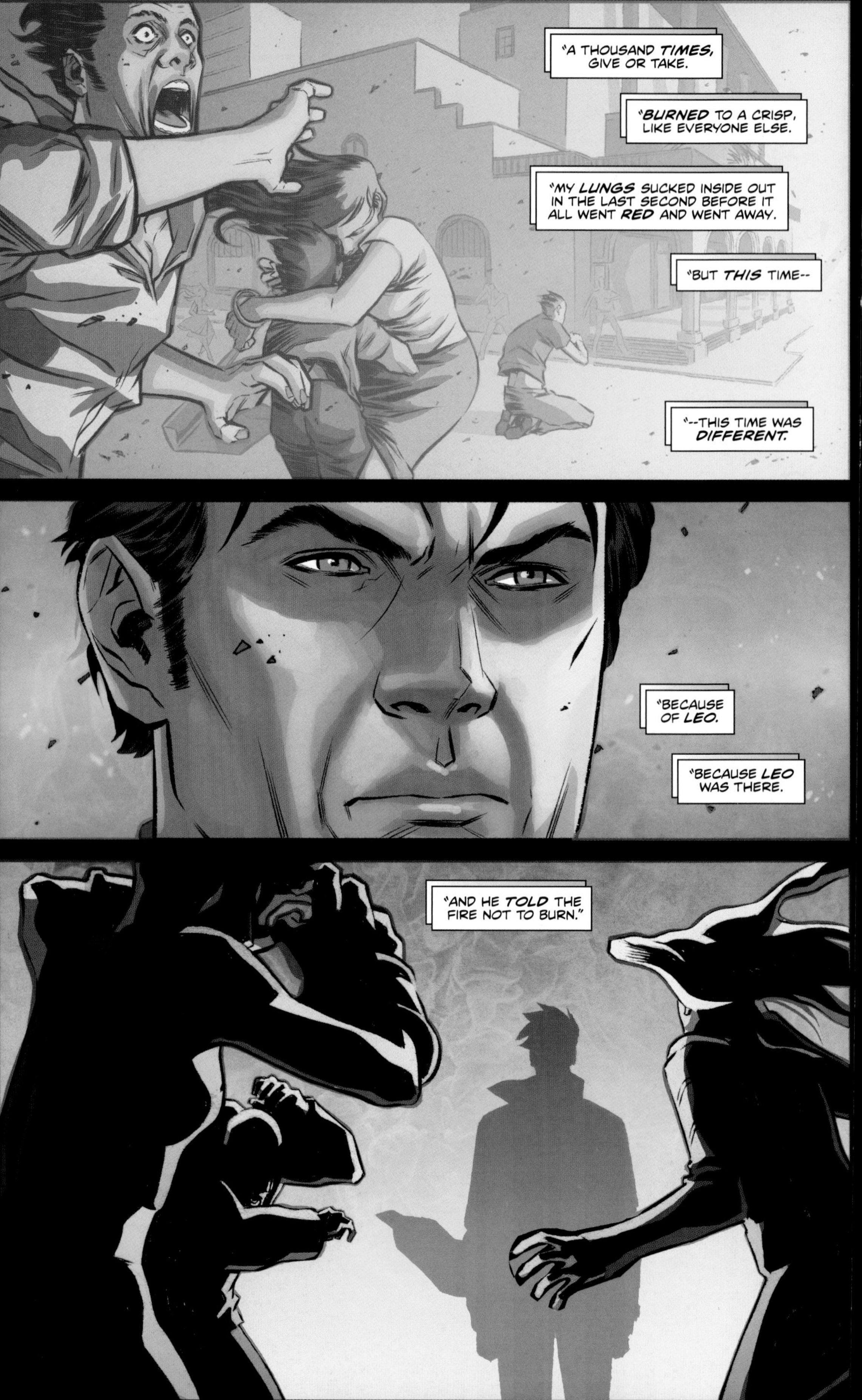
"A THOUSAND TIMES, GIVE OR TAKE.
"BURNED TO A CRISP, LIKE EVERYONE ELSE.
"MY LUNGS SUCKED INSIDE OUT IN THE LAST SECOND BEFORE IT ALL WENT RED AND WENT AWAY.
"BUT THIS TIME--
"--THIS TIME WAS DIFFERENT.
"BECAUSE OF LEO.
"BECAUSE LEO WAS THERE.
"AND HE TOLD THE FIRE NOT TO BURN."

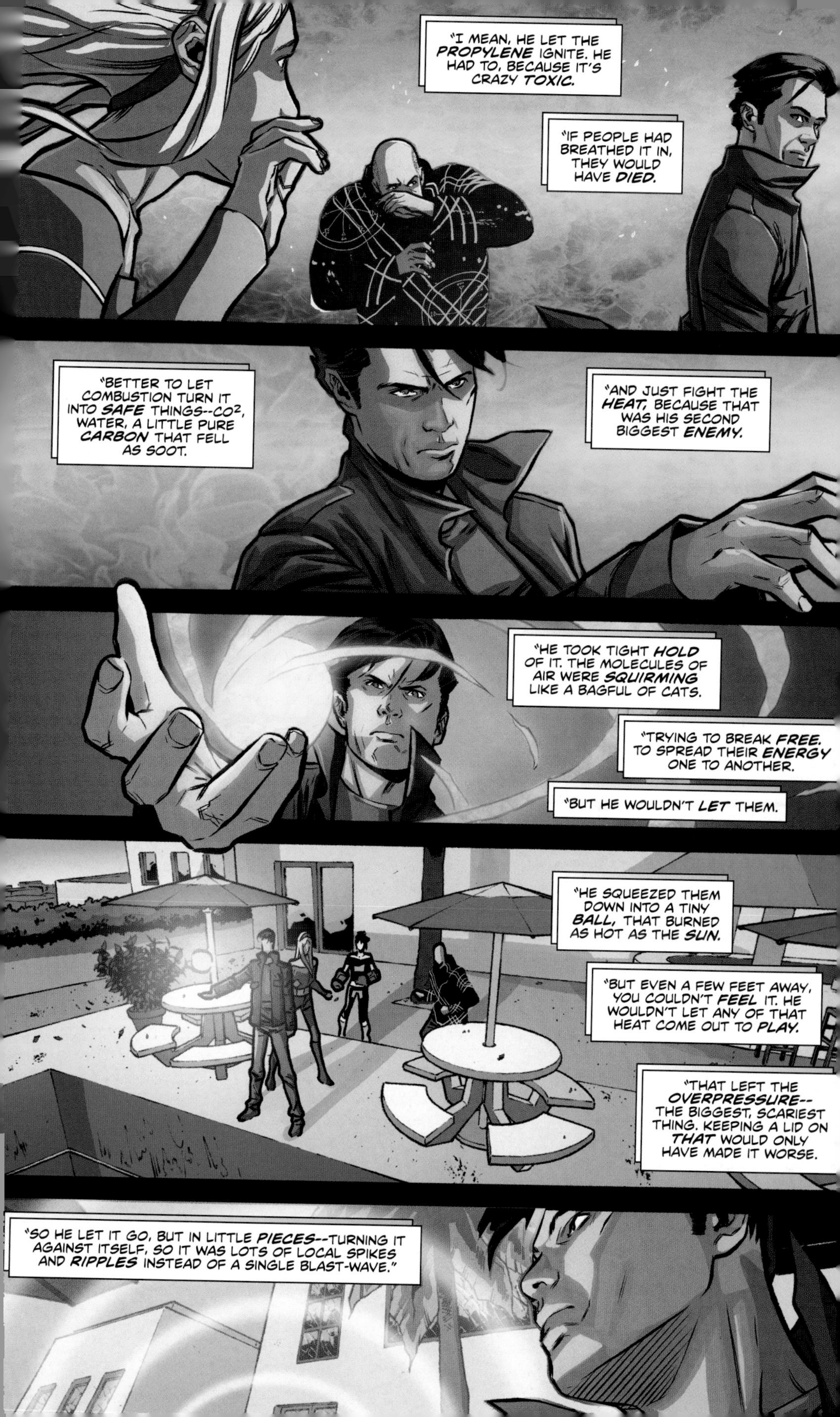
"I MEAN, HE LET THE *PROPYLENE* IGNITE. HE HAD TO, BECAUSE IT'S CRAZY *TOXIC.*
"IF PEOPLE HAD BREATHED IT IN, THEY WOULD HAVE *DIED.*
"BETTER TO LET COMBUSTION TURN IT INTO *SAFE* THINGS--CO_2, WATER, A LITTLE PURE *CARBON* THAT FELL AS SOOT.
"AND JUST FIGHT THE *HEAT,* BECAUSE THAT WAS HIS SECOND BIGGEST *ENEMY.*
"HE TOOK TIGHT *HOLD* OF IT. THE MOLECULES OF AIR WERE *SQUIRMING* LIKE A BAGFUL OF CATS.
"TRYING TO BREAK *FREE.* TO SPREAD THEIR *ENERGY* ONE TO ANOTHER.
"BUT HE WOULDN'T *LET* THEM.
"HE SQUEEZED THEM DOWN INTO A TINY *BALL,* THAT BURNED AS HOT AS THE *SUN.*
"BUT EVEN A FEW FEET AWAY, YOU COULDN'T *FEEL* IT. HE WOULDN'T LET ANY OF THAT HEAT COME OUT TO *PLAY.*
"THAT LEFT THE *OVERPRESSURE--* THE BIGGEST, SCARIEST THING. KEEPING A LID ON *THAT* WOULD ONLY HAVE MADE IT WORSE.
"SO HE LET IT GO, BUT IN LITTLE *PIECES*--TURNING IT AGAINST ITSELF, SO IT WAS LOTS OF LOCAL SPIKES AND *RIPPLES* INSTEAD OF A SINGLE BLAST-WAVE."

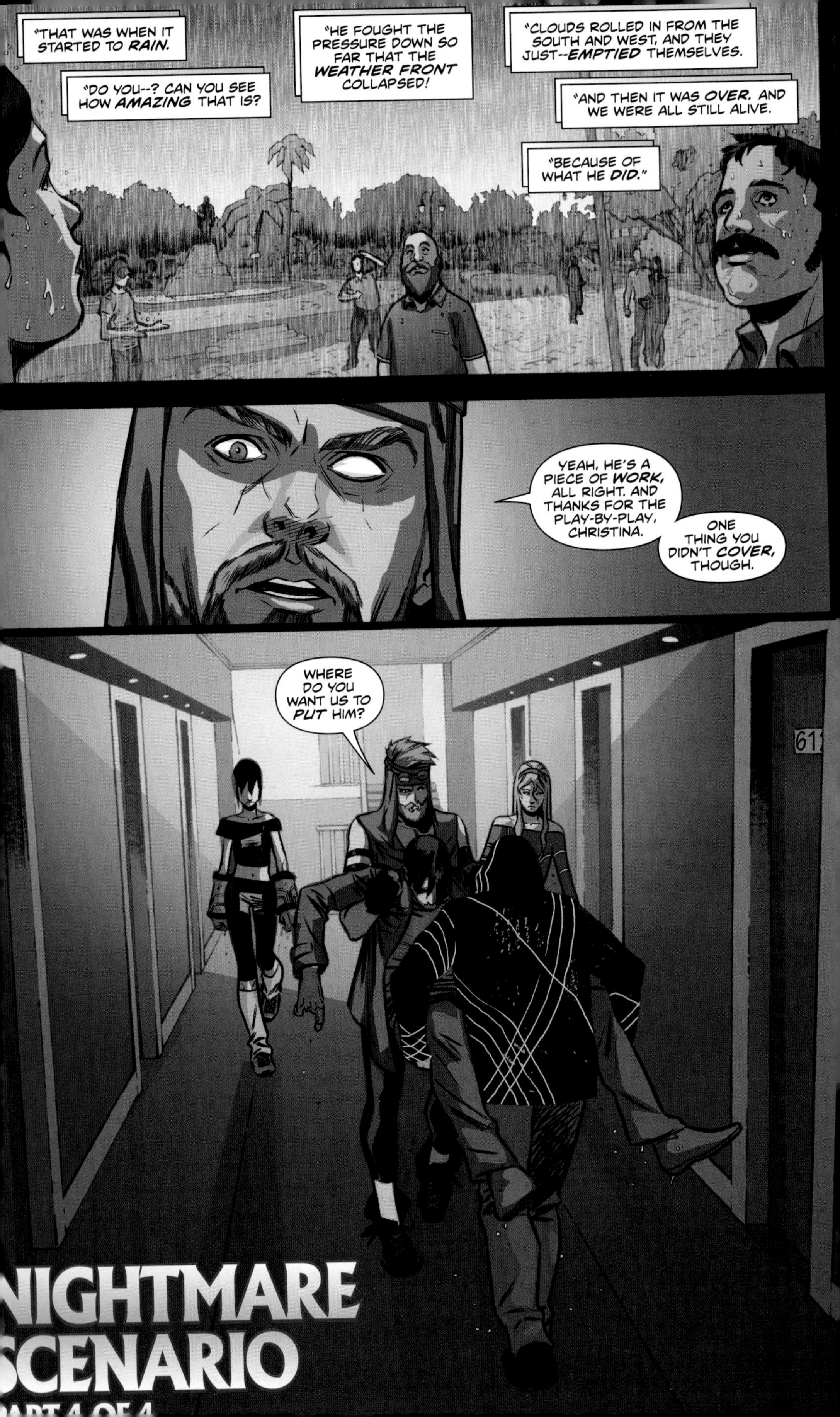
"THAT WAS WHEN IT STARTED TO *RAIN.*
"DO YOU--? CAN YOU SEE HOW *AMAZING* THAT IS?
"HE FOUGHT THE PRESSURE DOWN SO FAR THAT THE *WEATHER FRONT* COLLAPSED!
"CLOUDS ROLLED IN FROM THE SOUTH AND WEST, AND THEY JUST--*EMPTIED* THEMSELVES.
"AND THEN IT WAS *OVER.* AND WE WERE ALL STILL ALIVE.
"BECAUSE OF WHAT HE *DID.*"
YEAH, HE'S A PIECE OF *WORK,* ALL RIGHT. AND THANKS FOR THE PLAY-BY-PLAY, CHRISTINA.
ONE THING YOU DIDN'T *COVER,* THOUGH.
WHERE DO YOU WANT US TO *PUT* HIM?
61
NIGHTMARE SCENARIO

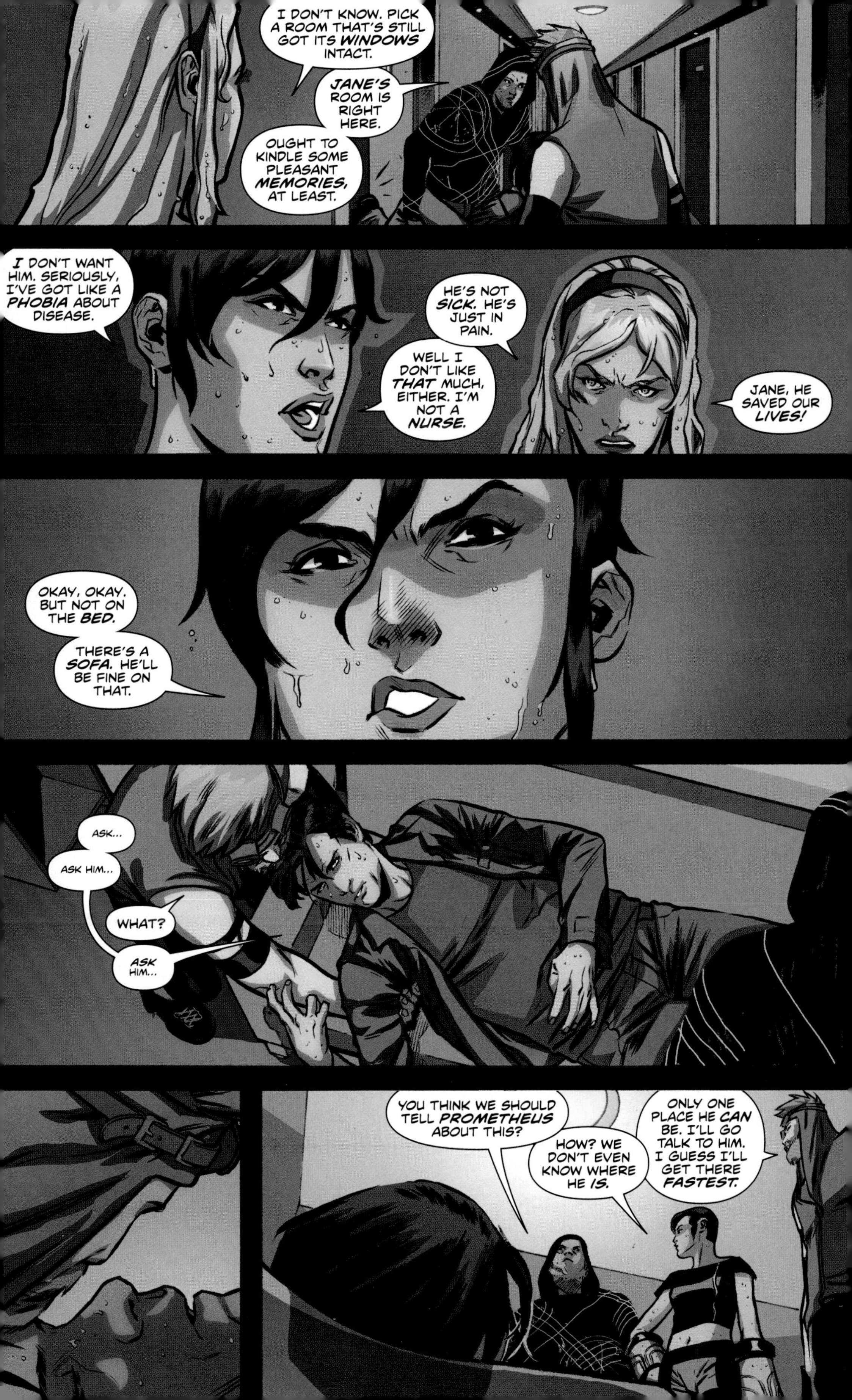
I DON'T KNOW. PICK A ROOM THAT'S STILL GOT ITS WINDOWS INTACT.
JANE'S ROOM IS RIGHT HERE.
OUGHT TO KINDLE SOME PLEASANT MEMORIES, AT LEAST.
I DON'T WANT HIM. SERIOUSLY, I'VE GOT LIKE A PHOBIA ABOUT DISEASE.
HE'S NOT SICK. HE'S JUST IN PAIN.
WELL I DON'T LIKE THAT MUCH, EITHER. I'M NOT A NURSE.
JANE, HE SAVED OUR LIVES!
OKAY, OKAY. BUT NOT ON THE BED.
THERE'S A SOFA. HE'LL BE FINE ON THAT.
ASK...
ASK HIM...
WHAT?
ASK HIM...
YOU THINK WE SHOULD TELL PROMETHEUS ABOUT THIS?
HOW? WE DON'T EVEN KNOW WHERE HE IS.
ONLY ONE PLACE HE CAN BE. I'LL GO TALK TO HIM. I GUESS I'LL GET THERE FASTEST.

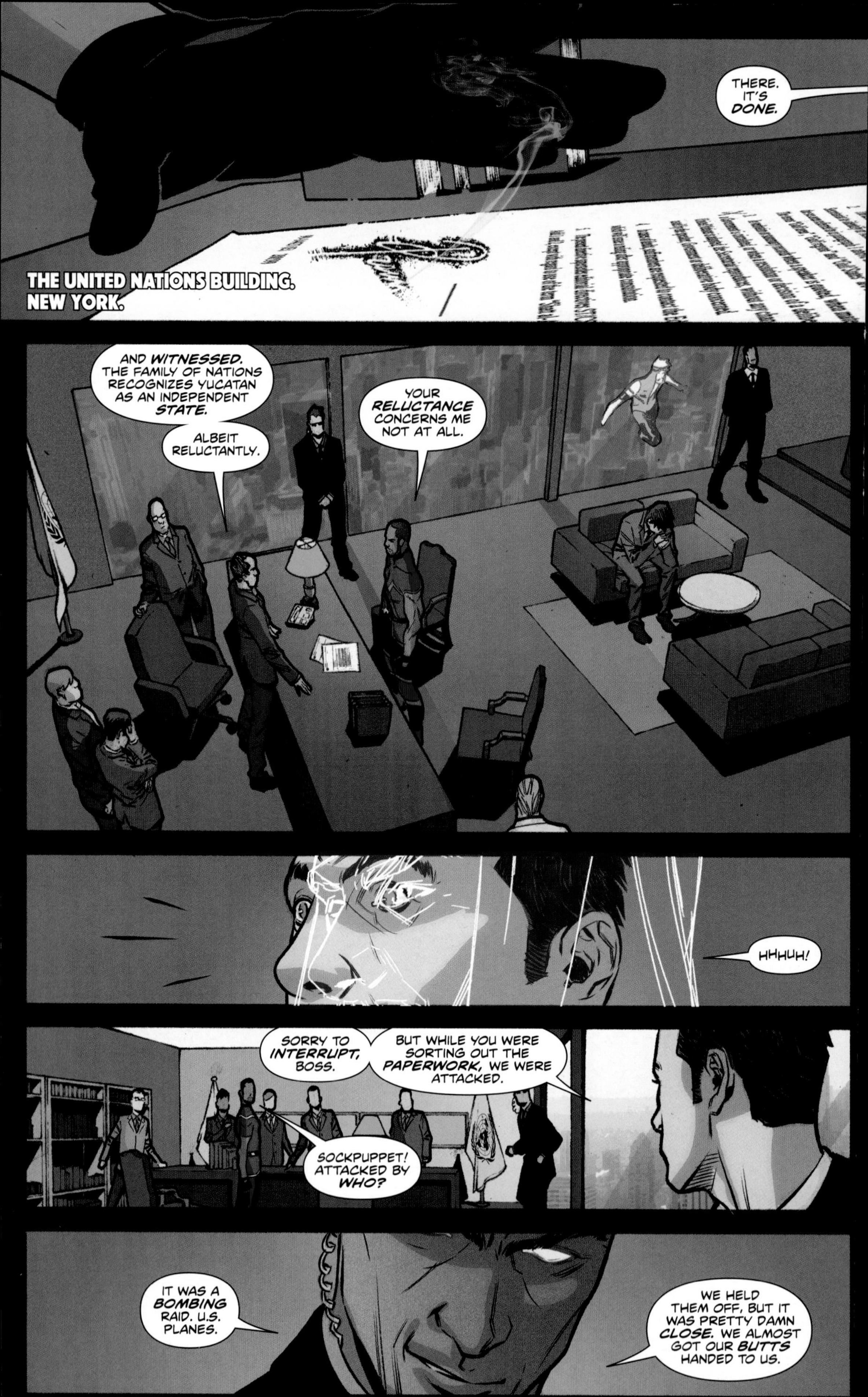
THERE. IT'S DONE.
THE UNITED NATIONS BUILDING. NEW YORK.
AND WITNESSED. THE FAMILY OF NATIONS RECOGNIZES YUCATAN AS AN INDEPENDENT STATE.
ALBEIT RELUCTANTLY.
YOUR RELUCTANCE CONCERNS ME NOT AT ALL.
HHHUH!
SORRY TO INTERRUPT, BOSS.
BUT WHILE YOU WERE SORTING OUT THE PAPERWORK, WE WERE ATTACKED.
SOCKPUPPET! ATTACKED BY WHO?
IT WAS A BOMBING RAID. U.S. PLANES.
WE HELD THEM OFF, BUT IT WAS PRETTY DAMN CLOSE. WE ALMOST GOT OUR BUTTS HANDED TO US.

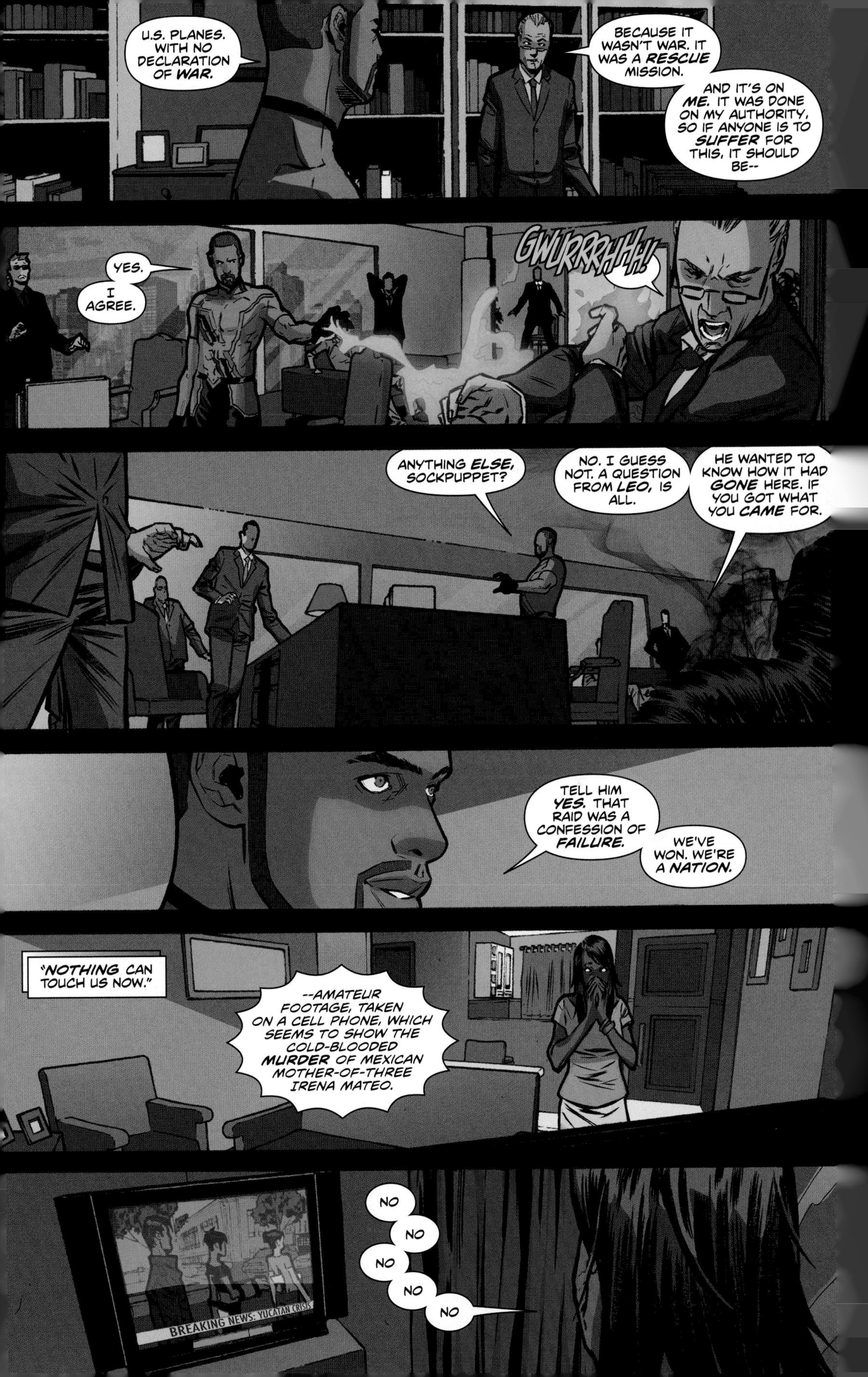
U.S. PLANES. WITH NO DECLARATION OF WAR.
BECAUSE IT WASN'T WAR. IT WAS A RESCUE MISSION.
AND IT'S ON ME. IT WAS DONE ON MY AUTHORITY, SO IF ANYONE IS TO SUFFER FOR THIS, IT SHOULD BE--
YES. I AGREE.
GWURRRHHH!
ANYTHING ELSE, SOCKPUPPET?
NO. I GUESS NOT. A QUESTION FROM LEO, IS ALL.
HE WANTED TO KNOW HOW IT HAD GONE HERE. IF YOU GOT WHAT YOU CAME FOR.
TELL HIM YES. THAT RAID WAS A CONFESSION OF FAILURE.
WE'VE WON. WE'RE A NATION.
"NOTHING CAN TOUCH US NOW."
--AMATEUR FOOTAGE, TAKEN ON A CELL PHONE, WHICH SEEMS TO SHOW THE COLD-BLOODED MURDER OF MEXICAN MOTHER-OF-THREE IRENA MATEO.
BREAKING NEWS: YUCATAN CRISIS
NO
NO
NO
NO
NO

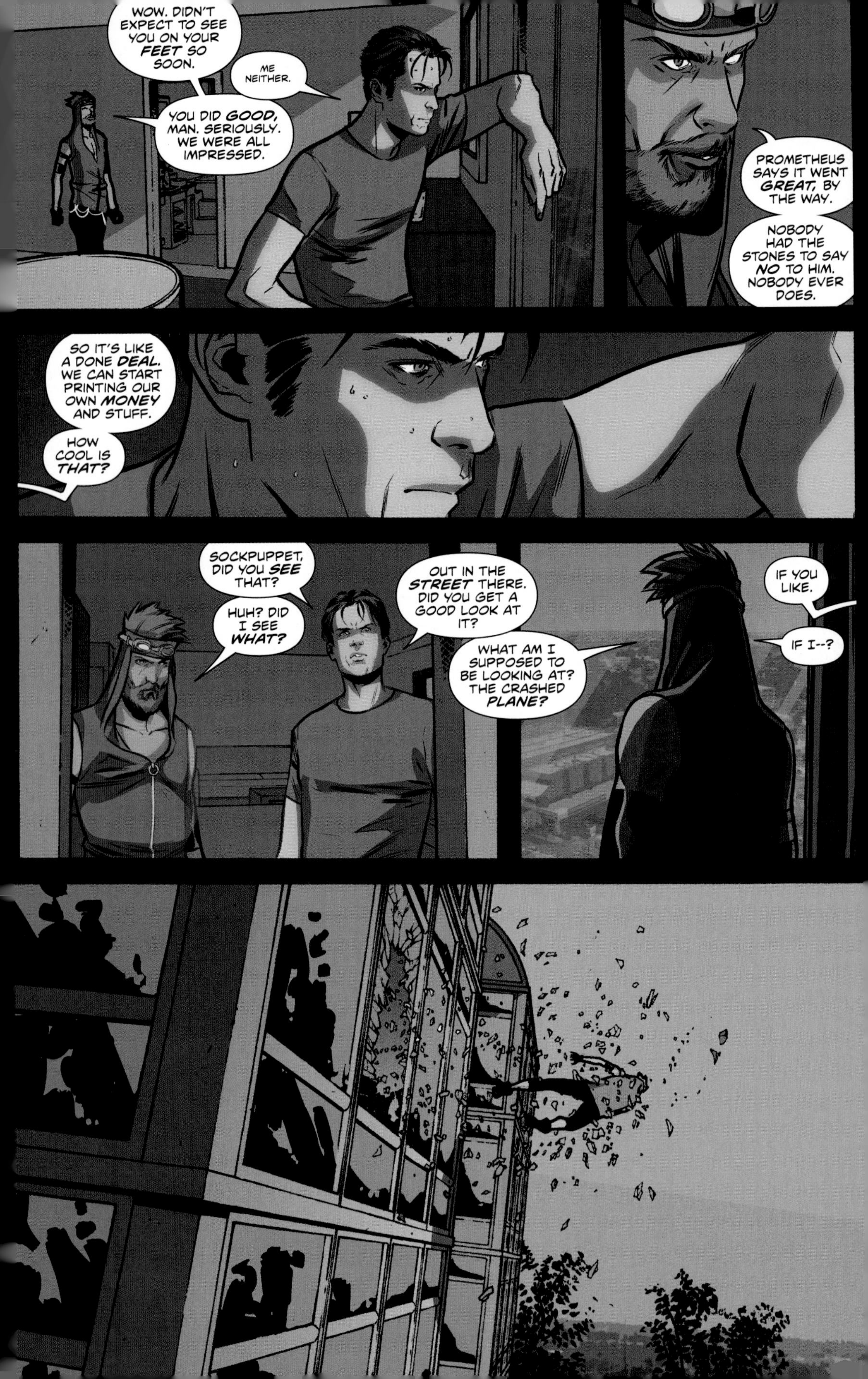
WOW. DIDN'T EXPECT TO SEE YOU ON YOUR FEET SO SOON.
ME NEITHER.
YOU DID GOOD, MAN. SERIOUSLY. WE WERE ALL IMPRESSED.
PROMETHEUS SAYS IT WENT GREAT, BY THE WAY.
NOBODY HAD THE STONES TO SAY NO TO HIM. NOBODY EVER DOES.
SO IT'S LIKE A DONE DEAL. WE CAN START PRINTING OUR OWN MONEY AND STUFF.
HOW COOL IS THAT?
SOCKPUPPET, DID YOU SEE THAT?
HUH? DID I SEE WHAT?
OUT IN THE STREET THERE. DID YOU GET A GOOD LOOK AT IT?
WHAT AM I SUPPOSED TO BE LOOKING AT? THE CRASHED PLANE?
IF YOU LIKE.
IF I--?

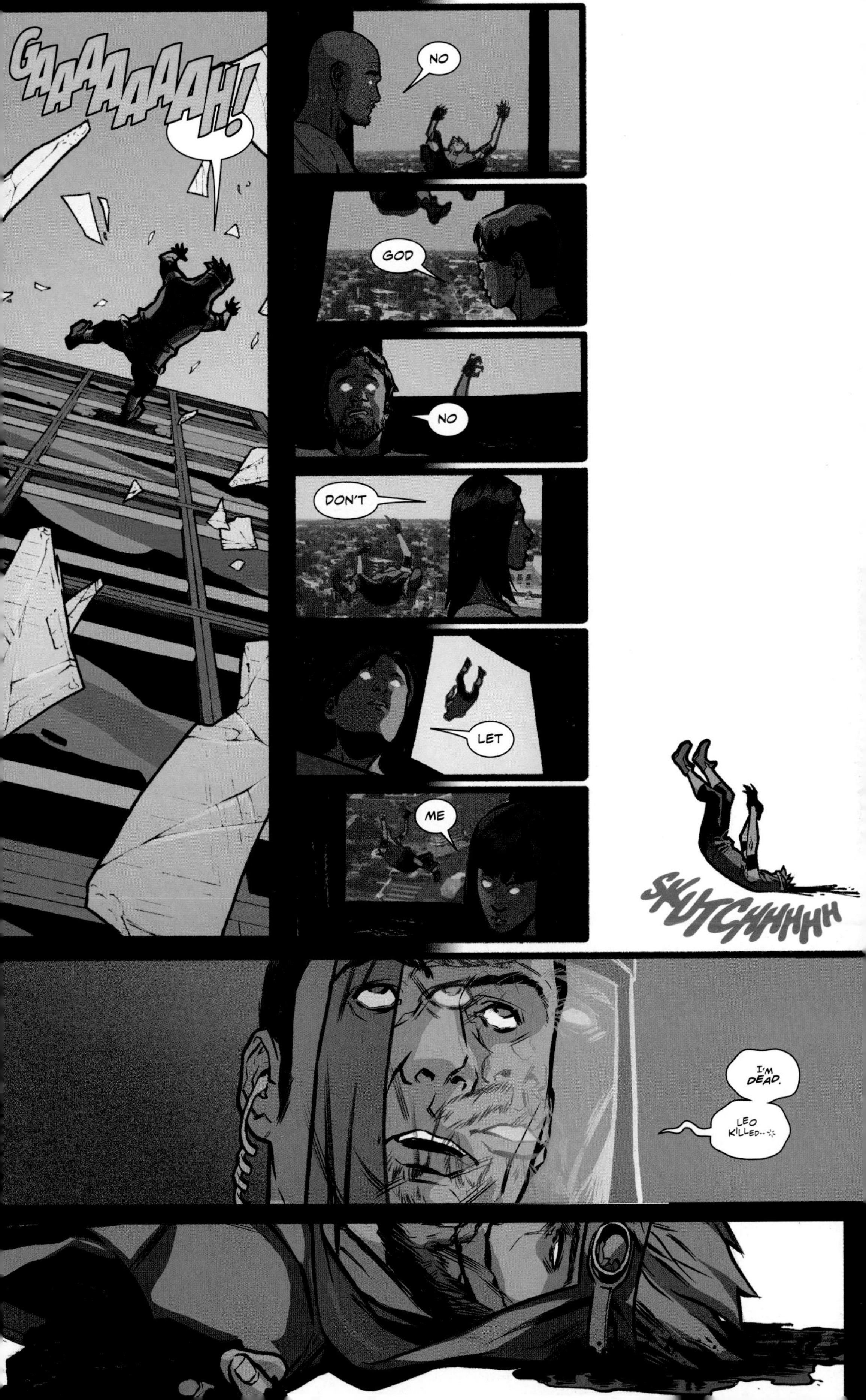
GAAAAAAAAH!
NO
GOD
NO
DON'T
LET
ME
SKLTCHHHHH
I'M DEAD.
LEO KILLED--

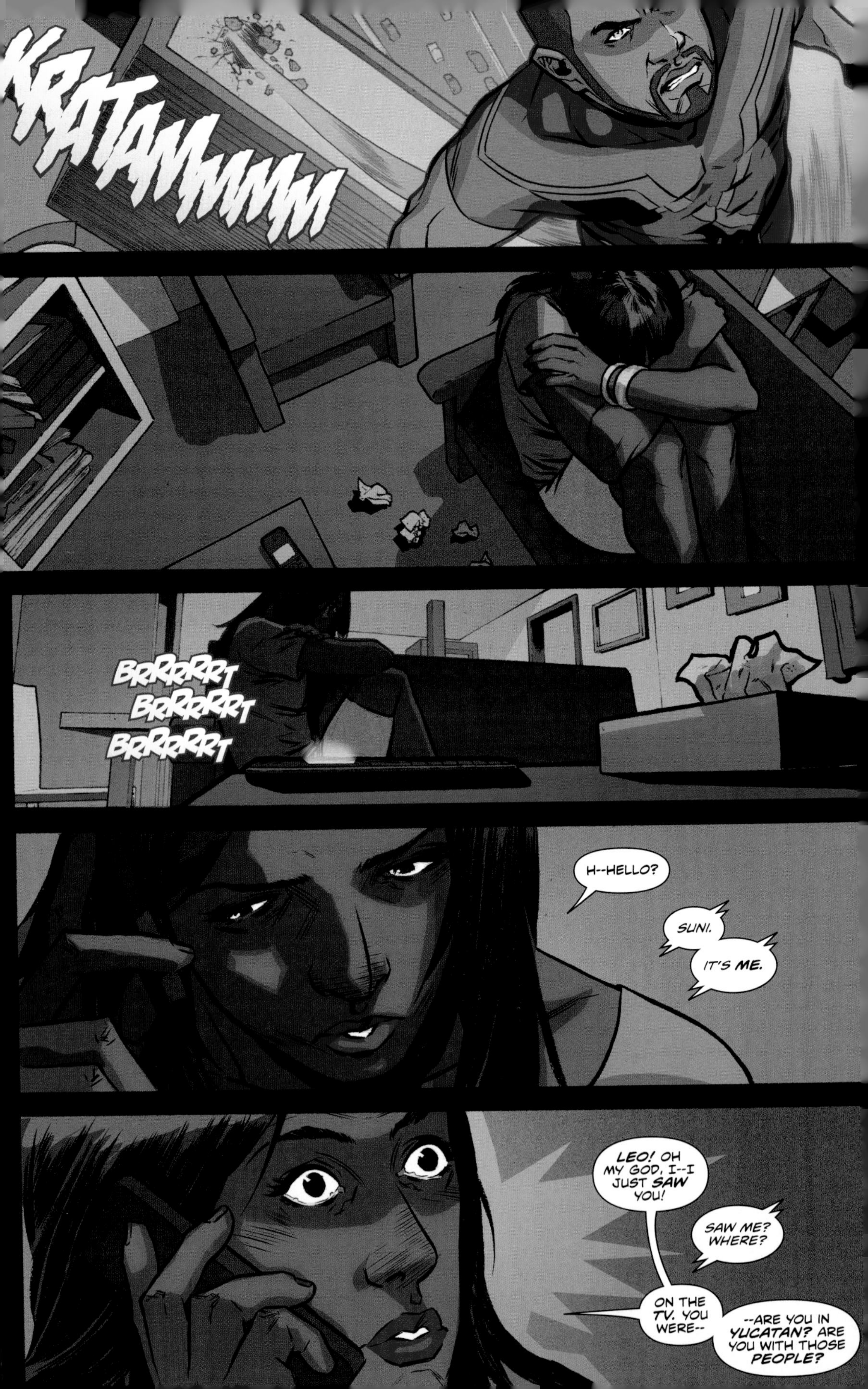
KRATAMMMMM
BRRRRRT
BRRRRRT
BRRRRRT
H--HELLO?
SUNI.
IT'S **ME.**
LEO! OH MY GOD, I--I JUST **SAW** YOU!
SAW ME? WHERE?
ON THE **TV.** YOU WERE--
--ARE YOU IN **YUCATAN?** ARE YOU WITH THOSE **PEOPLE?**

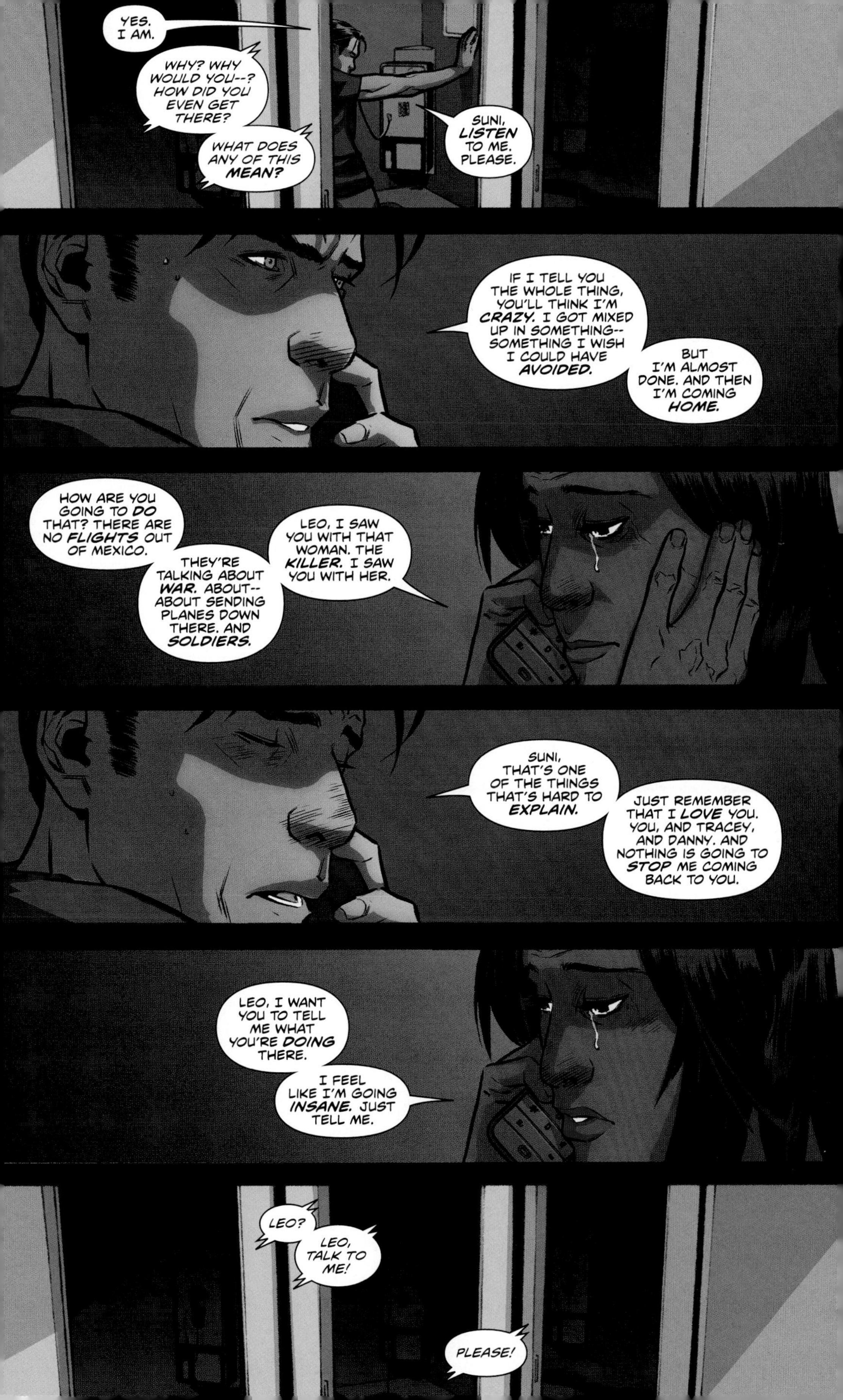
YES. I AM.
WHY? WHY WOULD YOU--? HOW DID YOU EVEN GET THERE?
WHAT DOES ANY OF THIS MEAN?
SUNI, LISTEN TO ME. PLEASE.
IF I TELL YOU THE WHOLE THING, YOU'LL THINK I'M CRAZY. I GOT MIXED UP IN SOMETHING-- SOMETHING I WISH I COULD HAVE AVOIDED.
BUT I'M ALMOST DONE. AND THEN I'M COMING HOME.
HOW ARE YOU GOING TO DO THAT? THERE ARE NO FLIGHTS OUT OF MEXICO.
THEY'RE TALKING ABOUT WAR. ABOUT-- ABOUT SENDING PLANES DOWN THERE. AND SOLDIERS.
LEO, I SAW YOU WITH THAT WOMAN. THE KILLER. I SAW YOU WITH HER.
SUNI, THAT'S ONE OF THE THINGS THAT'S HARD TO EXPLAIN.
JUST REMEMBER THAT I LOVE YOU. YOU, AND TRACEY, AND DANNY. AND NOTHING IS GOING TO STOP ME COMING BACK TO YOU.
LEO, I WANT YOU TO TELL ME WHAT YOU'RE DOING THERE.
I FEEL LIKE I'M GOING INSANE. JUST TELL ME.
LEO?
LEO, TALK TO ME!
PLEASE!

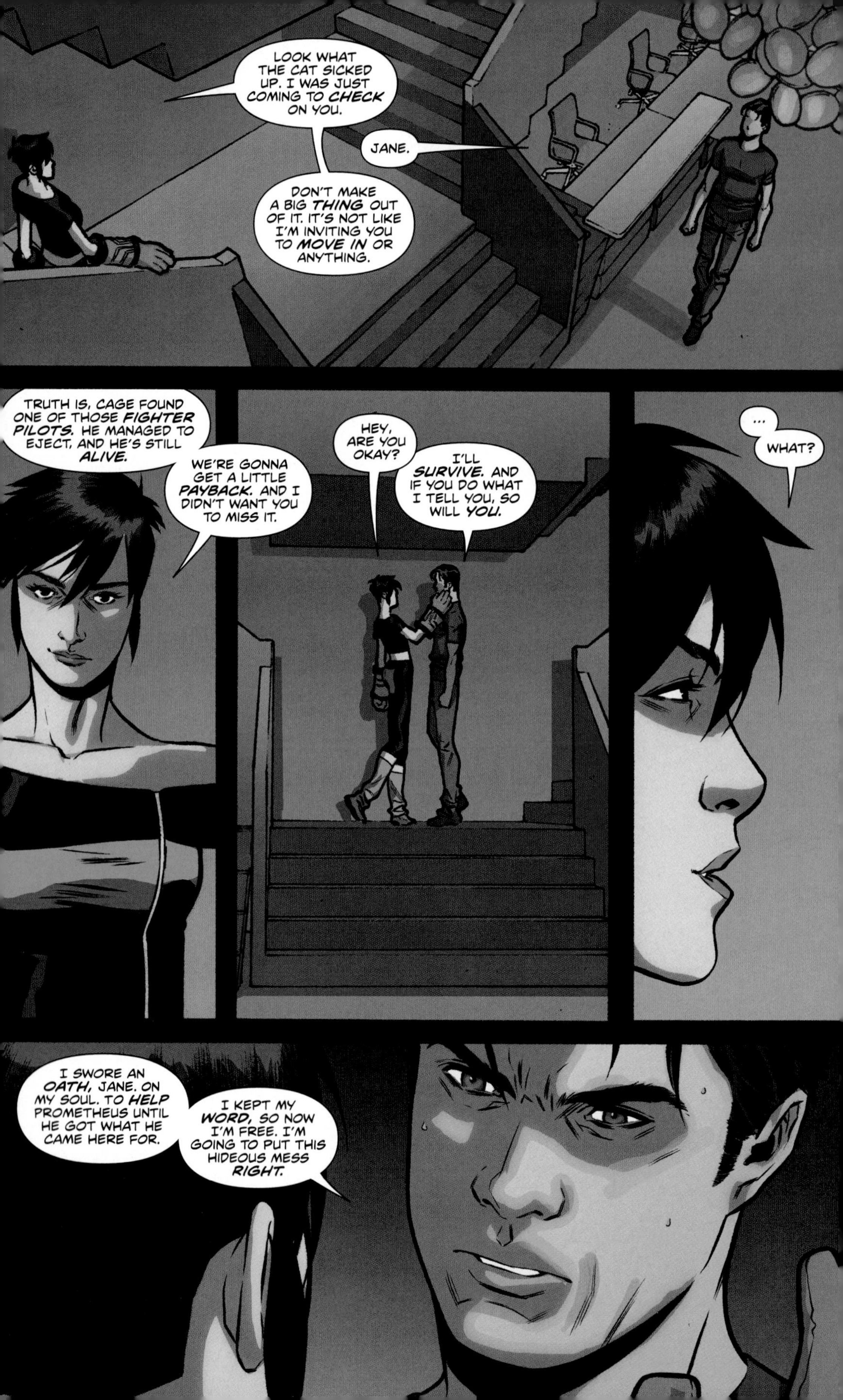
LOOK WHAT THE CAT SICKED UP. I WAS JUST COMING TO CHECK ON YOU.
JANE.
DON'T MAKE A BIG THING OUT OF IT. IT'S NOT LIKE I'M INVITING YOU TO MOVE IN OR ANYTHING.
TRUTH IS, CAGE FOUND ONE OF THOSE FIGHTER PILOTS. HE MANAGED TO EJECT, AND HE'S STILL ALIVE.
WE'RE GONNA GET A LITTLE PAYBACK. AND I DIDN'T WANT YOU TO MISS IT.
HEY, ARE YOU OKAY?
I'LL SURVIVE. AND IF YOU DO WHAT I TELL YOU, SO WILL YOU.
...
WHAT?
I SWORE AN OATH, JANE. ON MY SOUL. TO HELP PROMETHEUS UNTIL HE GOT WHAT HE CAME HERE FOR.
I KEPT MY WORD, SO NOW I'M FREE. I'M GOING TO PUT THIS HIDEOUS MESS RIGHT.

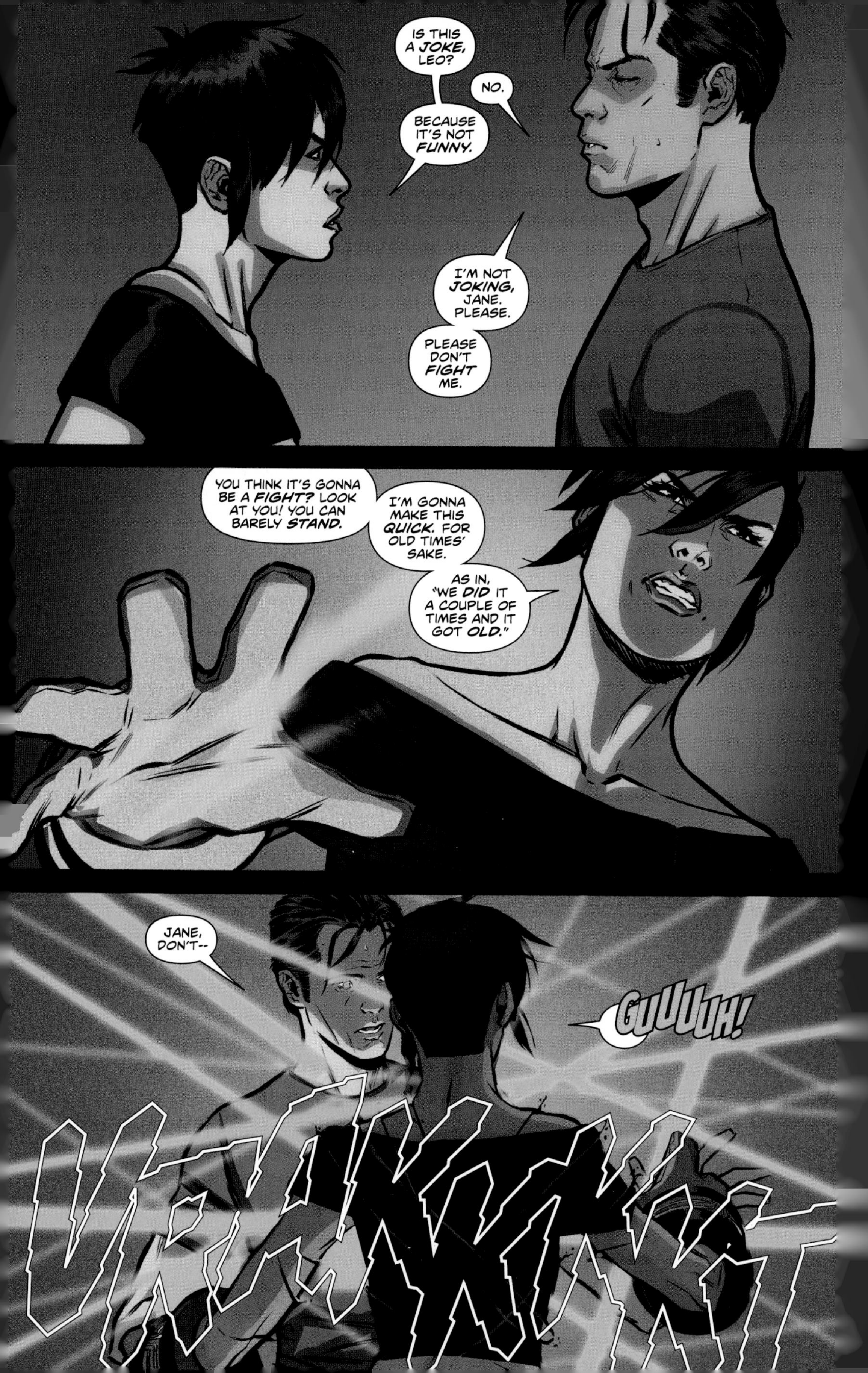
IS THIS A JOKE, LEO?
NO.
BECAUSE IT'S NOT FUNNY.
I'M NOT JOKING, JANE. PLEASE.
PLEASE DON'T FIGHT ME.
YOU THINK IT'S GONNA BE A FIGHT? LOOK AT YOU! YOU CAN BARELY STAND.
I'M GONNA MAKE THIS QUICK. FOR OLD TIMES' SAKE.
AS IN, "WE DID IT A COUPLE OF TIMES AND IT GOT OLD."
JANE, DON'T--
GUUUUH!
VRAKKKKT

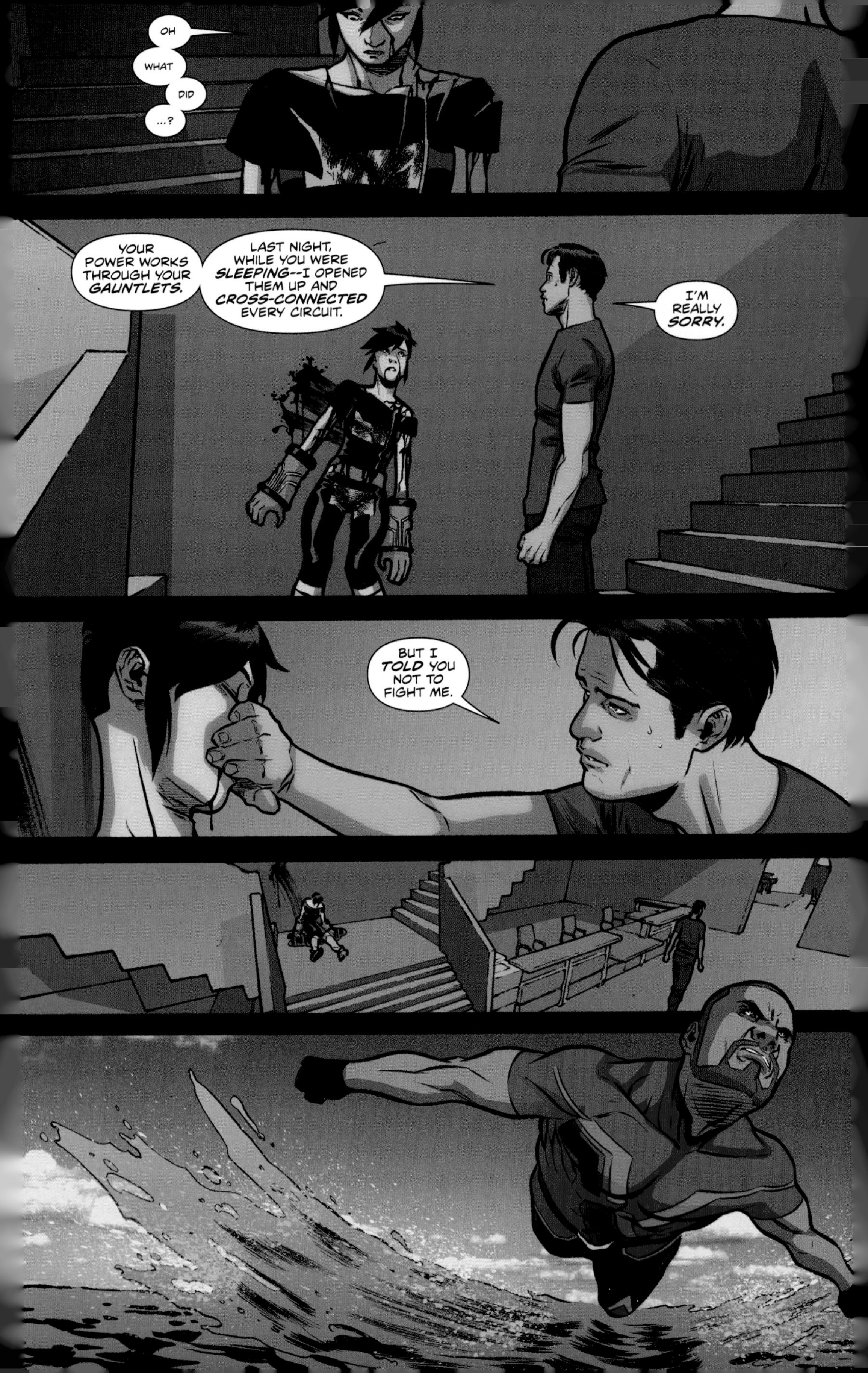
OH
WHAT
DID
...?
YOUR POWER WORKS THROUGH YOUR GAUNTLETS.
LAST NIGHT, WHILE YOU WERE SLEEPING--I OPENED THEM UP AND CROSS-CONNECTED EVERY CIRCUIT.
I'M REALLY SORRY.
BUT I TOLD YOU NOT TO FIGHT ME.

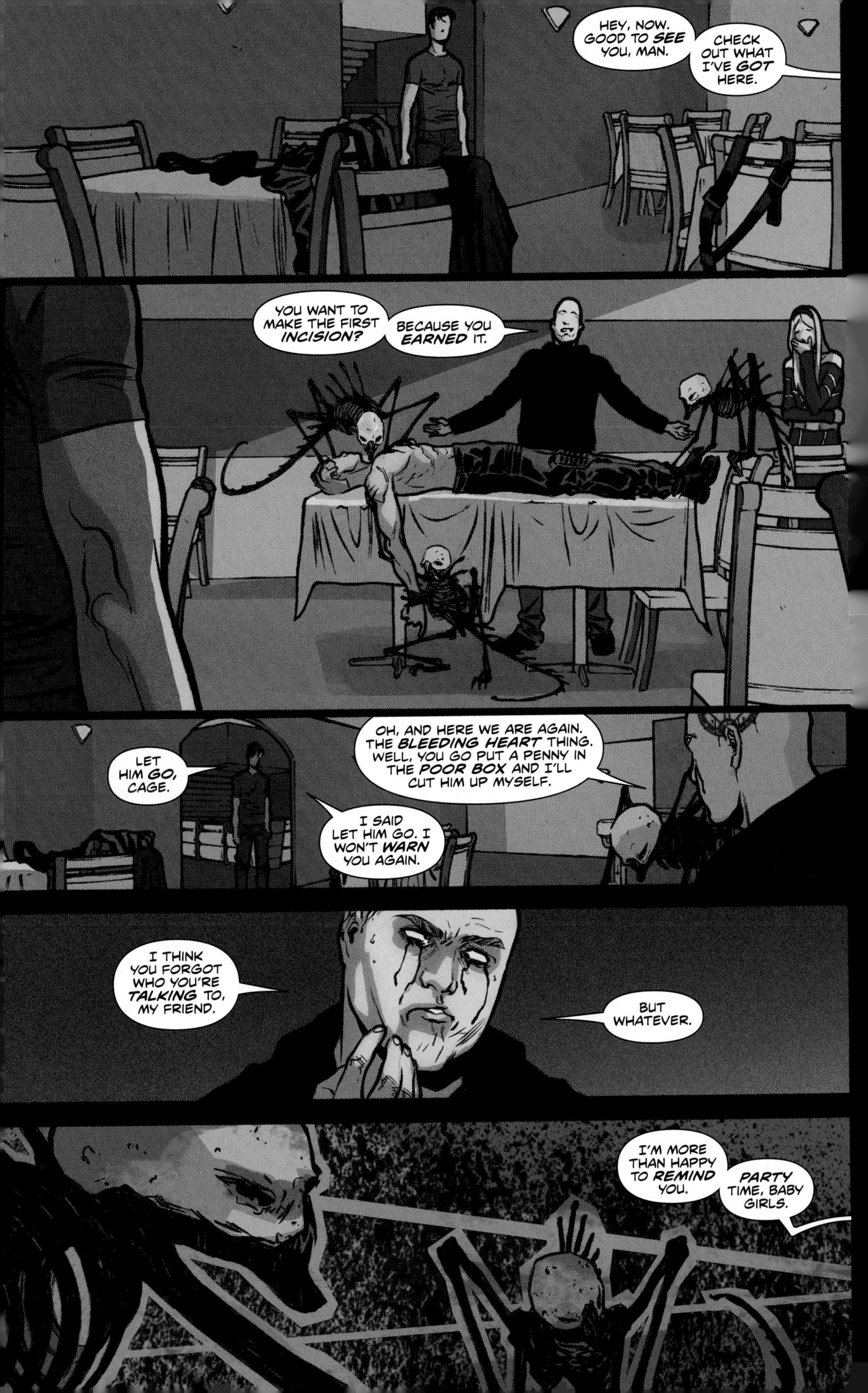
HEY, NOW. GOOD TO SEE YOU, MAN.
CHECK OUT WHAT I'VE GOT HERE.
YOU WANT TO MAKE THE FIRST INCISION?
BECAUSE YOU EARNED IT.
LET HIM GO, CAGE.
OH, AND HERE WE ARE AGAIN. THE BLEEDING HEART THING. WELL, YOU GO PUT A PENNY IN THE POOR BOX AND I'LL CUT HIM UP MYSELF.
I SAID LET HIM GO. I WON'T WARN YOU AGAIN.
I THINK YOU FORGOT WHO YOU'RE TALKING TO, MY FRIEND.
BUT WHATEVER.
I'M MORE THAN HAPPY TO REMIND YOU.
PARTY TIME, BABY GIRLS.

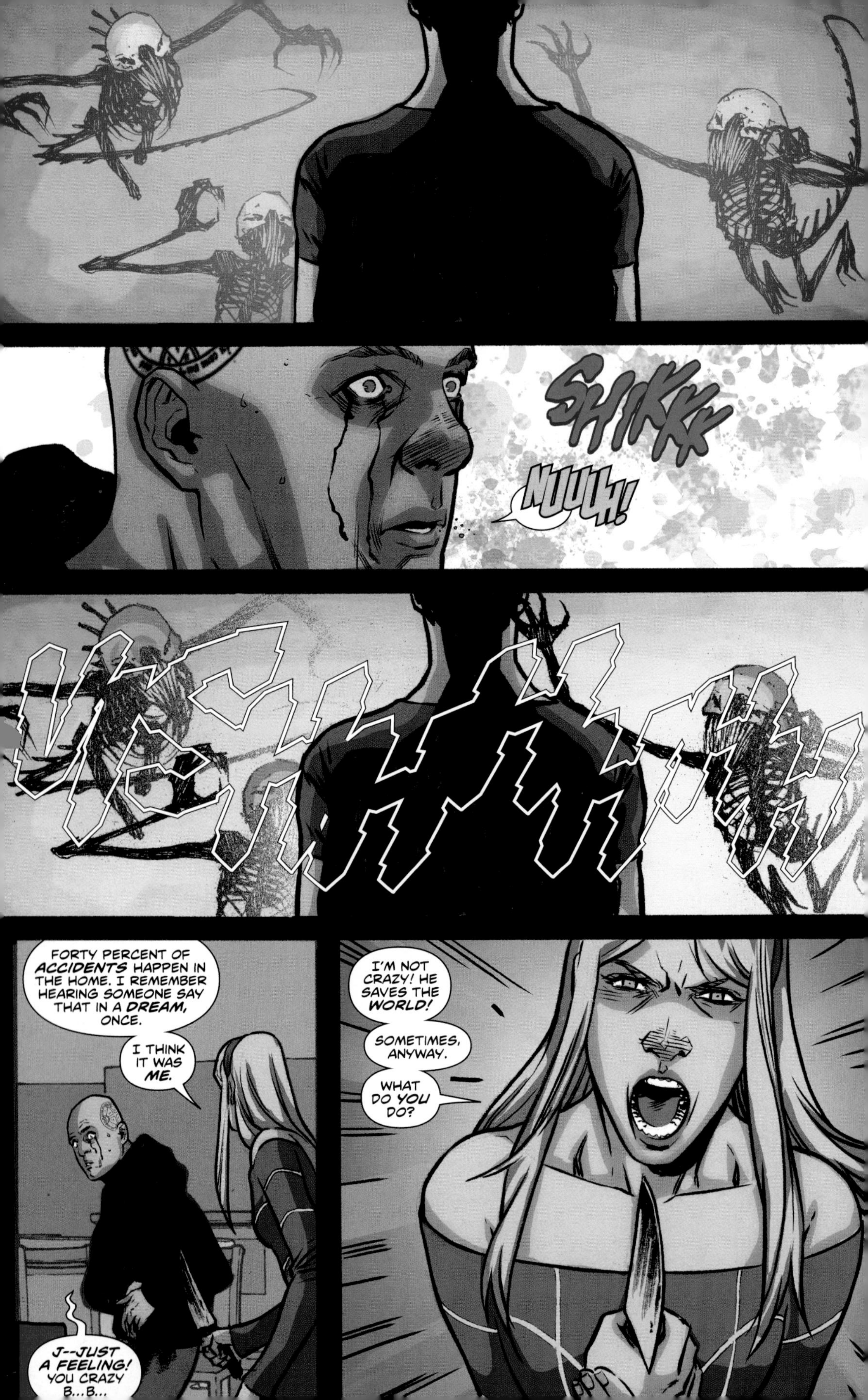
SHIKKK
NUUUH!
VRRRRRRM
FORTY PERCENT OF ACCIDENTS HAPPEN IN THE HOME. I REMEMBER HEARING SOMEONE SAY THAT IN A DREAM, ONCE.
I THINK IT WAS ME.
J--JUST A FEELING! YOU CRAZY B...B...
I'M NOT CRAZY! HE SAVES THE WORLD!
SOMETIMES, ANYWAY.
WHAT DO YOU DO?

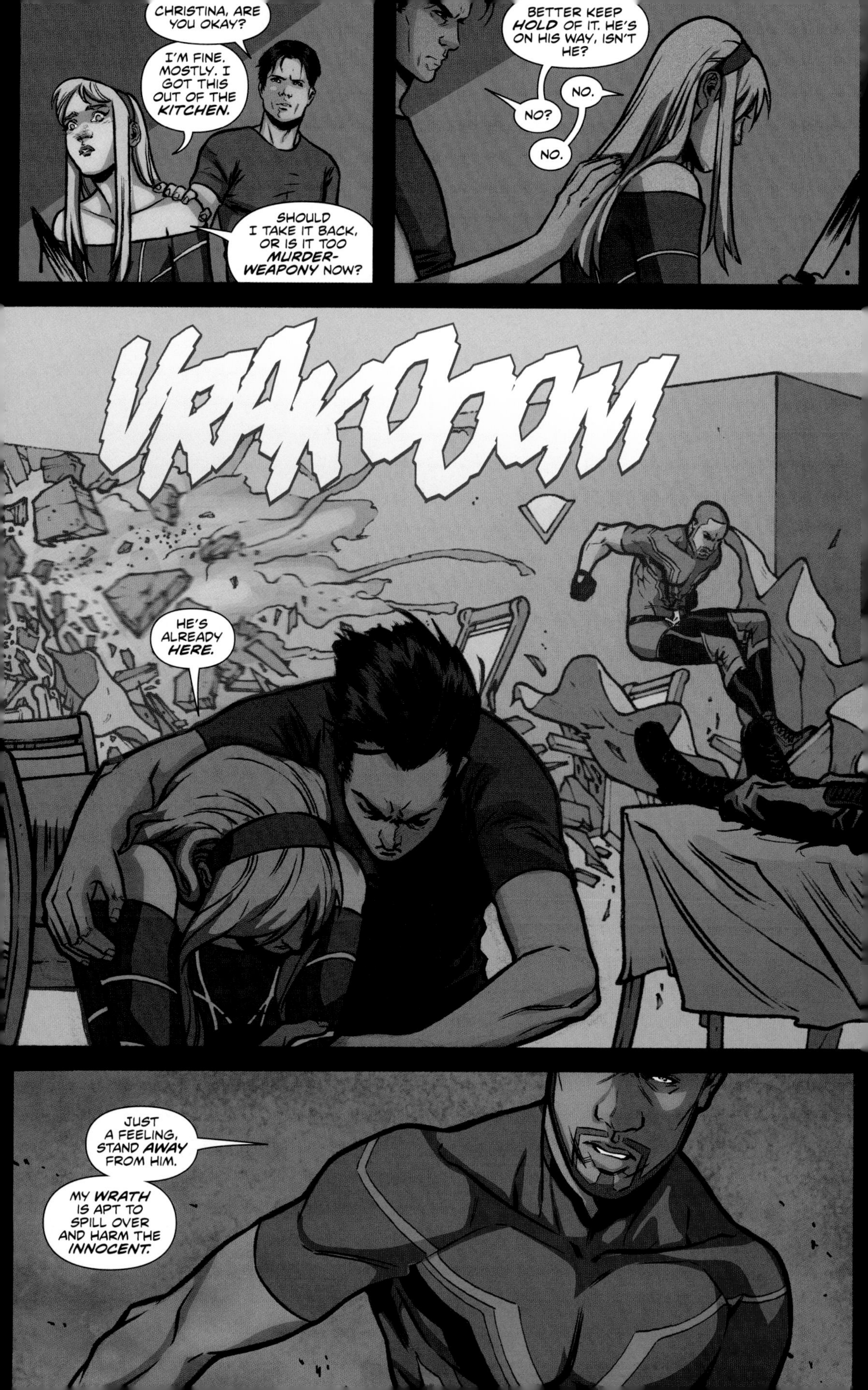
CHRISTINA, ARE YOU OKAY?
I'M FINE. MOSTLY. I GOT THIS OUT OF THE KITCHEN.
SHOULD I TAKE IT BACK, OR IS IT TOO MURDER-WEAPONY NOW?
BETTER KEEP HOLD OF IT. HE'S ON HIS WAY, ISN'T HE?
NO?
NO.
NO.
VRAKOOOM
HE'S ALREADY HERE.
JUST A FEELING, STAND AWAY FROM HIM.
MY WRATH IS APT TO SPILL OVER AND HARM THE INNOCENT.

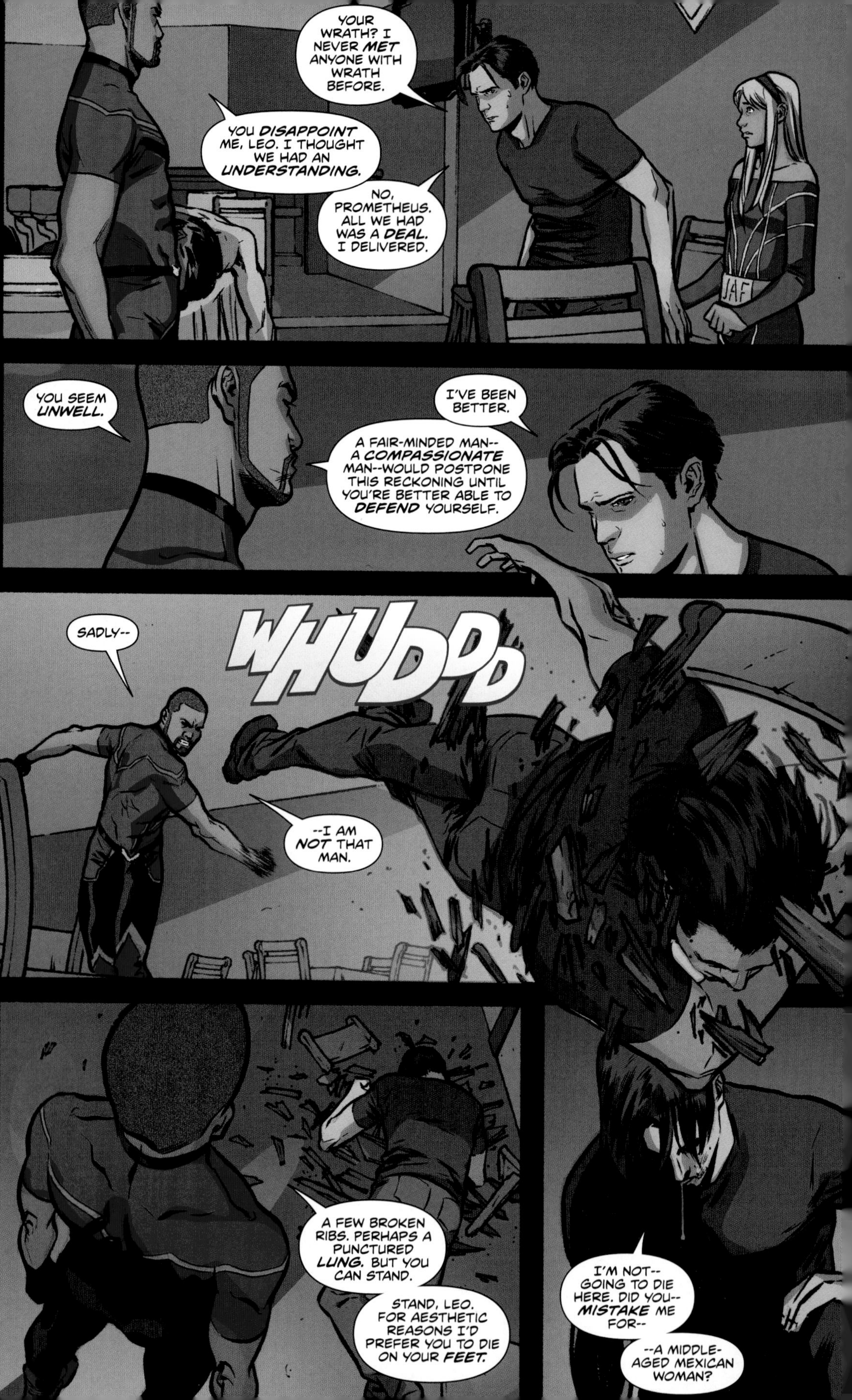
YOUR WRATH? I NEVER MET ANYONE WITH WRATH BEFORE.
YOU DISAPPOINT ME, LEO. I THOUGHT WE HAD AN UNDERSTANDING.
NO, PROMETHEUS. ALL WE HAD WAS A DEAL. I DELIVERED.
JAF
YOU SEEM UNWELL.
I'VE BEEN BETTER.
A FAIR-MINDED MAN--A COMPASSIONATE MAN--WOULD POSTPONE THIS RECKONING UNTIL YOU'RE BETTER ABLE TO DEFEND YOURSELF.
SADLY--
WHUDDD
--I AM NOT THAT MAN.
A FEW BROKEN RIBS. PERHAPS A PUNCTURED LUNG. BUT YOU CAN STAND.
STAND, LEO. FOR AESTHETIC REASONS I'D PREFER YOU TO DIE ON YOUR FEET.
I'M NOT--GOING TO DIE HERE. DID YOU--MISTAKE ME FOR--
--A MIDDLE-AGED MEXICAN WOMAN?

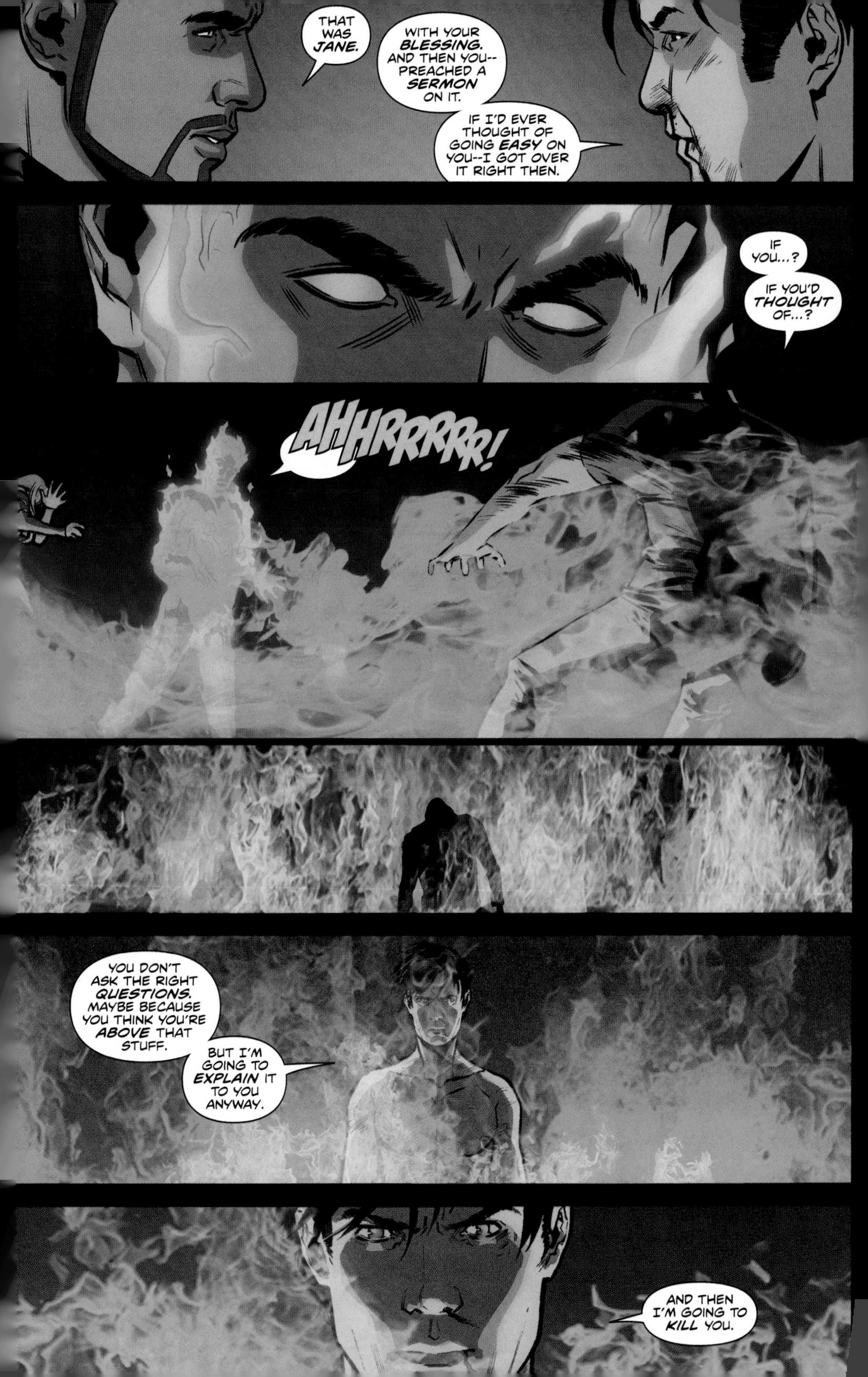
THAT WAS JANE.
WITH YOUR BLESSING. AND THEN YOU-- PREACHED A SERMON ON IT.
IF I'D EVER THOUGHT OF GOING EASY ON YOU--I GOT OVER IT RIGHT THEN.
IF YOU...?
IF YOU'D THOUGHT OF...?
AHHRRRRR!
YOU DON'T ASK THE RIGHT QUESTIONS. MAYBE BECAUSE YOU THINK YOU'RE ABOVE THAT STUFF.
BUT I'M GOING TO EXPLAIN IT TO YOU ANYWAY.
AND THEN I'M GOING TO KILL YOU.

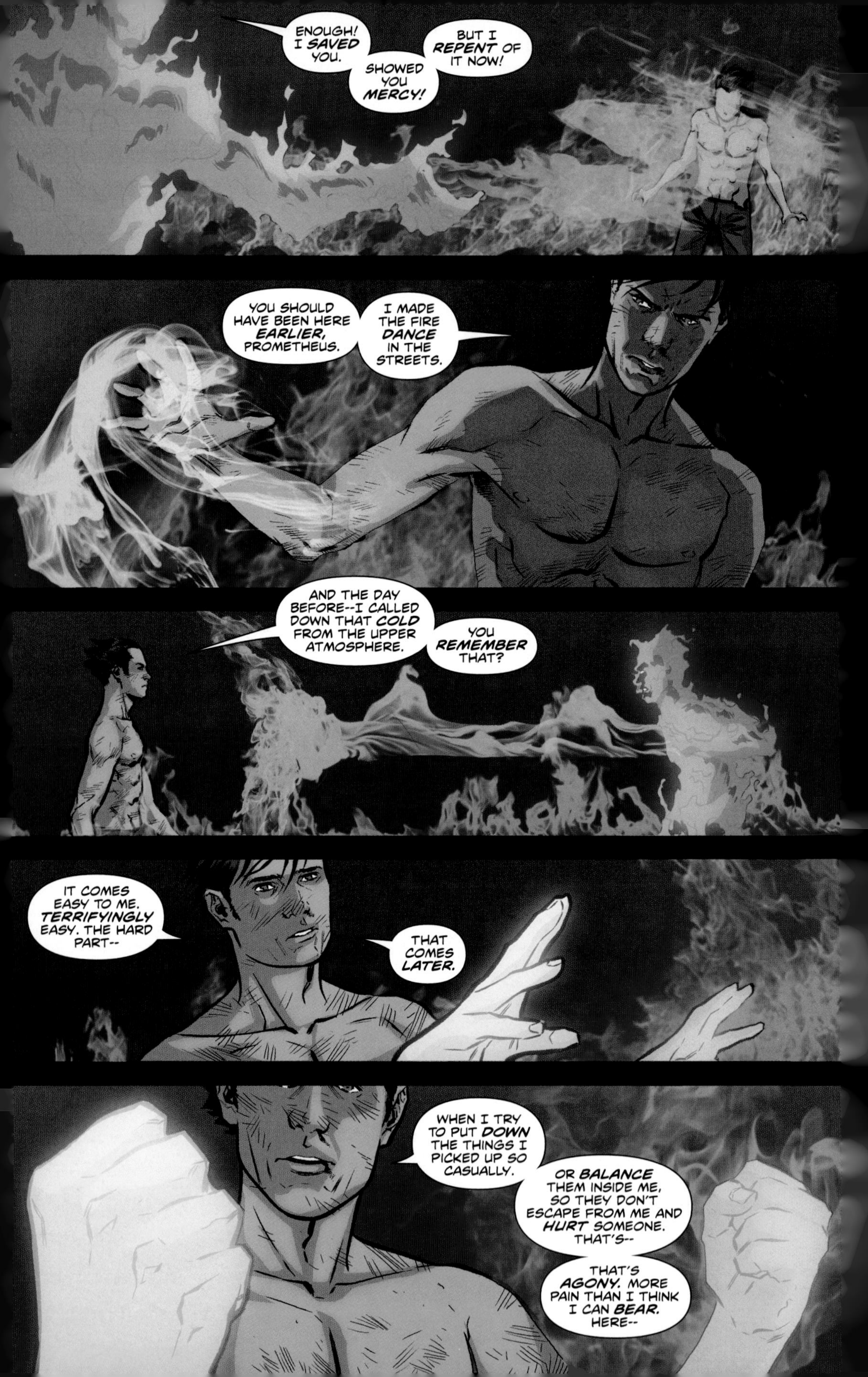
ENOUGH! I SAVED YOU.
SHOWED YOU MERCY!
BUT I REPENT OF IT NOW!
YOU SHOULD HAVE BEEN HERE EARLIER, PROMETHEUS.
I MADE THE FIRE DANCE IN THE STREETS.
AND THE DAY BEFORE--I CALLED DOWN THAT COLD FROM THE UPPER ATMOSPHERE.
YOU REMEMBER THAT?
IT COMES EASY TO ME. TERRIFYINGLY EASY. THE HARD PART--
THAT COMES LATER.
WHEN I TRY TO PUT DOWN THE THINGS I PICKED UP SO CASUALLY.
OR BALANCE THEM INSIDE ME, SO THEY DON'T ESCAPE FROM ME AND HURT SOMEONE. THAT'S--
THAT'S AGONY. MORE PAIN THAN I THINK I CAN BEAR. HERE--

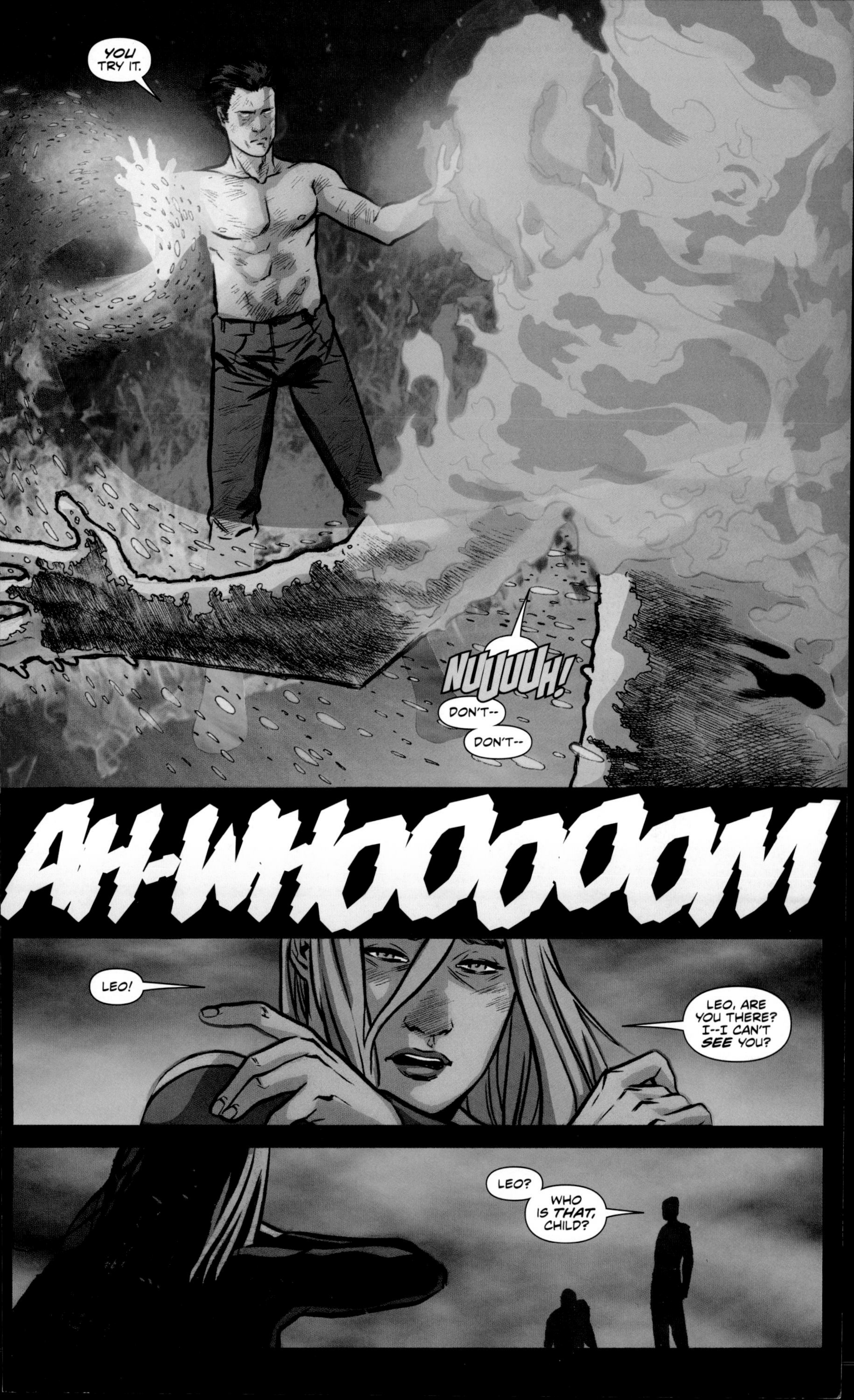
YOU TRY IT.
NUUUUH!
DON'T--
DON'T--
AH-WHOOOOOM
LEO!
LEO, ARE YOU THERE? I--I CAN'T SEE YOU?
LEO?
WHO IS THAT, CHILD?

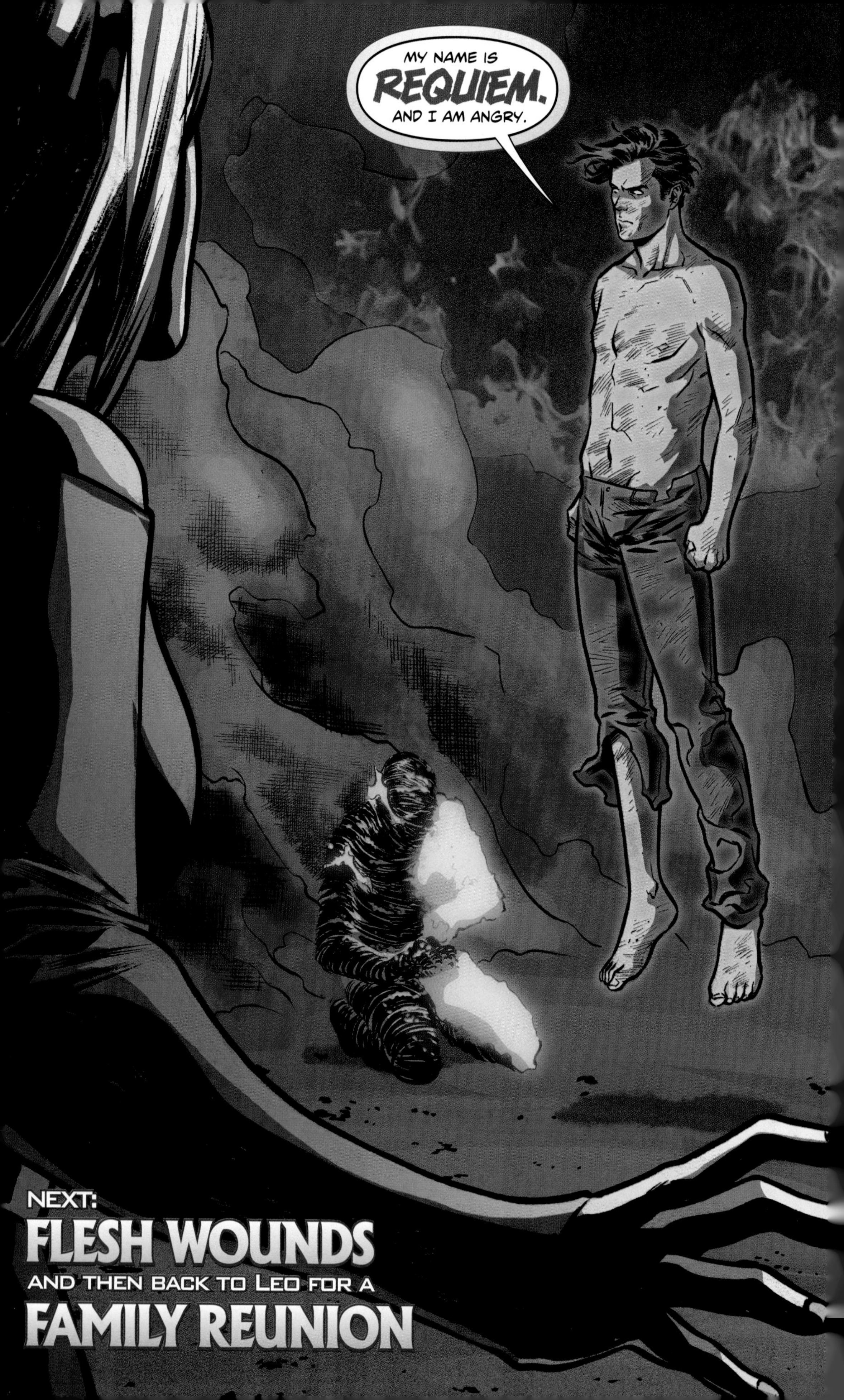
MY NAME IS REQUIEM. AND I AM ANGRY.
NEXT:
FLESH WOUNDS
AND THEN BACK TO LEO FOR A
FAMILY REUNION

COVER GALLERY

ISSUE FIVE
TOMMY LEE EDWARDS

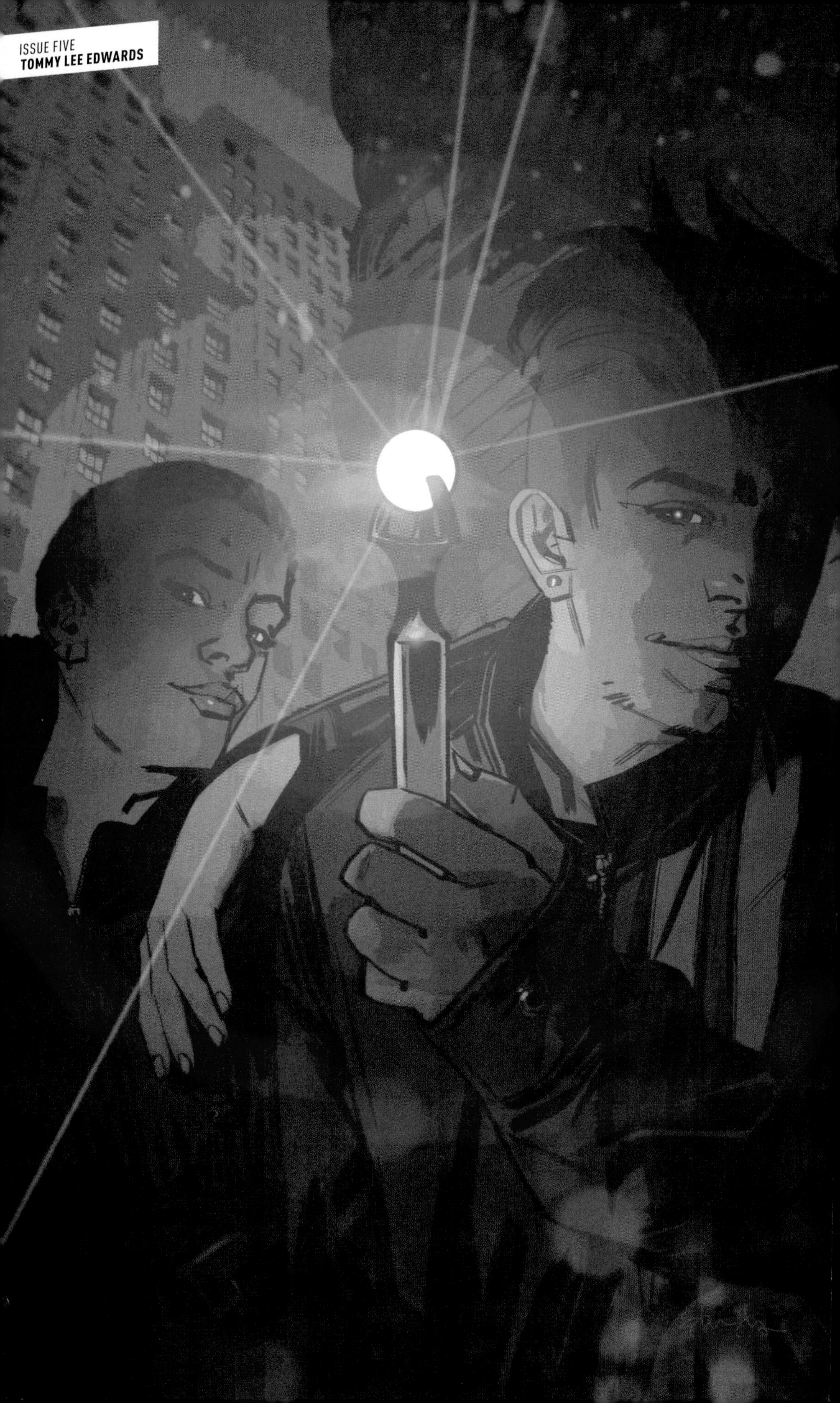

ISSUE FIVE
STEPHANIE HANS

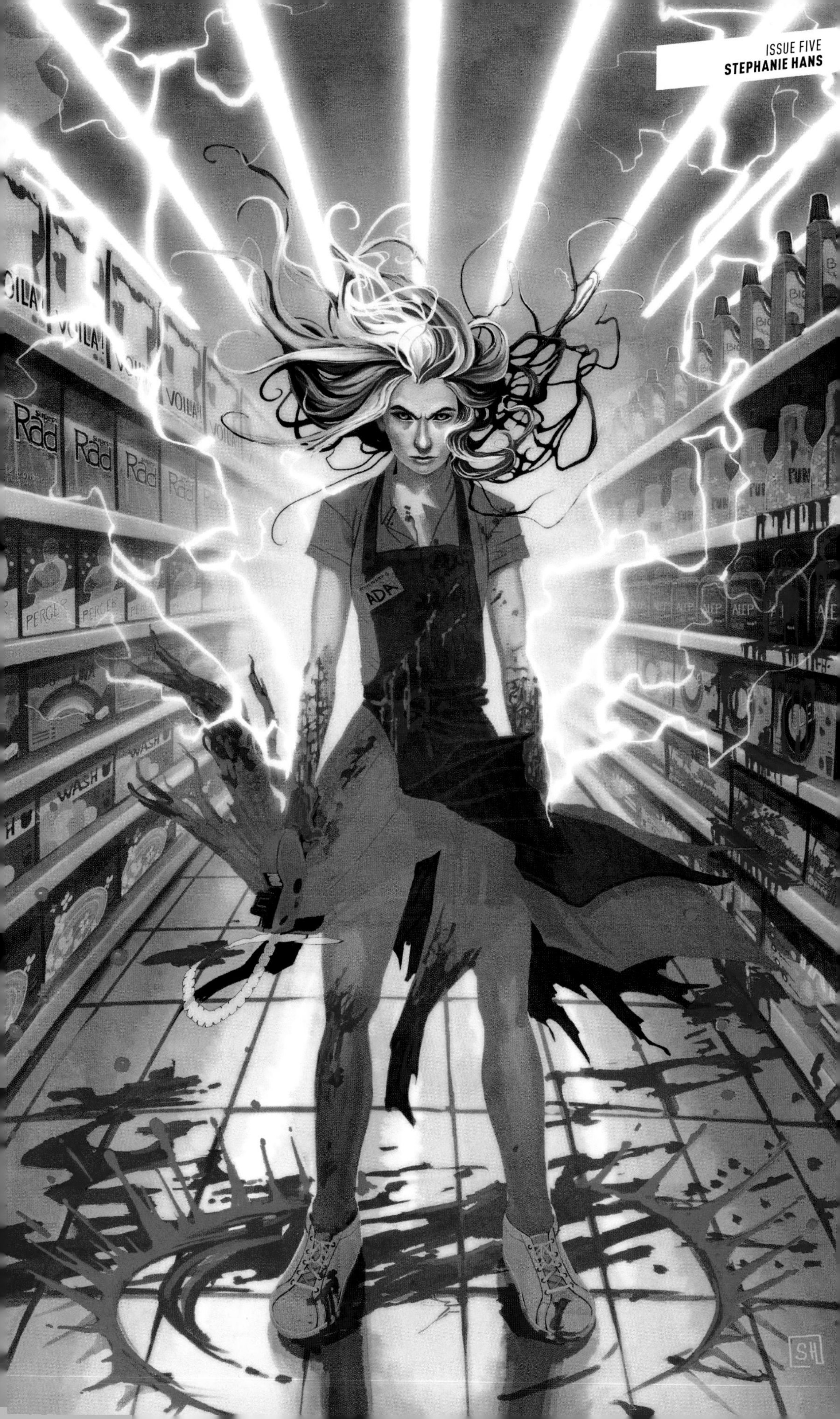
VOILA!
Rad
PERGER
WASH
ADA
PUR
ALEP
BIO
SH

ISSUE SIX
TOMMY LEE EDWARDS

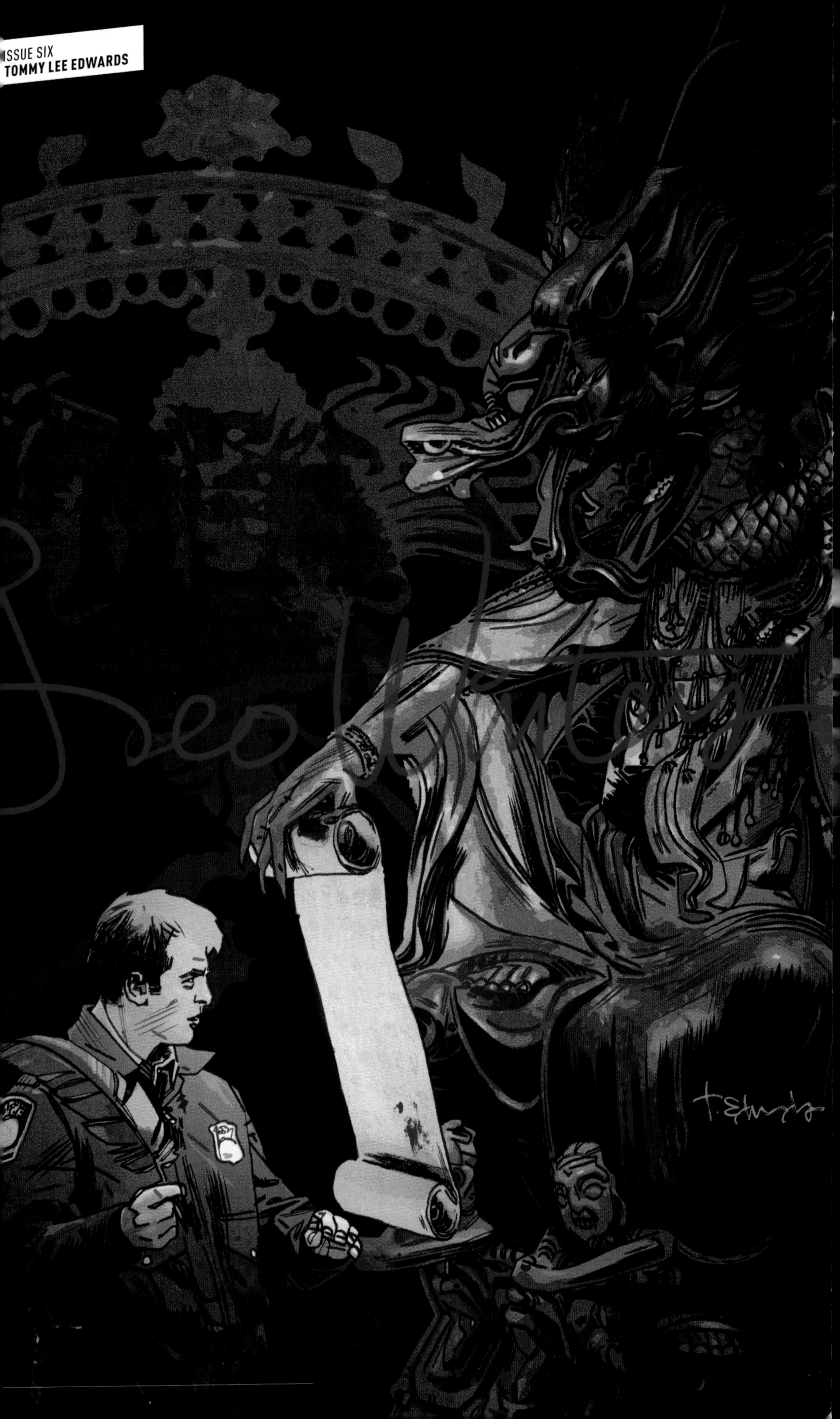

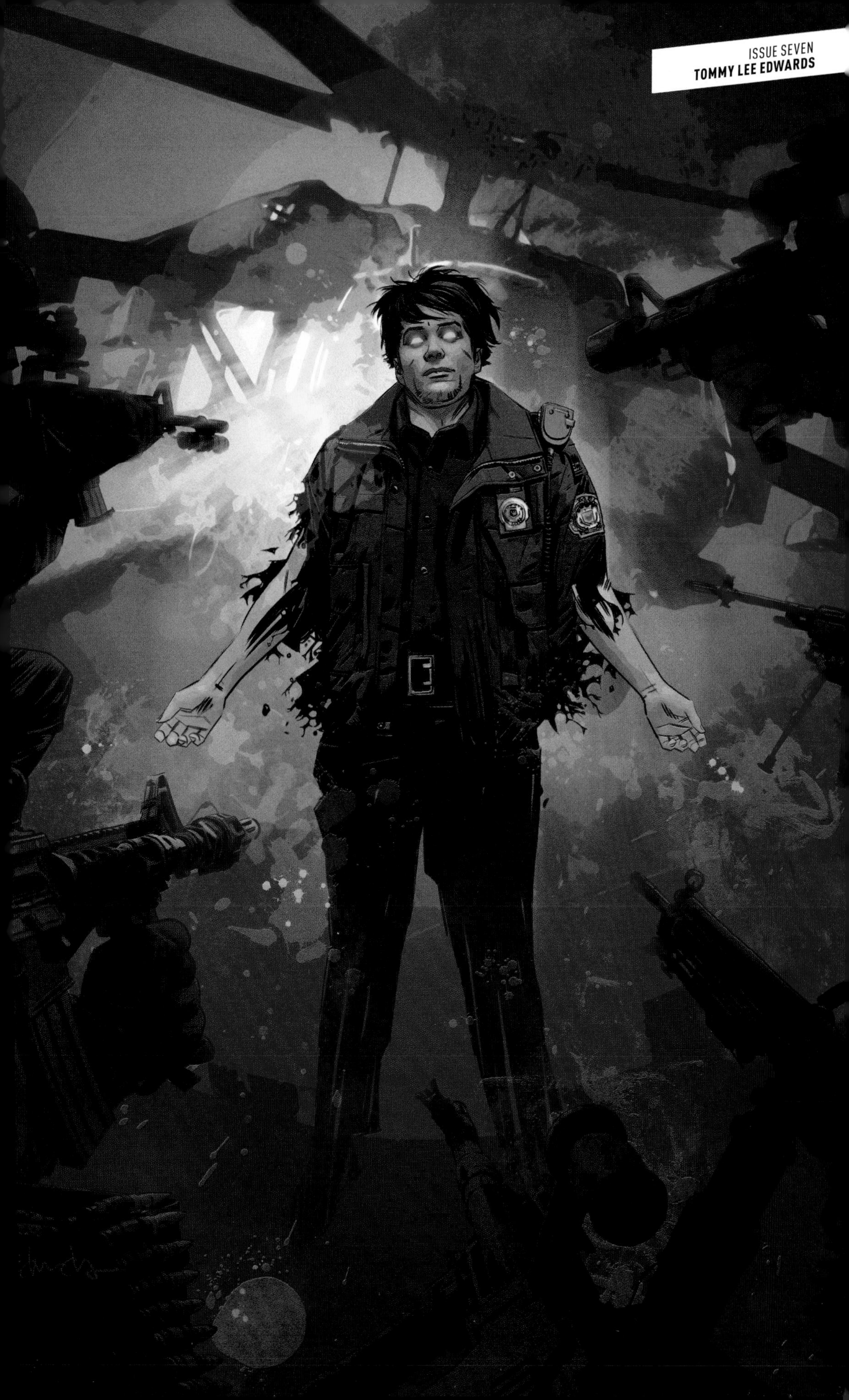

ISSUE SEVEN
TOMMY LEE EDWARDS

ISSUE EIGHT
TOMMY LEE EDWARDS

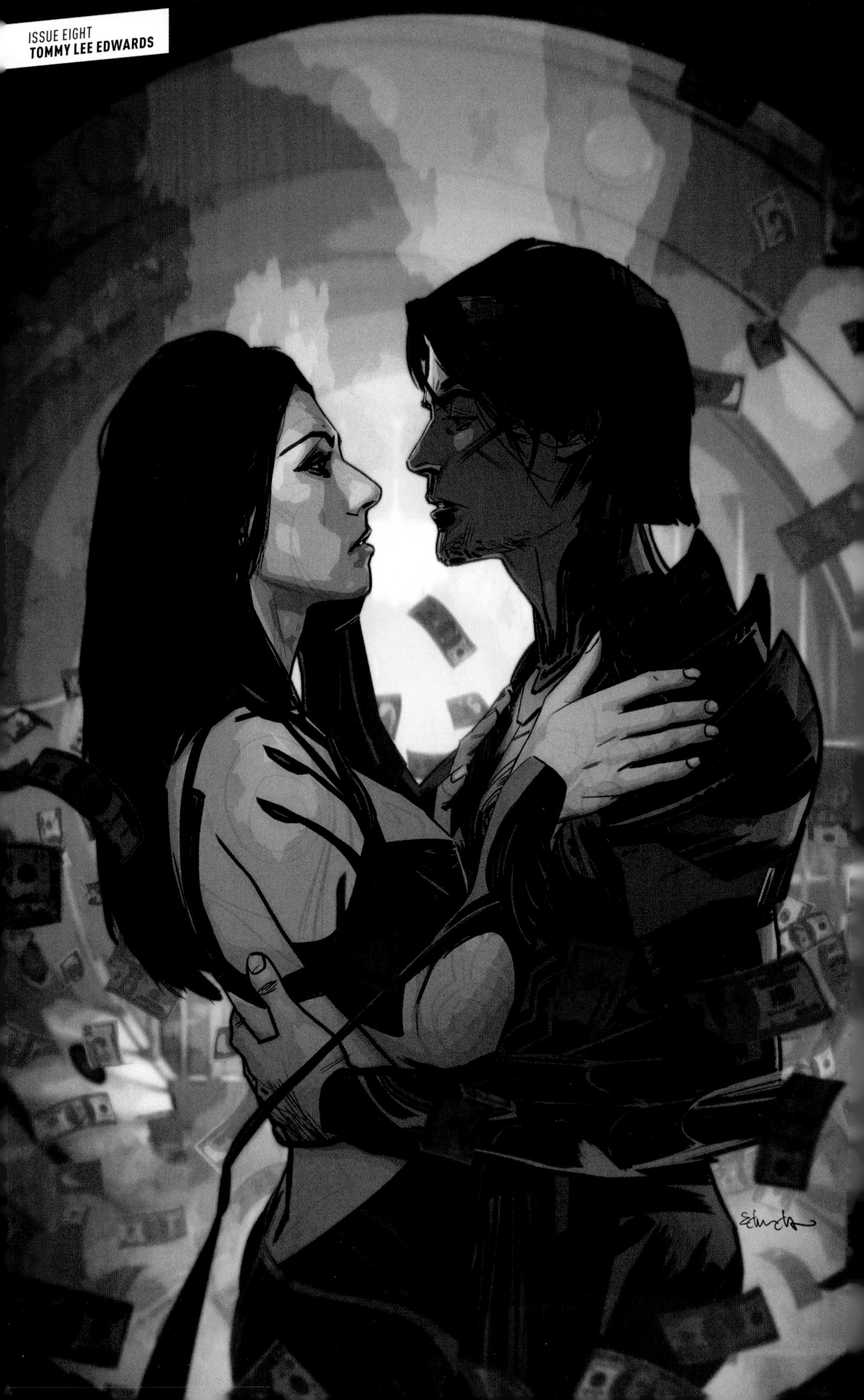

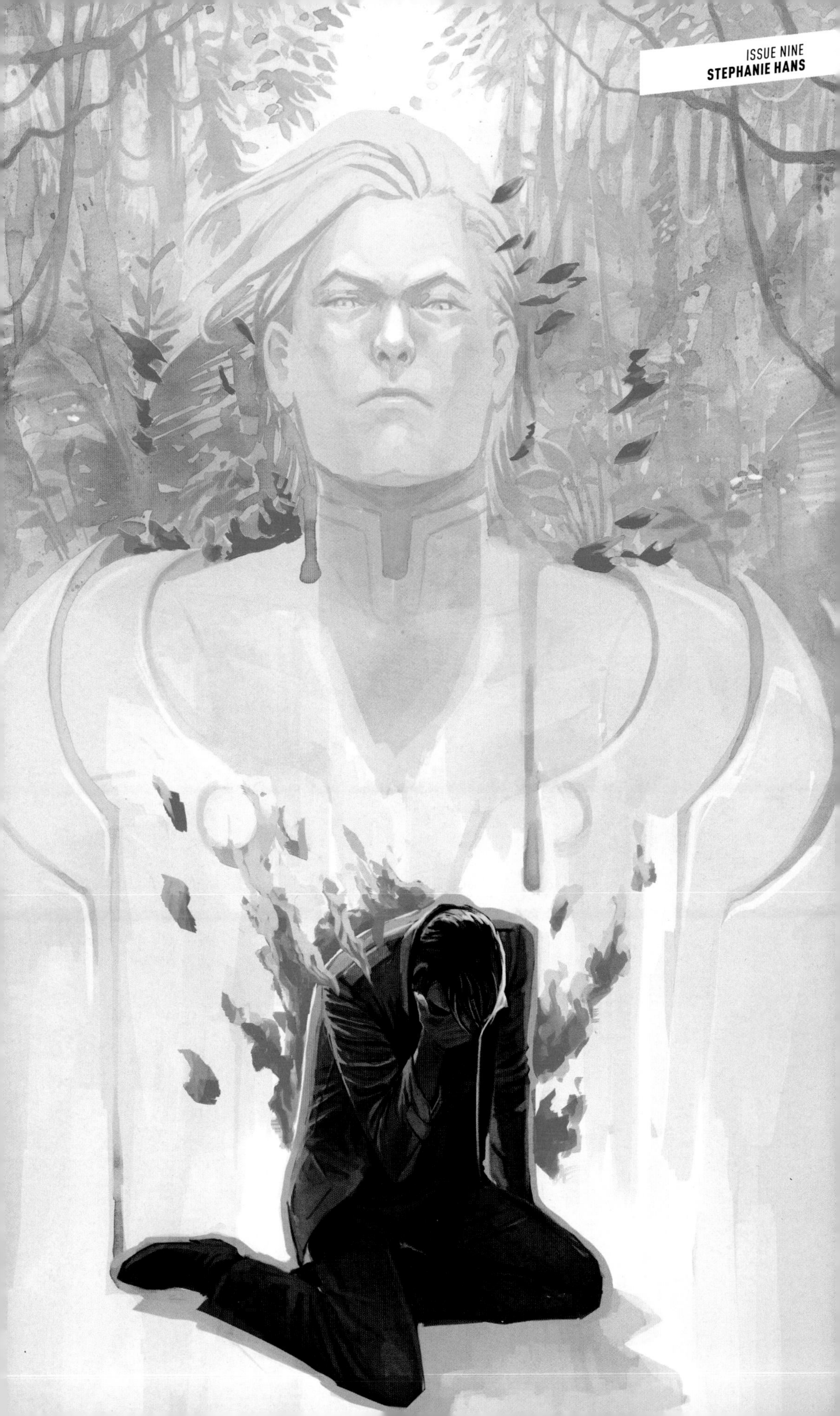

ISSUE NINE
STEPHANIE HANS

CHARACTER GALLERY
BY ELENA CASAGRANDE